**national
STATISTICS**

Family Spending

A report on the 2003-04 Expenditure and Food Survey

2004 edition

Editors: Catherine Gibbins

Office for National Statistics

palgrave
macmillan

First published 2005 by
PALGRAVE MACMILLAN
Houndmills, Basingstoke, Hampshire RG21 6XS and
175 Fifth Avenue, New York, NY 10010
Companies and representatives throughout the world.

PALGRAVE MACMILLAN is the global academic imprint of the Palgrave Macmillan division of St. Martin's Press, LLC and of Palgrave Macmillan Ltd. Macmillan® is a registered trademark in the United States, United Kingdom and other countries. Palgrave is a registered trademark in the European Union and other countries.

ISBN 1-4039-9072-7
ISSN 0965-1403

This book is printed on paper suitable for recycling and made from fully managed and sustained forest sources.

A catalogue record for this book is available from the British Library.

10   9   8   7   6   5   4   3   2   1
14 13 12 11 10 09 08 07 06 05

Printed and bound in Great Britain by Ashford Colour Press Ltd, Gosport.

A National Statistics publication

National Statistics are produced to high professional standards as set out in the National Statistics Code of Practice. They are produced free from political influence.

About the Office for National Statistics

The Office for National Statistics (ONS) is the government agency responsible for compiling, analysing and disseminating economic, social and demographic statistics about the United Kingdom. It also administers the statutory registration of births, marriages and deaths in England and Wales.

The Director of ONS is also the National Statistician and the Registrar General for England and Wales.

For enquiries about this publication, contact The Editor.
Tel: 020 7533 5407
E-mail: cathy.gibbins@ons.gov.uk

For general enquiries, contact the National Statistics Customer Contact Centre.
Tel: **0845 601 3034** (minicom: 01633 812399)
E-mail: info@statistics.gov.uk
Fax: 01633 652747
Post: Room D115, Government Buildings,
             Cardiff Road, Newport NP10 8XG

You can also find National Statistics on the Internet at
www.statistics.gov.uk

Contents

List of tables

4: Trends in household expenditure over time

Appendix A

Appendix B

List of Figures

Equivalised Income

Introduction

This report presents the latest information from the Expenditure and Food Survey (EFS) for the financial year April 2003 to March 2004.

The EFS is the result of the amalgamation of the Family Expenditure and National Food Surveys (FES and NFS).   Both surveys were well established and important sources of information for government and the wider community, charting changes and patterns in Britain's spending and food consumption since the 1950s. The Office for National Statistics (ONS) has overall project management and financial responsibility for the EFS while the Department for Environment, Food and Rural Affairs (DEFRA) sponsors the specialist food data.

The design of the EFS is based on the FES and the same questions were asked of the respondents. The survey continues to be primarily used to provide information for the Retail Prices Index; National Accounts estimates of household expenditure; the analysis of the effect of taxes and benefits, and trends in nutrition. However, the results are multi purpose, providing an invaluable supply of economic and social data.

The 2003-04 survey

In 2003-04 7,048 households in Great Britain took part in the EFS. The response rate was 58 per cent in both Great Britain and in Northern Ireland. The fieldwork was undertaken by the Office for National Statistics and the Northern Ireland Statistics and Research Agency.

Further details about the conduct of the survey are given in Appendix B.

The format of the Family Spending publication has changed this year and the tables of key results which previously were found in the main body of the report are now in Appendix A. This year's report focuses upon three principle topics: expenditure on housing; expenditure by children and the impact of equivalising income when calculating results. This change of style has been made to present increased detail and analysis about certain aspects of interest to survey users, while continuing to maintain the high level of reporting of EFS results. In future years it is intended to report on different aspects of the survey results in similar levels of detail.

Data quality and definitions

The results shown in this report are of the data collected by the EFS, following a process of validation and adjustment for non-response using weights that control for a number of factors. These issues are discussed in the section on reliability in Appendix B.

Figures in the report are subject to sampling variability. Standard errors for detailed expenditure items are presented in relative terms in Table A1 and are described in Appendix B, section B6. Figures shown for particular groups of households (e.g. income groups or household composition groups), regions or other sub-sets of the sample are subject to larger sampling variability, and are more sensitive to possible extreme values than are figures for the sample as a whole. In order to increase reliability, some tables are based on data collected across two or three-years.

The definitions used in the report are set out in Appendix B, section B4, and changes made since 1991 are described in section B5. Note particularly that housing benefit and council tax rebate (rates rebate in Northern Ireland), unlike other social security benefits, are not included in income but are shown as a reduction in housing costs.

Related data sources

Details of household consumption expenditure within the context of the UK National Accounts are produced as part of Consumer Trends (http://www.statistics.gov.uk/statbase/Product.asp?vlnk=242). This publication includes all expenditure by members of UK resident households. National Accounts figures draw on a number of sources including the EFS: figures shown in this report are therefore not directly comparable to National Accounts data. National Accounts data may be more appropriate for deriving long term trends on expenditure.

More detailed income information is available from the Family Resources Survey (FRS), conducted for the Department for Work and Pensions. Further information about food consumption, and in particular details of food quantities, is available from the Department for Environment, Food and Rural Affairs, who are continuing to produce their own report of the survey (http://statistics.defra.gov.uk/esg/publications/efs/default.asp).

In Northern Ireland, a companion survey to the GB EFS is conducted by the Central Survey Unit of the Northern Ireland Statistics and Research Agency (NISRA). Households in Northern Ireland are over-sampled so that separate analysis can be carried out, however these cases are given less weight when UK data are analysed. Results from this sample will be published in a separate report, The Northern Ireland Family Expenditure Survey Report for 2003-04. Further information and copies of this report can be obtained from:

Northern Ireland Statistics and Research Agency,
Central Survey Unit
McAuley House
2-14 Castle Street
Belfast BT1 1SY

Tel: 02890 348 214

Additional tabulations

This report gives a broad overview of the results of the survey, and provides more detailed information about some aspects of expenditure. However, many users of EFS data have very specific data requirements that may not appear in the desired form in this report. The ONS can provide more detailed analysis of the tables in this report, and can also provide additional tabulations to meet specific requests. A charge will be made to cover the cost of providing additional information.

The tables in Family Spending 2003-04 are available as Excel spreadsheets (with unrounded data).

Acknowledgements

A large scale survey is a collaborative effort and the authors wish to thank the interviewers and other ONS staff who contributed to the study. The survey would not be possible without the co-operation of the respondents who gave up their time to be interviewed and keep a diary of their spending. Their help is gratefully acknowledged.

Contact points

Please address all enquiries to:

Expenditure and Food Survey,
Office for National Statistics,
Room D1/23,
1, Drummond Gate,
London SW1V 2QQ.

Tel: 020 7533 5756

Fax: 020 7533 5300

Symbols and conventions used in this report

[ ]	Figures to be used with extra caution because based on fewer than 20 reporting households.
Rounding:	Individual figures have been rounded independently. The sum of component items does not therefore necessarily add to the totals shown.
Averages:	These are averages (means) for all households included in the column or row, and are not restricted to those households reporting expenditure on a particular item or income of a particular type.

Period covered: Financial year 2003-04 (1 April 2003 to 31 March 2004).

List of contributors

Editor:	Catherine Gibbins
Authors:	Georgina Julian
	Deborah Lader
Production team:	Kay Joseland
	Tim Samuels
	Sandy Lim
	Anwar Annut
	Deo Sande
	Mark Baines
	David Devore
	Karen Irving
	Ramona Franklyn
	Lynne Rhodes
	Tony King
	Christine Farmer
	Carole Abrahams
	Fiona Dawe
	Katherine Ralph
	Field team and interviewers
	Coders and Editors
Reviewers:	Francis Jones
	Craig Corbet
	Margaret Dolling
	Bev Botting
	ONS Press Office
Cover artwork:	ONS Design

Housing Expenditure

Chapter 1

Summary

The purpose of this chapter is to present an overview of all EFS data on housing costs. This includes expenditure which is classified as household consumption expenditure, in the National Accounts. Household consumption expenditure reported in Family Spending tables in Appendix A, under the section entitled 'housing, fuel and power', are combined with other expenditure items on housing which are not classified in this way and are consequently found in the table sections 'other expenditure items' or 'other items recorded'.

As this chapter concentrates on housing costs alone, it has excluded data relating to fuel and power consumption and has focused explicitly on costs associated with maintaining a house, such as rent, mortgage, council tax, maintenance and house insurance (see Table 1.1 for further detail of what is included).

Housing expenditure included:

Housing costs classified in COICOP category 'housing, fuel and power':

- Actual rentals for housing
    - net rent (gross rent *less* housing benefit, rebates and allowances received)
    - second dwelling rent
- Maintenance and repair of dwelling
    - central heating maintenance and repair
    - house maintenance and repair
    - paint, wallpaper, timber
    - equipment hire, small materials
- Water supply and miscellaneous services relating to dwelling
    - water charges
    - other regular housing payments including service charge for rent
    - refuse collection, including skip hire.

Housing costs found elsewhere in the COICOP classification system:

- Household Insurances
    - structural insurance
    - contents insurance
    - insurance for household appliances.

Housing costs not classified under COICOP:

Other expenditure items

- Housing: mortgage interest payments etc
    - mortgage interest payments
    - mortgage protection premiums
    - council tax, domestic rates
    - council tax, mortgage, insurance (second dwelling).

Other items recorded

- Purchase or alteration of dwellings (contracted out), mortgages
    - outright purchase of houses, flats etc. including deposits
    - capital repayment of mortgage
    - central heating installation
    - DIY improvements: double glazing, kitchen units, sheds etc
    - home improvements (contracted out)
    - bathroom fittings
    - purchase of materials for capital improvements
    - purchase of second dwelling.

Combining and presenting all data related to housing aids understanding of total housing costs for each household, rather than just those items which contribute to household consumption estimates.

Background

Since 2001-02, the **C**lassification **O**f **I**ndividual **CO**nsumption by **P**urpose (COICOP) has been used as a coding frame for expenditure items on the EFS. COICOP is the classification system used on Household Budget Surveys (HBS) across the EU. These surveys collect information on household consumption expenditure, which is then used to update the weights in the basket of goods and services used in consumer price indices. To ensure harmonisation across countries, all data has to comply with the European System of Accounts (ESA95) definitions and classifications and therefore the COICOP system must be used.

National Accounts use COICOP to provide a breakdown of household consumption expenditure with rent measured as either actual paid rent (in the case of tenants) or imputed rent (in the case of owner occupiers or those living rent free or largely free). This enables all dwelling services to be treated in the same way and prevents the need to change the measure of GDP of the economy each time a dwelling changes from tenanted to owner occupied and vice versa.

In line with national accounting definitions and conventions, additions to savings, investments or loans; repayments of loans and mortgage interest; cash grants or donations and other financial transactions, as well as house purchase and major renovations and alterations, are considered to be non-consumption expenditures. One problem therefore with the COICOP system is that it does not include expenditure related to housing such as mortgage interest payments, purchase or alteration of dwellings and mortgages . In Family Spending, these are shown under 'other expenditure items' and 'other items recorded'.

Family Spending reports on household expenditure and therefore does not report on goods and services provided for collective consumption to all members of a community, such as the National Health Service and the state education system. Tables presented in Appendix A of Family Spending report household consumption expenditure under the twelve COICOP headings. In addition to the COICOP categories of spending, these tables contain two sections referred to as 'other expenditure items' and 'other items recorded' under which non-consumption expenditures involved in housing costs can be found. It is also worth noting that Family Spending tables use rent net of service charges and any benefit receipts associated with housing when calculating total expenditure, a convention continued within this chapter. This convention ensures that rebates, benefits and allowances are excluded from the total calculation of household expenditure on rent.

The present Family Spending household expenditure tables in Appendix A contain a category called 'housing, fuel and power' under which all COICOP classified housing costs except insurance can be found. All expenditure is averaged across all households, including those reporting zero expenditure on a specific item. Therefore all households are deemed to pay a proportion of all housing costs. The impact of this is that all sample households are included when calculating both rent and mortgage interest, despite the fact that they are only actually likely to pay one or the other. In order to address this issue and explore housing costs further, some additional analysis was conducted that just looked at expenditure of renters and mortgage payers, see Tables 1.6 to 1.9 and Figures 1.7, 1.8 and 1.9.

Results

Using the new definition of housing expenditure, the average weekly expenditure on housing is £115.60 compared to £27.00 which is the total spent on housing under the COICOP heading of 'housing, fuel and power'.

Housing expenditure over time

Table 1.1 provides a comparison of housing costs over time, using data from the past three survey years (2001-02, 2002-03 and 2003-04). This table contains both average household consumption and non-consumption expenditure data. It also includes a total for all expenditure, both consumption and non-consumption spending, which is consequently greater than the average weekly household expenditure as detailed in the tables in Appendix A. This new total for all household spending is £591.90 per week, compared to £418.10 for household consumption expenditure alone.

Overall expenditure on housing was £115.60 per week for 2003-04, this equates to 20 per cent of all weekly (consumption and non-consumption) expenditure. The largest portion of this was the £38.80 spent on mortgages (interest, protection and capital repayment). Household alterations and improvements accounted for £22.80 per week, charges (including council tax or domestic rates, water charges, refuse collection) for £20.20 and net rent payments were £13.20 per week. As previously mentioned, these calculations average expenditure on all items, across all households in the sample and therefore every household is attributed a weekly expenditure on net rent and a mortgage.

There appears to be little difference in the various housing payments over the combined three year period, with the exception of the 2001-02 dataset which contained a relatively large incidence of 81 households making outright purchases of houses (23 primary and 58 secondary dwellings). This unusually large number of outright purchases, therefore reduces the percentage of spending in other areas of household housing costs. If however, these outliers are ignored, then spending on housing appears to be very similar each year for all categories.

Figure 1.1 shows the amount spent by each household per week on net rent, mortgage, charges, moving house, household maintenance and repair, household alterations and improvements and household insurances, over the combined three year period.

The greatest increase was seen in the household alterations and improvements category, where spending grew from £16.20 in 2001-02 to £18.90 per week in 2002-03 to £22.80 in the current year. Despite this being the greatest increase in the current survey year, it accounts for less than a one percent change in total spending. Spending on mortgages increased from £37.00 per week in 2001-02 to £37.30 in 2002-03 to £38.80 per week in the past year, although this accounted for a percentage change of less than 0.5 percent in total spending in the past survey year.

Figure **1.1**

Housing expenditure 2001-02 to 2003-04

£ per week

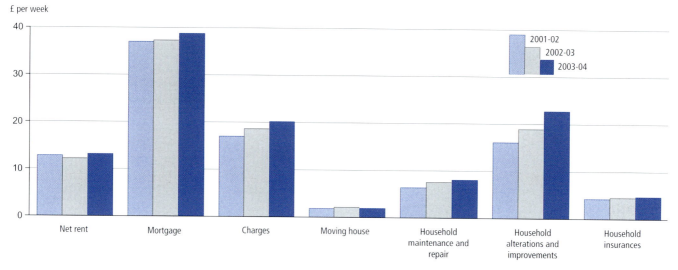

Expenditure by gross income

Table 1.2 shows expenditure on housing by gross income decile group. Figure 1.2 shows the amount spent per week on mortgage, net rent, household maintenance and repair and on household alterations and improvements, by gross income decile. In general terms, expenditure on all aspects of housing increased with income. The highest income group spent £292.20 per week, more than double the average weekly expenditure for all UK households (£115.60) and almost ten times that of the lowest income group who spent £29.70 per week. Figure 1.2 shows little increase in expenditure on net rent or household alterations and improvements, over income

deciles. However, this is not the case for mortgage and household maintenance and repair which both show a marked increase with income.

Expenditure by age of the household reference person

Figure 1.3 shows weekly spend on the top five housing expenditures: mortgage, net rent, household maintenance and repair, household alterations and improvements and charges, analysed by age of the household reference person. It shows that those aged more than 30 but less than 50, spend the most on their mortgages, spending £69.90 per week. Those older than 65 but less than 75 spent £2.50 per week, with those older than 75 spending the least at 60p. Those under the age of 30 spend three times as much as any other group on net rent. They spent £44.50 each week, compared to £14.10 by those aged more than 30 and under 50. All other age groups spent less than £6.50 each week on net rent.

Expenditure by region

Table 1.4 details the expenditure on all aspects of housing, by UK Countries and Government Office Regions. It is worth noting that spending on charges in Northern Ireland is exceptionally low, compared to the UK national average. Those living in this region spend £7.20, which is only 36 per cent of the UK national average for charges which is £20.20 per week. This is due to the fact that those living in Northern Ireland do not pay council tax but pay rates instead and these rates are much lower than council tax.

Figure 1.4 shows the percentage difference from the UK average net rent across regions within the UK. The average UK expenditure on net rent is £13.20, with only two regions

Figure **1.2**

Expenditure on selected items by gross income decile group, 2003-04

£ per week

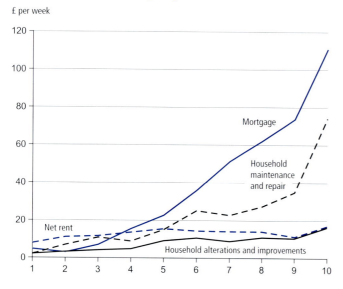

Figure 1.3

Expenditure on selected items by age of household reference person, 2003-04

£ per week

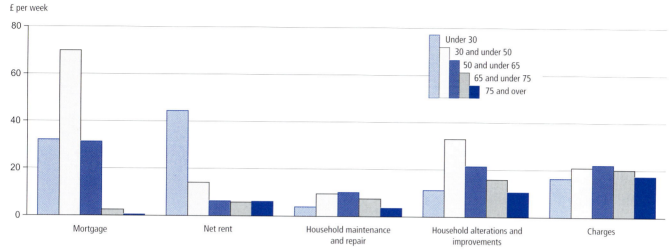

spending more than the average. Those renting in London spent more than double this amount at £31.30 and those living in the South East spend 18 per cent more than the average at £15.60. Those living in the North East pay £6.50 per week, which is 51 per cent less net rent than the UK average. With the exception of the North East of England, spending on rent in Wales, Northern Ireland and Scotland was lower than in all English regions. The average net rent in Wales was £7.10, 46 per cent below the UK average, in Northern Ireland it was £7.80, 41 per cent below the average and at £9.00 Scotland was 32 per cent less than the UK average.

Figure 1.5 demonstrates the regional differences throughout the UK in terms of spending on mortgages. The UK weekly

average spent on mortgages was £38.80 and four regions spent more than this. Those living in the South West spent 11 per cent more than the average at £43.20 per week, households in the East spent 21 per cent more at £46.80, those living in London spent £47.80 which is 23 per cent more than the average and those living in the South East spent the most, 31 per cent more than the average at £51.00 per week. Those living in the East Midlands (four per cent less) and West Midlands (five per cent less) spent just under the UK average on mortgages, at £37.40 and £36.70 respectively. Those living in the North East spent the least on their mortgages, £22.10 per week, which was 43 per cent less than the UK weekly average of £38.80.

Figure 1.4

Percentage change from UK average for net rent by UK Countries and Government Office Regions, 2003-04

Per cent

Figure 1.5

Percentage change from UK average for mortgage payments by UK Countries and Government Office Regions, 2003-04

Per cent

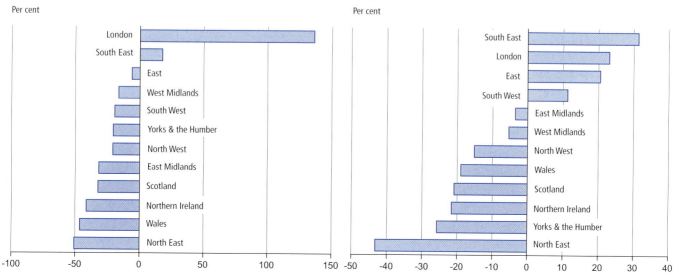

Figure 1.6

Expenditure on selected items by socio-economic class of household reference person, 2003-04

£ per week

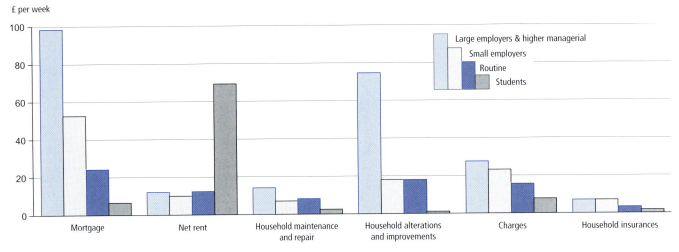

Expenditure by socio-economic characteristics

Table 1.5 includes the average weekly housing expenditure data by socio-economic group of the household reference person. This analysis makes use of the National Statistics Socio-Economic Classification (NS-SEC) when classifying the occupation of the household reference person. It clearly shows that those in the 'large employers and higher managerial' group spent the most on making outright purchases of primary dwellings, spending £6.90 per week, compared to £1.00 by 'small employers', 40p by 'intermediate' workers and 10p by those in 'lower managerial and professional' and 'lower supervisory' groups.

Students spent far more than any other group on net rent, £69.30, compared to the next nearest spenders on rent, 'higher professionals' who spent £18.50 per week. Those classified as 'large employers and higher managerial' spent the most per week on mortgages at £98.50, closely followed by the 'higher professional' group who spent £84.00. The two groups who spent the least on mortgages were the 'long term unemployed' who spent £2.70 per week and those in the 'occupation not stated and not classifiable' group, who spent just £1.40 per week on a mortgage.

Figure 1.6 shows the housing expenditure of four different socio-economic groups. It clearly shows the large amounts spent on mortgages by members of the 'large employers and higher managerial' group and the large amount spent on rent by students. It also shows that as spending on mortgages decreased, spending on charges (which includes council tax or domestic rates, water charges and refuse collections) also decreased.

Analysis of rent and mortgage data by renters and mortgage holders alone

In order to explore further the actual costs of running a household in the UK, some additional analysis was conducted. This analysis is the only incidence in the Family Spending publication where spending is averaged over only those households which spend money on the item concerned. Therefore figures for rent are averaged over those 2,018 households which spent money on rent and mortgage figures are calculated based only on the 2,838 households which paid mortgages. There are a total of 7,048 households in the 2003-04 sample, which equates to 29 per cent of households paying rent, 40 per cent paying mortgages and 31 per cent of households not paying rent or mortgage.

Tables 1.6 and 1.7 include data relating to expenditure on rent by renters and mortgages by mortgage holders alone. This type of analysis should produce a more accurate reflection of what people actually spent on their rent or mortgage each week, as the results of the question are only based on the answers given by those people who actually paid rent or a mortgage.

Figure 1.7 and Table 1.8 show the new amounts spent on net rent and mortgages, divided by gross income decile. One apparent anomaly is that a relatively large amount was spent on mortgages by those in the lowest decile, (£76.50 per week) which was almost double what was spent by those in the second decile (£39.50) and an amount of spending not surpassed until the seventh decile (who spent £86.00 per week on mortgages). This could be due to households in this category having a temporarily low income for example if the household reference person had recently left work, either

Figure **1.7**

Expenditure on net rent and mortgages[1] by gross income decile group, 2003-04

£ per week

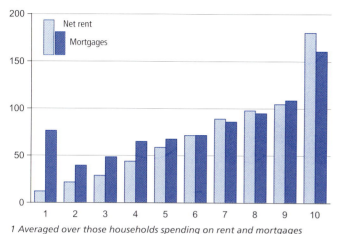

1 Averaged over those households spending on rent and mortgages respectively

through redundancy or for other reasons and continued to pay their mortgage. It is also possible that this category contains a number of households with a self-employed reference person, who report both a low income and high spending on their mortgage.

Analysing rent by those who pay rent and amounts spent on mortgages by mortgage holders alone, made little difference to the overall national picture (Table 1.9), although the East moved above the UK national average of £45.80, in this

analysis. Figure 1.8 shows the expenditure on net rent by UK Countries and Government Office Region. The most expensive three regions for renters were London (£79.70), the South East (£67.90) and the East (£48.70). The North East remained the cheapest area to rent at a weekly cost of £21.20 (under half the national average), this was followed by Scotland (£26.90), Northern Ireland (£27.10) and Wales (£27.10). Therefore the four regions with the lowest rent remained the same, as in the analysis of household expenditure by region (see Figure 1.4), although their order changed slightly.

In this new analysis Figure 1.9 shows the expenditure on mortgages, by those paying a mortgage, by UK Countries and Government Office Regions. The UK national average in this analysis was £97.20 per week, a figure only exceeded in four regions, the most expensive being London (£133.90), followed by the South East (£119.20), the East (£115.30) and the South West (£109.50). The region with the lowest expenditure on mortgages was the North East with a weekly average of £57.80, followed by Yorkshire and the Humber and Northern Ireland, where £73.70 was the weekly average, and Scotland where £75.50 was spent on mortgages each week. All of these regions remain in the same order as in the analysis of household expenditure by region, the only changes are in the order of regions in the middle of the mortgage expenditure range where West Midlands (£94.10) changes place with the East Midlands (where £88.30 per week is now spent) and Wales (£82.40) exceeds the cost of the North West (£80.20).

Figure **1.8**

Expenditure on net rent[1] by UK Countries and Government Office Regions, 2003-04

£ per week

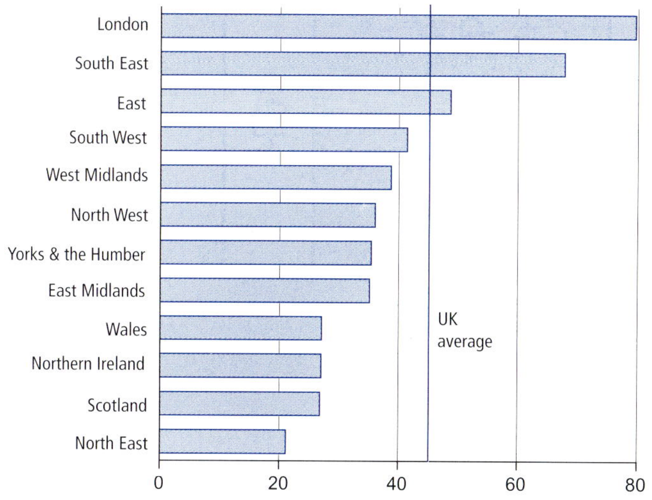

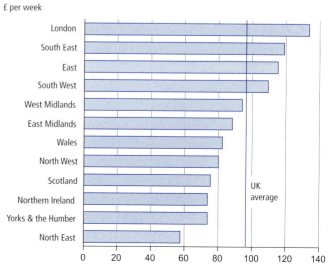

1 Averaged over those households spending on rent

Figure **1.9**

Expenditure on mortgages[1] by UK Countries and Government Office Regions, 2003-04

£ per week

1 Averaged over those households spending on mortgages

Table **1.1**

Housing expenditure, 2001-02 to 2003-04

	2001-02			2002-03			2003-04		
	£ per week	% of total expend-iture	% of housing expend-iture	£ per week	% of total expend-iture	% of housing expend-iture	£ per week	% of total expend-iture	% of housing expend-iture
Grossed number of households (thousands)	24,890			24,346			24,670		
Total number of households in sample	7,473			6,927			7,048		
Total number of persons in sample	18,122			16,586			16,965		
Total number of adults in sample	13,446			12,450			12,617		
Weighted average number of persons per household	2.4			2.4			2.4		
Primary dwelling									
Rent	**21.60**	*3*	*12*	**21.60**	*4*	*21*	**23.50**	*4*	*20*
Gross rent	21.60	3	12	21.60	4	21	23.50	4	20
less housing benefit, rebates & allowances received	8.70	1	5	9.40	2	9	10.20	2	9
Net rent	12.90	2	7	12.20	2	12	13.20	2	11
Mortgage	**37.00**	*6*	*20*	**37.30**	*7*	*36*	**38.80**	*7*	*34*
Mortgage interest payments	25.00	4	13	24.50	4	24	24.20	4	21
Mortgage protection premiums	1.30	0	1	1.40	0	1	1.50	0	1
Capital repayment of mortgage	10.80	2	6	11.40	2	11	13.10	2	11
Outright purchase, including deposits	**19.60**	*3*	*11*	**0.20**	*0*	*0*	**0.50**	*0*	*0*
Secondary dwelling	**71.00**	*11*	*38*	**1.90**	*0*	*2*	**5.10**	*1*	*4*
Rent	0.10	0	0	0.00	0	0	0.00	0	0
Council tax, mortgage, insurance (secondary dwelling)	0.30	0	0	0.40	0	0	0.70	0	1
Purchase of second dwelling	70.60	11	38	1.50	0	1	4.30	1	4
Charges	**17.10**	*3*	*9*	**18.60**	*3*	*18*	**20.20**	*3*	*17*
Council tax, domestic rates	12.40	2	7	13.20	2	13	14.70	2	13
Water charges	4.10	1	2	4.60	1	4	4.80	1	4
Other regular housing payments, including service charge for rent	0.60	0	0	0.70	0	1	0.70	0	1
Refuse collection, including skip hire	0.00	0	0	0.10	0	0	0.10	0	0
Moving house	**1.90**	*0*	*1*	**2.20**	*0*	*2*	**2.00**	*0*	*2*
Property transaction - purchase and sale	0.80	0	0	0.80	0	1	0.90	0	1
Property transaction - sale only	0.60	0	0	0.70	0	1	0.50	0	0
Property transaction - purchase only	0.40	0	0	0.50	0	1	0.50	0	0
Property transaction - other payments	0.10	0	0	0.10	0	0	0.10	0	0
Household maintenance and repair	**6.50**	*1*	*3*	**7.50**	*1*	*7*	**8.20**	*1*	*7*
Central heating maintenance and repair	0.90	0	1	1.10	0	1	1.10	0	1
House maintenance and repair	3.10	0	2	4.10	1	4	4.20	1	4
Paint, wallpaper, timber	1.60	0	1	1.30	0	1	1.40	0	1
Equipment hire, small materials	0.90	0	0	1.00	0	1	1.50	0	1
Household alterations and improvements	**16.20**	*3*	*9*	**18.90**	*3*	*18*	**22.80**	*4*	*20*
Central heating installation	1.00	0	1	0.90	0	1	1.20	0	1
DIY improvements: Double Glazing, Kitchen Units, Sheds etc.	1.70	0	1	1.10	0	1	3.00	1	3
Home improvements - contracted out	11.90	2	6	15.70	3	15	17.10	3	15
Bathroom fittings	0.70	0	0	0.60	0	1	0.70	0	1
Purchase of materials for Capital Improvements	0.90	0	0	0.70	0	1	0.70	0	1
Household insurances	**4.30**	*1*	*2*	**4.50**	*1*	*4*	**4.80**	*1*	*4*
Structure	2.00	0	1	2.10	0	2	2.30	0	2
Contents	2.20	0	1	2.20	0	2	2.40	0	2
Household applicances	0.10	0	0	0.10	0	0	0.20	0	0
Housing expenditure	**186.60**	*29*	*100*	**103.20**	*18*	*100*	**115.60**	*20*	*100*
Total expenditure[1]	**646.10**			**566.40**			**591.90**		

1 This total includes all categories recorded in the EFS, including those outside the 'COICOP' total expenditure

Table **1.2**

Housing expenditure by gross income decile group, 2003-04

Average weekly household expenditure (£)

	Gross income decile group										
	1	2	3	4	5	6	7	8	9	10	All
Grossed number of households (thousands)	2,468	2,467	2,468	2,464	2,470	2,465	2,467	2,467	2,468	2,465	24,670
Total number of households in sample	703	720	729	729	715	719	712	687	681	653	7,048
Total number of persons in sample	930	1,212	1,457	1,461	1,730	1,899	1,997	2,062	2,093	2,124	16,965
Total number of adults in sample	781	924	1,142	1,169	1,296	1,354	1,440	1,452	1,522	1,537	12,617
Weighted average number of persons per household	1.3	1.6	1.9	1.9	2.4	2.6	2.7	2.9	3.0	3.2	2.4
Primary dwelling											
Rent	**47.30**	**37.10**	**29.70**	**22.60**	**21.20**	**16.70**	**15.30**	**14.60**	**11.80**	**18.20**	**23.50**
Gross rent	47.30	37.10	29.70	22.60	21.20	16.70	15.30	14.60	11.80	18.20	23.50
less *housing benefit, rebates & allowances received*	39.30	25.80	17.90	8.80	5.50	2.20	1.10	0.50	0.20	1.00	10.20
Net rent	8.00	11.20	11.80	13.80	15.70	14.60	14.30	14.20	11.50	17.30	13.20
Mortgage	**4.90**	**3.10**	**7.20**	**15.60**	**22.70**	**36.10**	**51.50**	**62.20**	**73.90**	**111.10**	**38.80**
Mortgage interest payments	3.30	2.10	5.10	10.70	14.40	23.30	32.20	37.80	45.50	67.20	24.20
Mortgage protection premiums	0.10	0.10	0.20	0.60	1.00	1.90	2.40	2.90	2.90	3.10	1.50
Capital repayment of mortgage	1.50	0.90	1.80	4.30	7.30	10.90	16.90	21.60	25.50	40.70	13.10
Outright purchase, including deposits	**0.60**	**0.00**	**0.00**	**0.00**	**0.00**	**0.10**	**0.20**	**0.00**	**3.10**	**0.60**	**0.50**
Secondary dwelling	**0.00**	**0.00**	**0.10**	**7.20**	**1.30**	**0.60**	**1.80**	**5.50**	**4.50**	**29.90**	**5.10**
Rent	0.00	0.00	0.00	0.00	0.00	0.00	0.00	0.00	0.40	0.00	0.00
Council tax, mortgage, insurance (second dwelling)	0.00	0.00	0.00	0.30	0.00	0.20	0.20	0.80	1.00	4.50	0.70
Purchase of second dwelling	0.00	0.00	0.10	6.90	1.20	0.40	1.60	4.60	3.20	25.40	4.30
Charges	**9.50**	**12.50**	**15.40**	**19.30**	**20.60**	**22.40**	**22.90**	**23.80**	**25.40**	**30.50**	**20.20**
Council tax, domestic rates	4.60	7.60	10.20	13.70	15.10	16.30	17.30	18.30	19.80	23.60	14.70
Water charges	3.90	4.10	4.20	4.50	4.80	5.00	5.00	5.10	5.30	6.00	4.80
Other regular housing payments, including service charge for rent	1.00	0.80	0.80	0.90	0.70	0.80	0.50	0.40	0.30	0.90	0.70
Refuse collection, including skip hire	0.00	0.00	0.10	0.20	0.00	0.30	0.10	0.10	0.00	0.00	0.10
Moving house	**0.70**	**0.40**	**1.00**	**0.80**	**2.40**	**2.90**	**2.20**	**2.90**	**3.10**	**3.80**	**2.00**
Property transaction - purchase and sale	0.30	0.10	0.60	0.30	1.40	1.10	0.70	1.30	1.60	1.70	0.90
Property transaction - sale only	0.00	0.20	0.30	0.20	0.60	0.70	0.60	0.60	0.60	0.90	0.50
Property transaction - purchase only	0.40	0.10	0.10	0.30	0.30	0.70	0.60	0.90	0.70	1.00	0.50
Property transaction - other payments	0.00	0.00	0.00	0.10	0.20	0.30	0.30	0.10	0.20	0.20	0.10
Household maintenance and repair	**2.10**	**3.30**	**4.30**	**4.90**	**9.20**	**10.80**	**8.90**	**11.00**	**10.60**	**16.40**	**8.20**
Central heating maintenance and repair	0.40	0.30	0.90	1.10	1.00	1.10	1.10	1.70	1.10	2.10	1.10
House maintenance and repair	1.20	2.00	1.90	2.40	6.50	4.50	4.50	4.40	5.80	8.90	4.20
Paint, wallpaper, timber	0.40	0.50	0.70	0.70	1.00	1.20	2.40	2.60	2.20	2.10	1.40
Equipment hire, small materials	0.10	0.40	0.70	0.70	0.70	4.10	0.90	2.20	1.60	3.30	1.50
Household alterations and improvements	**2.10**	**7.00**	**10.90**	**8.90**	**15.10**	**25.20**	**22.80**	**27.40**	**34.80**	**74.10**	**22.80**
Central heating installation	0.40	0.40	0.90	0.50	1.10	1.10	1.60	1.40	1.80	2.80	1.20
DIY improvements: Double Glazing, Kitchen Units etc.	0.10	2.50	1.40	1.90	1.20	6.60	4.60	2.30	2.40	7.50	3.00
Home improvements - contracted out	1.60	3.90	6.70	6.10	11.90	13.80	14.60	20.70	29.50	62.70	17.10
Bathroom fittings	0.00	0.20	1.60	0.10	0.50	2.20	0.50	1.40	0.30	0.50	0.70
Purchase of materials for Capital Improvements	0.00	0.00	0.30	0.40	0.30	1.60	1.60	1.60	0.80	0.70	0.70
Household insurances	**1.80**	**2.10**	**3.00**	**4.10**	**4.10**	**5.20**	**6.10**	**6.50**	**6.60**	**8.50**	**4.80**
Structure	0.80	1.00	1.40	1.90	2.00	2.40	2.70	3.30	3.20	4.10	2.30
Contents	1.00	1.10	1.50	2.00	2.10	2.50	2.80	3.20	3.20	4.30	2.40
Household appliances	0.00	0.00	0.10	0.20	0.00	0.30	0.60	0.10	0.20	0.10	0.20
Housing expenditure	**29.70**	**39.70**	**53.70**	**74.80**	**91.20**	**117.70**	**130.60**	**153.40**	**173.60**	**292.20**	**115.60**
Total expenditure[1]	**150.20**	**188.80**	**258.60**	**364.40**	**449.10**	**554.50**	**664.20**	**791.20**	**953.10**	**1546.10**	**591.90**

1 This total includes all categories recorded in the EFS, including those outside the 'COICOP' total expenditure

Table **1.3**

Housing expenditure by age of household reference person, 2003-04

Average weekly household expenditure (£)

	Under 30	30 and under 50	50 and under 65	65 and under 75	75 or over	All
Grossed number of households (thousands)	2,538	9,640	6,125	3,278	3,088	24,670
Total number of households in sample	682	2,877	1,725	965	799	7,048
Total number of persons in sample	1,598	8,860	3,765	1,602	1,140	16,965
Total number of adults in sample	1,154	5,354	3,388	1,588	1,133	12,617
Weighted average number of persons per household	2.3	3.0	2.2	1.7	1.4	2.4
Primary dwelling						
Rent	**59.90**	**23.10**	**14.70**	**15.00**	**20.70**	**23.50**
Gross rent	59.90	23.10	14.70	15.00	20.70	23.50
less housing benefit, rebates and allowances received	15.40	9.10	8.30	9.20	14.40	10.20
Net rent	44.50	14.10	6.40	5.80	6.30	13.20
Mortgage	**32.20**	**69.90**	**31.40**	**2.50**	**0.60**	**38.80**
Mortgage interest payments	20.50	42.60	20.50	1.90	0.40	24.20
Mortgage protection premiums	1.60	2.70	1.20	0.10	0.00	1.50
Capital repayment of mortgage	10.20	24.60	9.70	0.60	0.10	13.10
Outright purchase, including deposits	**0.10**	**1.00**	**0.30**	**0.00**	**0.00**	**0.50**
Secondary dwelling	**4.60**	**9.90**	**1.90**	**1.80**	**0.10**	**5.10**
Rent	0.00	0.10	0.00	0.10	0.00	0.00
Council tax, mortgage, insurance (secondary dwelling)	0.20	1.00	0.20	1.70	0.10	0.70
Purchase of second dwelling	4.40	8.90	1.70	0.00	0.00	4.30
Charges	**16.50**	**20.90**	**22.20**	**20.10**	**17.50**	**20.20**
Council tax, domestic rates	10.80	15.40	16.50	14.80	11.80	14.70
Water charges	4.80	4.90	5.10	4.40	4.10	4.80
Other regular housing payments, including service charge for rent	1.00	0.50	0.50	0.90	1.60	0.70
Refuse collection, including skip hire	0.00	0.10	0.20	0.00	0.00	0.10
Moving house	**2.30**	**3.00**	**1.30**	**1.70**	**0.50**	**2.00**
Property transaction - purchase and sale	0.60	1.30	0.50	1.40	0.20	0.90
Property transaction - sale only	0.20	0.80	0.30	0.20	0.10	0.50
Property transaction - purchase only	1.20	0.70	0.30	0.10	0.10	0.50
Property transaction - other payments	0.30	0.20	0.10	0.00	0.10	0.10
Household maintenance and repair	**4.10**	**9.50**	**10.30**	**7.50**	**3.70**	**8.20**
Central heating maintenance and repair	0.30	1.10	1.20	1.70	0.80	1.10
House maintenance and repair	2.40	4.00	6.10	4.10	2.40	4.20
Paint, wallpaper, timber	1.00	2.00	1.50	0.80	0.30	1.40
Equipment hire, small materials	0.40	2.40	1.50	0.90	0.20	1.50
Household alterations and improvements	**11.40**	**33.00**	**21.50**	**15.80**	**10.60**	**22.80**
Central heating installation	1.00	1.40	1.40	0.70	0.70	1.20
DIY improvements: Double Glazing, Kitchen Units, Sheds etc.	1.70	4.20	2.20	1.60	3.70	3.00
Home improvements - contracted out	7.40	25.70	16.80	11.30	5.30	17.10
Bathroom fittings	0.10	0.70	0.70	1.30	0.90	0.70
Purchase of materials for Capital Improvements	1.30	1.00	0.40	1.00	0.10	0.70
Household insurances	**3.10**	**5.40**	**5.70**	**4.40**	**3.00**	**4.80**
Structure	1.10	2.50	2.90	2.20	1.50	2.30
Contents	1.70	2.70	2.60	2.10	1.50	2.40
Household appliances	0.20	0.20	0.20	0.10	0.00	0.20
Housing expenditure	**118.90**	**166.70**	**100.90**	**59.70**	**42.20**	**115.60**
Total expenditure[1]	**549.50**	**781.60**	**629.00**	**352.60**	**215.30**	**591.90**

1 This total includes all categories recorded in the EFS, including those outside the 'COICOP' total expenditure

Table 1.4

Housing expenditure by UK Countries and Government Office Regions, 2003-04

Average weekly household expenditure (£)

	North East	North West	Yorks & the Humber	East Midlands	West Midlands	East	London
Grossed number of households (thousands)	1,078	2,894	2,159	1,760	2,146	2,284	2,889
Total number of households in sample	313	743	596	497	571	606	639
Total number of persons in sample	2,460	6,610	4,897	4,147	5,207	5,361	7,192
Total number of adults in sample	1,893	5,108	3,858	3,220	3,945	4,203	5,515
Weighted average number of persons per household	2.3	2.3	2.3	2.4	2.4	2.3	2.5
Primary dwelling							
Rent	**19.30**	**21.60**	**19.40**	**17.80**	**20.80**	**20.50**	**47.10**
Gross rent	19.30	21.60	19.40	17.80	20.80	20.50	47.10
less housing benefit, rebates and allowances received	12.80	11.10	8.80	8.70	9.70	8.10	15.90
Net rent	6.50	10.50	10.50	9.10	11.10	12.40	31.30
Mortgage	**22.10**	**33.00**	**28.80**	**37.40**	**36.70**	**46.80**	**47.80**
Mortgage interest payments	14.90	20.40	18.90	22.20	22.80	27.60	31.30
Mortgage protection premiums	1.20	1.50	1.20	1.40	1.50	1.60	1.50
Capital repayment of mortgage	5.90	11.10	8.70	13.80	12.50	17.60	15.00
Outright purchase, including deposits	**0.00**	**0.10**	**0.00**	**0.00**	**0.00**	**0.90**	**0.20**
Secondary dwelling	**0.80**	**12.20**	**0.70**	**10.30**	**1.80**	**3.10**	**2.60**
Rent	0.00	0.00	0.00	0.00	0.10	0.00	0.00
Council tax, mortgage, insurance (secondary dwelling)	0.00	0.20	0.10	0.50	1.40	2.30	1.00
Purchase of second dwelling	0.80	12.00	0.60	9.80	0.30	0.70	1.60
Charges	**16.60**	**19.30**	**18.30**	**19.10**	**18.90**	**21.90**	**22.80**
Council tax, domestic rates	11.90	13.80	12.70	14.10	14.00	16.00	16.10
Water charges	4.30	4.80	4.90	4.60	4.70	5.40	4.30
Other regular housing payments, including service charge for rent	0.30	0.60	0.40	0.40	0.20	0.50	1.80
Refuse collection, including skip hire	0.00	0.00	0.20	0.00	0.00	0.00	0.50
Moving house	**1.40**	**1.60**	**1.00**	**1.70**	**0.80**	**2.70**	**2.30**
Property transaction - purchase and sale	0.40	0.70	0.30	0.80	0.40	1.80	0.60
Property transaction - sale only	0.50	0.40	0.10	0.40	0.00	0.40	0.60
Property transaction - purchase only	0.50	0.40	0.50	0.30	0.30	0.40	0.70
Property transaction - other payments	0.10	0.10	0.20	0.10	0.10	0.00	0.30
Household maintenance and repair	**5.40**	**7.70**	**6.50**	**6.50**	**6.90**	**8.20**	**10.50**
Central heating maintenance and repair	0.50	0.80	1.20	0.80	1.10	1.10	1.30
House maintenance and repair	2.60	4.30	3.20	3.60	2.80	5.40	4.30
Paint, wallpaper, timber	1.30	1.40	1.00	1.50	1.60	1.10	1.70
Equipment hire, small materials	0.90	1.20	1.00	0.70	1.40	0.60	3.20
Household alterations and improvements	**24.70**	**20.70**	**17.20**	**27.80**	**23.30**	**29.90**	**22.90**
Central heating installation	0.40	1.10	1.40	1.10	0.80	1.00	1.10
DIY improvements: Double Glazing, Kitchen Units, Sheds etc.	13.30	4.60	0.50	6.70	3.90	0.80	1.50
Home improvements - contracted out	10.50	13.00	13.90	19.40	16.90	26.80	19.40
Bathroom fittings	0.40	0.40	0.40	0.40	0.50	1.00	0.20
Purchase of materials for Capital Improvements	0.10	1.50	1.10	0.20	1.10	0.30	0.60
Household insurances	**3.90**	**4.40**	**4.40**	**4.70**	**4.50**	**5.40**	**5.90**
Structure	1.90	2.10	2.10	2.30	2.30	2.40	2.70
Contents	1.80	2.20	2.20	2.20	2.20	2.80	3.00
Household appliances	0.20	0.10	0.10	0.20	0.00	0.20	0.20
Housing expenditure	**81.40**	**109.50**	**87.40**	**116.60**	**104.10**	**131.40**	**146.30**
Total expenditure[1]	**446.40**	**568.20**	**536.50**	**559.40**	**557.40**	**653.10**	**700.30**

1 This total includes all categories recorded in the EFS, including those outside the 'COICOP' total expenditure

Table 1.4 (cont.)

Housing expenditure by UK Countries and Government Office Regions, 2003-04

Average weekly household expenditure (£)

	South East	South West	England	Wales	Scotland	Northern Ireland	United Kingdom
Grossed number of households (thousands)	3,368	2,164	20,742	1,189	2,102	637	24,670
Total number of households in sample	898	652	5,515	370	548	616	7,049
Total number of persons in sample	7,893	4,870	48,638	2,875	4,959	1,678	58,149
Total number of adults in sample	6,154	3,837	37,732	2,136	3,833	1,190	44,891
Weighted average number of persons per household	2.3	2.3	2.3	2.4	2.4	2.6	2.4
Primary dwelling							
Rent	**23.90**	**19.60**	**24.40**	**16.20**	**19.70**	**17.10**	**23.50**
Gross rent	23.90	19.60	24.40	16.20	19.70	17.10	23.50
less housing benefit, rebates and allowances received	8.30	9.00	10.30	9.10	10.70	9.30	10.20
Net rent	15.60	10.70	14.20	7.10	9.00	7.80	13.20
Mortgage	**51.00**	**43.20**	**40.30**	**31.50**	**30.70**	**30.40**	**38.80**
Mortgage interest payments	32.00	25.40	25.10	20.50	18.80	18.90	24.20
Mortgage protection premiums	1.70	1.60	1.50	1.50	1.50	1.90	1.50
Capital repayment of mortgage	17.20	16.20	13.70	9.40	10.50	9.70	13.10
Outright purchase, including deposits	**0.10**	**3.50**	**0.50**	**0.10**	**0.00**	**0.70**	**0.50**
Secondary dwelling	**4.70**	**4.80**	**4.80**	**19.60**	**0.60**	**0.90**	**5.10**
Rent	0.00	0.00	0.00	0.70	0.00	0.00	0.00
Council tax, mortgage, insurance (secondary dwelling)	0.50	1.00	0.80	0.10	0.00	0.40	0.70
Purchase of second dwelling	4.10	3.70	4.00	18.70	0.60	0.50	4.30
Charges	**23.60**	**21.80**	**20.70**	**17.20**	**20.90**	**7.20**	**20.20**
Council tax, domestic rates	17.40	15.50	15.00	11.50	15.60	6.90	14.70
Water charges	4.90	5.60	4.90	5.40	5.10	0.00	4.80
Other regular housing payments, including service charge for rent	1.30	0.60	0.80	0.40	0.20	0.40	0.70
Refuse collection, including skip hire	0.00	0.00	0.10	0.00	0.00	0.00	0.10
Moving house	**3.70**	**2.80**	**2.10**	**2.20**	**1.20**	**0.80**	**2.00**
Property transaction - purchase and sale	2.10	0.70	1.00	1.00	0.60	0.30	0.90
Property transaction - sale only	0.70	1.20	0.50	0.90	0.10	0.10	0.50
Property transaction - purchase only	0.70	0.70	0.50	0.30	0.40	0.20	0.50
Property transaction - other payments	0.20	0.20	0.20	0.10	0.10	0.10	0.10
Household maintenance and repair	**11.20**	**8.10**	**8.30**	**10.50**	**5.40**	**8.00**	**8.20**
Central heating maintenance and repair	1.30	1.20	1.10	0.80	1.70	0.40	1.10
House maintenance and repair	6.80	4.30	4.40	5.00	2.20	2.60	4.20
Paint, wallpaper, timber	1.60	1.30	1.40	1.80	1.00	1.70	1.40
Equipment hire, small materials	1.60	1.30	1.40	2.90	0.50	3.30	1.50
Household alterations and improvements	**26.70**	**23.90**	**24.10**	**18.30**	**15.30**	**16.60**	**22.80**
Central heating installation	1.70	1.30	1.20	2.00	1.10	0.40	1.20
DIY improvements: Double Glazing, Kitchen Units, Sheds etc.	4.40	0.50	3.40	2.10	0.30	0.90	3.00
Home improvements - contracted out	17.80	20.20	17.90	13.90	13.10	13.00	17.10
Bathroom fittings	2.30	0.40	0.80	0.00	0.50	2.10	0.70
Purchase of materials for Capital Improvements	0.50	1.40	0.80	0.20	0.30	0.20	0.70
Household insurances	**5.40**	**4.50**	**4.90**	**4.20**	**4.30**	**3.90**	**4.80**
Structure	2.70	2.20	2.40	2.20	1.80	1.90	2.30
Contents	2.40	2.20	2.40	2.00	2.30	2.00	2.40
Household appliances	0.30	0.10	0.20	0.00	0.20	0.00	0.20
Housing expenditure	**141.90**	**123.30**	**120.00**	**110.70**	**87.30**	**76.30**	**115.60**
Total expenditure[1]	**682.80**	**575.30**	**603.80**	**529.70**	**526.30**	**538.50**	**591.90**

1 This total includes all categories recorded in the EFS, including those outside the 'COICOP' total expenditure

Table **1.5**

Housing expenditure by socio-economic class of household reference person, 2003-04

Average weekly household expenditure (£)

	Large employers & higher managerial	Higher professional	Lower managerial & professional	Intermediate	Small employers	Lower supervisory
Grossed number of households (thousands)	1,208	1,589	4,919	1,682	1,582	1,979
Total number of households in sample	337	451	1,398	496	461	563
Total number of persons in sample	948	1,223	3,688	1,205	1,330	1,578
Total number of adults in sample	672	857	2,663	846	939	1,099
Weighted average number of persons per household	2.7	2.6	2.6	2.4	2.8	2.7
Primary dwelling						
Rent	**14.00**	**19.50**	**18.80**	**25.50**	**16.30**	**16.50**
Gross rent	14.00	19.10	18.80	25.50	16.30	16.50
less housing benefit, rebates and allowances received	1.90	0.60	2.30	7.10	6.30	5.20
Net rent	12.20	18.50	16.50	18.40	10.00	11.2
Mortgage	**98.50**	**84.00**	**67.00**	**45.70**	**52.60**	**47.60**
Mortgage interest payments	57.60	52.40	40.70	28.70	34.30	30.10
Mortgage protection premiums	2.50	2.60	2.70	1.40	2.20	2.40
Capital repayment of mortgage	38.40	28.90	23.60	15.50	16.10	15.10
Outright purchase, including deposits	**6.90**	**0.00**	**0.10**	**0.40**	**1.00**	**0.10**
Secondary dwelling	**3.50**	**8.00**	**12.80**	**10.60**	**2.50**	**5.60**
Rent	0.00	0.40	0.10	0.00	0.00	0.00
Council tax, mortgage, insurance (secondary dwelling)	1.50	2.90	0.90	0.00	0.00	0.00
Purchase of second dwelling	2.00	4.70	11.90	10.60	2.50	5.60
Charges	**27.70**	**25.60**	**23.90**	**20.50**	**23.10**	**20.50**
Council tax, domestic rates	21.10	19.80	18.00	14.70	17.80	14.90
Water charges	5.50	5.30	5.20	4.90	5.00	4.90
Other regular housing payments, including service charge for rent	0.90	0.50	0.50	0.80	0.30	0.60
Refuse collection, including skip hire	0.10	0.00	0.20	0.10	0.00	0.00
Moving house	**4.90**	**3.70**	**3.00**	**2.30**	**1.70**	**2.00**
Property transaction - purchase and sale	1.30	2.30	1.20	0.40	0.90	1.10
Property transaction - sale only	1.90	0.50	0.70	0.70	0.20	0.50
Property transaction - purchase only	1.40	0.60	0.80	0.90	0.40	0.40
Property transaction - other payments	0.20	0.30	0.30	0.20	0.10	0.10
Household maintenance and repair	**14.20**	**12.30**	**12.70**	**7.30**	**7.10**	**7.30**
Central heating maintenance and repair	1.50	1.80	1.50	1.20	0.60	0.70
House maintenance and repair	8.20	6.00	5.80	3.90	3.90	2.60
Paint, wallpaper, timber	2.60	1.40	2.20	1.60	1.60	1.80
Equipment hire, small materials	1.80	3.00	3.20	0.70	0.90	2.30
Household alterations and improvements	**74.70**	**37.40**	**37.80**	**18.20**	**18.10**	**15.50**
Central heating installation	2.40	2.40	1.70	0.70	2.00	1.10
DIY improvements: Double Glazing, Kitchen Units, Sheds etc.	18.80	0.80	4.10	1.80	1.20	2.10
Home improvements - contracted out	51.20	31.80	29.60	14.40	14.20	11.20
Bathroom fittings	0.20	1.50	0.80	1.20	0.30	0.60
Purchase of materials for Capital Improvements	2.10	1.00	1.60	0.10	0.40	0.50
Household insurances	**7.10**	**6.90**	**6.40**	**4.80**	**7.00**	**4.70**
Structure	3.50	3.40	2.90	2.40	3.60	2.30
Contents	3.50	3.40	3.10	2.40	3.30	2.30
Household appliances	0.10	0.10	0.40	0.10	0.10	0.10
Housing expenditure	**249.70**	**196.40**	**180.20**	**128.20**	**123.00**	**114.40**
Total expenditure[1]	**1217.30**	**1052.90**	**865.60**	**599.10**	**653.40**	**603.10**

1 This total includes all categories recorded in the EFS, including those outside the 'COICOP' total expenditure

Table **1.5** (cont.)

Housing expenditure by socio-economic class of household reference person, 2003-04

Average weekly household expenditure (£)

	Semi-routine	Routine	Long-term unemployed	Students	Occupation not stated & not classifiable	All groups
Grossed number of households (thousands)	2,500	2,328	492	306	6,085	24,670
Total number of households in sample	730	690	157	83	1,682	7,048
Total number of persons in sample	1,908	1,852	460	205	2,568	16,965
Total number of adults in sample	1,295	1,280	251	169	2,546	12,617
Weighted average number of persons per household	2.6	2.6	2.8	2.4	1.5	2.4
Primary dwelling						
Rent	**37.20**	**31.70**	**68.10**	**82.50**	**18.50**	**23.50**
Gross rent	37.20	31.70	68.10	82.50	18.40	23.50
less housing benefit, rebates and allowances received	19.90	19.20	58.00	13.20	12.90	10.20
Net rent	17.40	12.50	10.10	69.30	5.50	13.2
Mortgage	**21.30**	**24.30**	**2.70**	**6.50**	**1.40**	**38.80**
Mortgage interest payments	13.80	16.20	2.00	4.70	1.00	24.20
Mortgage protection premiums	1.40	1.20	0.10	0.20	0.00	1.50
Capital repayment of mortgage	6.10	6.90	0.50	1.60	0.30	13.1
Outright purchase, including deposits	**0.00**	**0.00**	**0.00**	**0.00**	**0.00**	**0.50**
Secondary dwelling	**2.10**	**0.40**	**0.00**	**0.10**	**1.00**	**5.10**
Rent	0.00	0.00	0.00	0.00	0.00	0.00
Council tax, mortgage, insurance (secondary dwelling)	0.10	0.10	0.00	0.10	1.00	0.70
Purchase of second dwelling	2.00	0.30	0.00	0.00	0.00	4.30
Charges	**16.80**	**15.70**	**8.10**	**7.80**	**18.30**	**20.20**
Council tax, domestic rates	11.40	10.70	3.10	2.90	12.80	14.70
Water charges	4.60	4.70	4.60	4.10	4.20	4.80
Other regular housing payments, including service charge for rent	0.50	0.30	0.40	0.80	1.30	0.70
Refuse collection, including skip hire	0.20	0.00	0.00	0.00	0.00	0.10
Moving house	**1.20**	**1.40**	**0.00**	**0.20**	**1.10**	**2.00**
Property transaction - purchase and sale	0.60	0.50	0.00	0.00	0.70	0.90
Property transaction - sale only	0.30	0.30	0.00	0.00	0.20	0.50
Property transaction - purchase only	0.30	0.60	0.00	0.10	0.10	0.50
Property transaction - other payments	0.10	0.00	0.00	0.10	0.10	0.10
Household maintenance and repair	**3.40**	**8.30**	**1.70**	**2.60**	**5.70**	**8.20**
Central heating maintenance and repair	0.40	0.70	0.00	0.70	1.30	1.10
House maintenance and repair	1.40	5.60	0.60	1.80	3.40	4.20
Paint, wallpaper, timber	1.20	1.30	0.80	0.10	0.50	1.40
Equipment hire, small materials	0.50	0.80	0.20	0.00	0.50	1.50
Household alterations and improvements	**8.20**	**18.00**	**1.10**	**1.10**	**12.20**	**22.80**
Central heating installation	0.70	1.10	0.00	0.00	0.60	1.20
DIY improvements: Double Glazing, Kitchen Units, Sheds etc.	0.60	3.00	0.20	0.00	2.20	3.00
Home improvements - contracted out	6.50	12.10	0.80	1.10	8.30	17.10
Bathroom fittings	0.20	1.50	0.00	0.00	0.60	0.70
Purchase of materials for Capital Improvements	0.20	0.20	0.10	0.00	0.50	0.70
Household insurances	**3.40**	**3.40**	**0.90**	**1.70**	**3.60**	**4.80**
Structure	1.50	1.50	0.40	0.40	1.70	2.30
Contents	1.70	1.70	0.50	1.40	1.70	2.40
Household appliances	0.20	0.20	0.00	0.00	0.10	0.20
Housing expenditure	**73.80**	**83.90**	**24.60**	**89.30**	**48.80**	**115.60**
Total expenditure[1]	**434.60**	**425.90**	**220.80**	**407.80**	**272.10**	**591.90**

1 This total includes all categories recorded in the EFS, including those outside the 'COICOP' total expenditure

Table **1.6**

Expenditure on rent by renters, 2001-02 to 2003-04

	2001-02		2002-03		2003-04	
	£[1]	% of total expenditure	£[1]	% of total expenditure	£[1]	% of total expenditure
Grossed number of households (thousands)	7,090		6,953		7,128	
Total number of households in sample	2,162		1,970		2,018	
Total number of persons in sample	5,061		4,493		4,534	
Total number of adults in sample	3,446		3,103		3,179	
Weighted average number of persons per household	2.3		2.3		2.2	
Total expenditure for renters	**370.90**		**330.20**		**346.30**	
Rent	**74.10**	*20*	**75.60**	*23*	**81.20**	*23*
Gross rent	74.10	*20*	75.60	*23*	81.20	*23*
less housing benefit, rebates and allowances received	30.50	*8*	32.90	*10*	35.40	*10*
Net rent	43.60	*12*	42.70	*13*	45.80	*13*

1 Average weekly household expenditure

Table **1.7**

Expenditure on mortgages by mortgage holders, 2001-02 to 2003-04

	2001-02		2002-03		2003-04	
	£[1]	% of total expenditure	£[1]	% of total expenditure	£[1]	% of total expenditure
Grossed number of households (thousands)	10,071		9,954		9,814	
Total number of households in sample	3,133		2,810		2,838	
Total number of persons in sample	8,915		7,951		8,186	
Total number of adults in sample	6,199		5,516		5,570	
Weighted average number of persons per household	2.8		2.8		2.8	
Total expenditure for mortgage payers	**962.60**		**816.10**		**864.60**	
Mortgage	**88.20**	*9*	**90.60**	*11*	**97.20**	*11*
Mortgage interest payments	59.50	*6*	59.60	*7*	60.50	*7*
Mortgage protection premiums	3.00	*0*	3.30	*0*	3.80	*0*
Capital repayment of mortgage	25.70	*3*	27.70	*3*	32.90	*4*

1 Average weekly household expenditure

Table **1.8**

Expenditure on rent and mortgages by renters and mortgage holders by gross income decile group, 2003-04

Average weekly household expenditure (£)

	Gross income decile group										
	1	2	3	4	5	6	7	8	9	10	All
Primary dwelling											
Grossed number of households (thousands)	1,641	1,280	1,010	774	660	502	396	358	272	236	7,128
Total number of households in sample	466	376	304	224	188	143	111	91	66	49	2,018
Total number of persons in sample	642	722	689	551	551	425	339	269	200	146	4,534
Total number of adults in sample	517	480	461	360	368	281	236	202	159	115	3,179
Weighted average number of persons per household	1.4	1.9	2.2	2.3	2.8	2.9	3.0	2.9	3.0	3.0	2.2
Rent by renters	**71.20**	**71.40**	**72.50**	**71.80**	**79.50**	**82.10**	**95.60**	**101.10**	**106.60**	**190.40**	**81.20**
Gross rent	71.20	71.40	72.50	71.80	79.50	82.10	95.60	101.10	106.60	190.40	81.20
less housing benefit, rebates & allowances rec'd	59.10	49.80	43.60	27.90	20.70	10.60	6.60	3.30	2.00	10.00	35.40
Net rent	12.10	21.70	28.90	43.90	58.70	71.60	89.00	97.80	104.60	180.50	45.80
Grossed number of households (thousands)	157	190	363	590	827	1,228	1,476	1,606	1,671	1,704	9,814
Total number of households in sample	48	57	110	180	253	362	435	459	467	467	2,838
Total number of persons in sample	68	105	226	348	643	1,011	1,267	1,444	1,495	1,579	8,186
Total number of adults in sample	58	79	165	272	423	665	854	952	1,021	1,081	5,570
Weighted average number of persons per household	1.3	1.8	2.0	1.9	2.5	2.7	2.8	3.0	3.1	3.3	2.8
Mortgage by mortgage holders	**76.50**	**39.50**	**48.50**	**64.90**	**67.50**	**71.70**	**86.00**	**94.90**	**108.60**	**160.60**	**97.20**
Mortgage interest payments	50.90	27.40	34.40	44.40	42.80	46.30	53.80	57.70	66.90	97.20	60.50
Mortgage protection premiums	2.00	1.00	1.60	2.50	3.00	3.80	4.00	4.40	4.20	4.50	3.80
Capital repayment of mortgage	23.60	11.20	12.50	18.00	21.70	21.60	28.20	32.80	37.50	58.90	32.90

Table **1.9**

Expenditure on rent and mortgages by renters and mortgage holders by UK Countries and Government Office Regions, 2003-04

Average weekly household expenditure (£)

	North East	North West	Yorks & the Humber	East Midlands	West Midlands	East	London
Primary dwelling							
Grossed number of households (thousands)	332	841	641	454	614	582	1,135
Total number of households in sample	97	217	173	125	163	154	255
Total number of persons in sample	216	470	375	278	389	360	602
Total number of adults in sample	144	323	280	200	261	262	418
Weighted average number of persons per household	2.1	2.1	2.1	2.1	2.3	2.3	2.4
Rent for renters	**62.90**	**74.20**	**65.20**	**69.10**	**72.60**	**80.60**	**120.00**
Gross rent	62.90	74.20	65.20	69.10	72.60	80.60	120.00
less housing benefit, rebates and allowances received	41.70	38.10	29.70	33.80	33.90	31.90	40.40
Net rent	21.20	36.10	35.50	35.20	38.80	48.70	79.70
Grossed number of households (thousands)	403	1,187	842	741	837	927	1,023
Total number of households in sample	115	304	237	212	225	246	226
Total number of persons in sample	319	821	661	603	679	708	631
Total number of adults in sample	221	580	450	419	452	493	439
Weighted average number of persons per household	2.7	2.7	2.7	2.8	3.0	2.8	2.8
Mortgage for mortgage holders	**57.80**	**80.20**	**73.70**	**88.30**	**94.10**	**115.30**	**133.90**
Mortgage interest payments	39.20	49.70	48.40	52.50	58.30	68.00	87.60
Mortgage protection premiums	3.30	3.60	3.00	3.40	3.80	4.00	4.30
Capital repayment of mortgage	15.30	26.90	22.30	32.40	32.00	43.30	42.00

Average weekly household expenditure (£)

	South East	South West	England	Wales	Scotland	Northern Ireland	United Kingdom
Primary dwelling							
Grossed number of households (thousands)	774	558	5,930	312	703	183	7,128
Total number of households in sample	206	170	1,560	98	183	177	2,018
Total number of persons in sample	462	369	3,521	243	382	388	4,534
Total number of adults in sample	335	257	2,480	150	274	275	3,179
Weighted average number of persons per household	2.1	2.1	2.2	2.3	2.1	2.2	2.2
Rent for renters	**104.00**	**76.10**	**85.50**	**61.90**	**58.90**	**59.60**	**81.20**
Gross rent	104.00	76.10	85.50	61.90	58.90	59.60	81.20
less housing benefit, rebates and allowances received	36.10	34.70	35.90	34.80	32.00	32.50	35.40
Net rent	67.90	41.40	49.60	27.10	26.90	27.10	45.80
Grossed number of households (thousands)	1,440	848	8,248	454	852	260	9,814
Total number of households in sample	399	259	2,223	148	218	249	2,838
Total number of persons in sample	1,183	743	6,348	445	610	783	8,186
Total number of adults in sample	787	514	4,355	287	430	498	5,570
Weighted average number of persons per household	2.8	2.8	2.8	2.9	2.8	3.2	2.8
Mortgage for mortgage holders	**119.20**	**109.50**	**101.00**	**82.40**	**75.50**	**73.70**	**97.20**
Mortgage interest payments	74.80	64.40	62.80	53.60	46.10	45.70	60.50
Mortgage protection premiums	4.10	4.10	3.80	4.10	3.60	4.60	3.80
Capital repayment of mortgage	40.30	41.00	34.40	24.70	25.80	23.40	32.90

Children's Expenditure

Chapter 2

Background

EFS has been collecting data from children (aged 7 to 15) since 1995-96. These data have been incorporated into household expenditure tables in Family Spending since 1998-99.

This analysis looks at children's spending data from 2002-03 and 2003-04, collected from 4,167 children aged 7 to 15 years. Children are asked to record everything that they buy with their own money for themselves or for others, in a young person's expenditure diary. They are asked to exclude items bought for other people with other people's money. Two years data were used to increase the sample size.

All children aged 7 to 15 years in the households selected to participate in the EFS were asked to complete a diary. In 2002-03 and 2003-04, a total of 4,336 children in the UK were invited to complete a diary and 4,167 did so, giving a response rate of 96 per cent. As an incentive, children are given a £5 payment upon return of a completed diary.

Reporting on Children's Expenditure

This is the only part of Family Spending where EFS results are reported unweighted. As this chapter looks at spending of children as a group overall, rather than looking at expenditure by households, household weights cannot be applied to the data.

When reporting children's expenditure on food and drinks, purchases have been collated into two groups, those of 'confectionery, snacks and drinks' and those grouped together as 'other food purchases'. The category of 'other food purchases' contains any spending on takeaway meals or school dinners, this will include food purchased at school, in shops or takeaways which does not fall into the category of 'confectionery, drinks and snacks'.

It has not been possible to extract the exact amount spent on school dinners in any further detail as we currently do not ask households the number and frequency of children purchasing school dinners or taking packed lunches to school with them. We also do not currently ask parents to state the amount that

Table **2.1**

Percentage distribution of children's expenditure[1]: by gender, age and type of purchase, 2002-03 to 2003-04 combined

United Kingdom   Per cent

	7 to 9			10 to 12			13 to 15			All		
	Males	Females	All	Males	Females	All	Males	Females	All	Males	Females	Children
Confectionery, snacks and drinks	18	21	20	21	21	21	17	15	16	18	18	18
Other food purchases (inc. takeaways & school dinners)	16	16	16	20	18	19	19	16	18	19	17	18
Clothing and footwear	8	10	9	6	17	12	13	25	19	10	20	15
Personal care	1	2	1	1	3	2	1	6	3	1	4	3
Magazines, newspapers, books and stationery	6	10	8	6	7	7	3	5	4	5	6	6
Music	2	4	3	3	3	3	6	5	5	4	4	4
Other entertainment (videos, DVDs)	2	2	2	2	1	2	2	1	1	2	1	2
Games, toys, hobbies, pets	35	17	26	23	8	15	14	3	8	20	7	13
of which: computer software and games*	15	4	9	10	2	6	10	0	5	11	1	6
Sporting and cultural activities	6	7	7	7	7	7	8	6	7	8	6	7
Travel	1	0	1	2	2	2	3	3	3	3	2	2
Mobile phones and charges	0	1	1	2	3	3	5	7	6	3	5	4
Other expenditure	4	10	7	6	10	8	8	10	9	7	10	9
All expenditure (=100%)	100	100	100	100	100	100	100	100	100	100	100	100
Total number of children in sample	662	679	1341	691	723	1414	700	712	1412	2053	2114	4167

1 Children aged 7 to 15

* Computer software and games is a sub-category of games, toys, hobbies and pets and therefore is not included when calculating total expenditure

Table **2.2**

Children's expenditure[1]: by gender, age and type of purchase, 2002-03 to 2003-04 combined

United Kingdom   £ per week

	7 to 9			10 to 12			13 to 15			All		
	Males	Females	All	Males	Females	All	Males	Females	All	Males	Females	Children
Confectionery, snacks and drinks	1.30	1.50	1.40	2.20	2.40	2.30	3.20	3.20	3.20	2.30	2.40	2.30
Other food purchases												
(inc. takeaways & school dinners)	1.10	1.20	1.10	2.10	2.10	2.10	3.80	3.40	3.60	2.30	2.20	2.30
Clothing and footwear	0.50	0.70	0.60	0.70	2.00	1.30	2.50	5.30	3.90	1.20	2.70	2.00
Personal care	0.00	0.10	0.10	0.10	0.40	0.30	0.20	1.20	0.70	0.10	0.60	0.30
Magazines, newspapers, books and stationery	0.40	0.70	0.60	0.70	0.90	0.80	0.60	1.10	0.90	0.60	0.90	0.70
Music	0.10	0.30	0.20	0.30	0.40	0.30	1.20	1.00	1.10	0.60	0.50	0.60
Other entertainment (videos, DVDs)	0.10	0.20	0.20	0.20	0.10	0.20	0.40	0.20	0.30	0.30	0.20	0.20
Games, toys, hobbies, pets	2.40	1.20	1.80	2.50	0.90	1.70	2.60	0.50	1.60	2.50	0.90	1.70
*of which: computer software and games**	*1.00*	*0.30*	*0.60*	*1.10*	*0.20*	*0.70*	*1.80*	*0.10*	*1.00*	*1.30*	*0.20*	*0.80*
Sporting and cultural activities	0.40	0.50	0.50	0.80	0.80	0.80	1.60	1.20	1.40	0.90	0.80	0.90
Travel	0.10	0.00	0.00	0.30	0.30	0.30	0.60	0.60	0.60	0.30	0.30	0.30
Mobile phones and charges	0.00	0.10	0.10	0.20	0.40	0.30	0.90	1.50	1.20	0.40	0.70	0.50
Other expenditure	0.30	0.70	0.50	0.70	1.10	0.90	1.60	2.20	1.90	0.90	1.40	1.10
All expenditure (£ per week)[2]	6.80	7.20	7.00	10.80	11.70	11.30	19.30	21.50	20.40	12.40	13.60	13.00
Total number of children in sample	662	679	1341	691	723	1414	700	712	1412	2053	2114	4167

1 Children aged 7 to 15
2 Rounded to the nearest 10p
* Computer software and games is a sub-category of games, toys, hobbies and pets and therefore is not included when calculating total expenditure

they spend on school dinners for each child. As a consequence of the EFS being a household expenditure survey, there is a limit to the level of detail that can be extracted from the data at a personal level. However in due course, as alterations are made to the survey instruments to contribute to the ongoing attempts to improve quality, some of these issues may well be addressed.

Expenditure on 'computer software and games', while reported independently in this chapter, is included within expenditure on 'games, toys, hobbies and pets' totals, in all the charts and tables, see Figure 2.8 for more information.

Results

Average expenditure of all children

On average, children spent £13.00 per week in 2002-03 and 2003-04. Girls spent £13.60, compared to boys, who spent £12.40. Table 2.1 shows the percentage spent on various items, by children aged 7 to 9, 10 to 12 and 13 to 15. The top four categories that children spent their money on were 'confectionery, snacks and drinks', 'other food purchases',

'clothing and footwear' and 'games, toys, hobbies and pets'. Confectionery, snacks and drinks were amongst the top three choices for all age groups, regardless of gender.

Table 2.2 details the weekly expenditure by boys and girls on the different types of purchases. On average girls spent more than boys at all ages. Children between the ages of 7 and 9, spent an average of £7.00 per week, with boys spending £6.80 and girls £7.20. Those aged between 10 and 12 spent on average £11.30 each week. Again girls spent more than boys, spending £11.70 compared to boys who spent £10.80. Teenage girls (aged between 13 and 15) spent £21.50 per week and boys of the same age spent £19.30, producing an average spend for this age group of £20.40 per week.

Spending by all children aged 7 to 9, 10 to 12 and 13 to 15

Figures 2.1 to 2.3 (overleaf) show the spending of all children, within each age group, by gender. Figure 2.1 shows the spending of children aged 7 to 9. For many categories of expenditure at this age, the differences in spending between genders is not very noticeable. Girls spent slightly more than

Figure 2.1

Expenditure on selected items by gender for 7 to 9 year olds, 2002-03 to 2003-04

£ per week

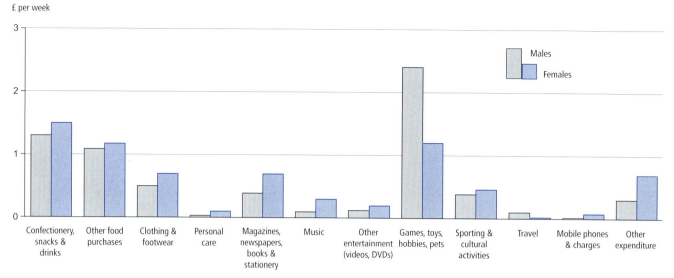

boys on most things, except travel (10p per week by boys, less than 10p by girls) and games, toys, hobbies and pets where boys spent substantially more, £2.40 each week which is twice as much as the £1.20 spent by girls of this age.

Figure 2.2 shows the amount spent per week by 10 to 12 year old children. Spending patterns are similar to the younger age group, with the one exception of girls' spending on clothing and footwear which has seen a sharp increase. Girls in this age group spent £2.00 per week on clothing and footwear, more than twice as much as the 70p weekly spent by boys. In contrast, boys spending was over twice as large as girls' on games, toys, hobbies and pets, £2.50 compared to 90p. The only other things that boys and girls in this age group, spent more than £2.00 per week on was confectionery, snacks and

drinks (£2.40 by girls, £2.20 by boys) and other food purchases (£2.10 by boys and girls).

Figure 2.3 shows the amount spent by teenagers, aged 13 to 15, each week. By this age children's spending was slightly different, boys and girls spent the same amount on confectionery, snacks and drinks (£3.20 per week) and on travel (60p per week). However, boys were now spending more than girls in five categories of expenditure: other food purchases; music; other entertainment; games, toys, hobbies and pets and sporting and cultural activities. Girls were still spending more than boys in the remaining five categories: clothing and footwear; personal care; magazines, newspapers, books and stationery; mobile phones and charges and other expenditure.

Figure 2.2

Expenditure on selected items by gender for 10 to 12 year olds, 2002-03 to 2003-04

£ per week

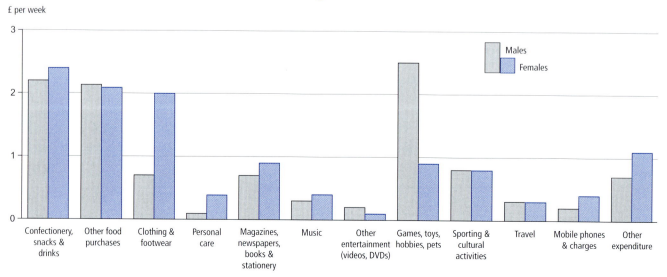

Figure 2.3

Expenditure on selected items by gender for 13 to 15 year olds, 2002-03 to 2003-04

£ per week

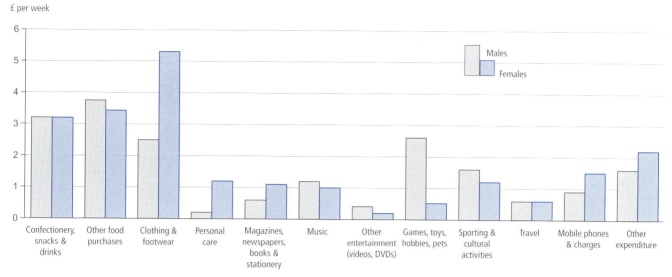

Boys' spending

Figure 2.4 shows the percentage distribution of boys expenditure on the different types of purchases by age group (7 to 9, 10 to 12 and 13 to 15 years). It shows that older boys spent less as a proportion of total spending on games, toys, hobbies and pets (36%, 23% and 14% in each age group). It also shows that older boys spent a greater percentage of their money on other food purchases (16%, 20% and 20%); music (2%, 3% and 6%) and mobile phones and charges (0.3%, 2% and 5%).

Figure 2.5 (overleaf) shows the percentage spent by boys of different ages on food, appearance, entertainment products, entertainment activities, travel, mobile phones and other

spending. Food (confectionery, snacks, drinks and other food purchases) and entertainment activities (toys, games, hobbies and pets, and sport and culture) accounted for over half of all spending by boys at all ages.

Girls' spending

Figure 2.6 (overleaf) details the percentage distribution of girls expenditure on the different types of purchases by age groups, 7 to 9, 10 to 12 and 13 to 15 years. It shows that older girls spent proportionately more on takeaway meals (8%, 10% and 11%), clothing and footwear (10%, 17% and 25%) and mobile phones and charges (1%, 3% and 7%).

Figure 2.4

Percentage of total expenditure on selected items by age for boys, 2002-03 to 2003-04

Per cent

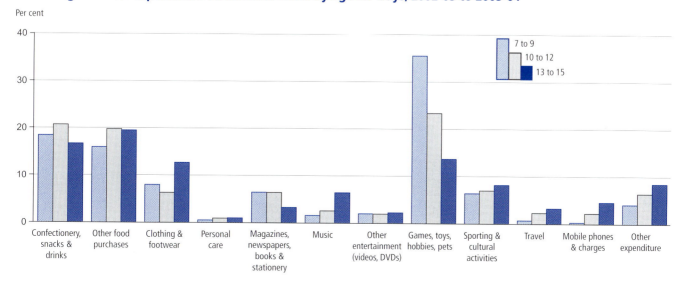

Figure 2.5

Percentage of total expenditure on selected categories by boys, 2002-03 to 2003-04

Per cent

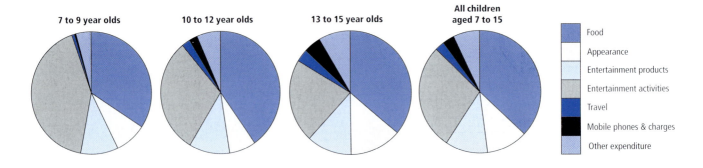

Figure 2.7 details the percentage spend of girls in each age group on food, appearance, entertainment products, entertainment activities, travel, mobile phones and all other spending. Food (confectionery, snacks, drinks and other food) and appearance (clothing, footwear and personal care) accounted for the two most popular areas of girls' spending. Seven to 9 year olds spent almost half their money (49 per cent) on these items (37 per cent on food and 11 per cent on appearance), 10 to 12 year olds spent 59 per cent on them (38 per cent on food and 20 per cent on appearance) and teenage girls aged 13 to 15 spent 61 per cent of their available money on these items, approximately half of which was spent on food (31 per cent) and half of which was spent on appearance (30 per cent).

Gender differences in spending by age

Figure 2.8 combines male and female spending by age on games, toys, hobbies and pets with spending on computer

software and games. Spending on computer software and games is one type of spending within the games, toys, hobbies and pets category of expenditure and it accounted for a large proportion of boys spending. Teenage boys (aged 13 to 15) spent 14 per cent of their available money on games, toys, hobbies and pets and 68 per cent of this spending was accounted for by computer software and games. However, younger boys (aged 7 to 12 years) spent 43 per cent of the money that they spent on the toy category in general, on computer games and software.

Older girls spent less on toys overall and they also spent smaller proportions of their expenditure on computer software and games. Girls aged 7 to 9 spent 27 per cent of the money that they spent on games, toys, hobbies and pets on computer software and games, yet for 10 to 12 year old girls it accounted for only 25 per cent of their toy spending and even less for teenage girls aged 13 to 15, for whom it counted for 20 per cent of their spending on toys.

Figure 2.6

Percentage of total expenditure on selected items by age for girls, 2002-03 to 2003-04

Per cent

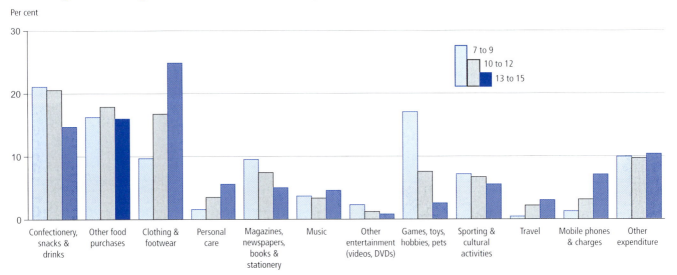

Figure **2.7**

Percentage of total expenditure on selected categories by girls, 2002-03 to 2003-04

Per cent

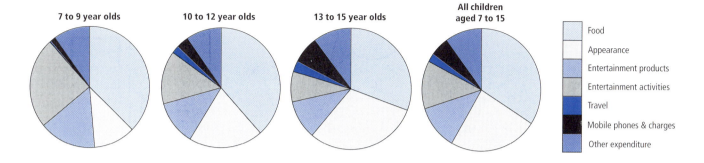

Figure 2.9 shows children's expenditure on clothing and footwear by age and gender. It shows that as children got older, girls spent substantially more in this category than boys. Girls aged 7 to 9 spent 70p per week on clothing and footwear, this more than doubled to £2.00 when aged 10 to 12 and this figure more than doubled again to £5.30 per week by 13 to 15 years of age. Boys spending is similar in the younger age groups, 50p of 7 to 9 year olds and 70p of 10 to 12 year olds spending per week, however this increased to £2.50 amongst 13 to 15 year olds.

Table 2.3 looks in some detail at children's spending in the category 'sporting and cultural activities'. It shows that overall boys use the largest amount of their money spent in this category (29 per cent) on participant sports, whereas girls tended to spend their money on club or disco entrance fees (27 per cent).

Boys aged 7 to 9 and 10 to 12 spent 34 per cent of the money they spend on sports and culture, on participant sports such as rugby, football, hockey, karate and swimming, this decreased to 26 per cent amongst 13 to 15 year olds. However, older boys spent more on bicycles and bicycle accessories (0 per cent of 7 to 9 year olds, 10 per cent of 10 to 12 years olds and 16 per cent of 13 to 15 year old boys' sports and culture spending).

Girls aged 7 to 9 spent their money on fees for leisure classes (eg dancing, music, art and horse riding lessons) which accounted for 38 per cent of their sports and culture spending and on club or disco entrance fees, 28 per cent. Girls spending on leisure classes decreased with age (26 per cent of spending in this category when aged 10 to 12, compared with only 6 per cent when aged 13 to 15). Girls spending on club or disco entrance fees appears to account for a large proportion of their sports and cultural activities spending at all ages, 28 per cent when aged 7 to 9, down to 19 per cent when aged 10 to 12 and rising again to 32 per cent when aged 13 to 15 years.

Figure **2.8**

Expenditure on games, toys, hobbies & pets and on computer software & games by age and gender, 2002-03 to 2003-04

£ per week

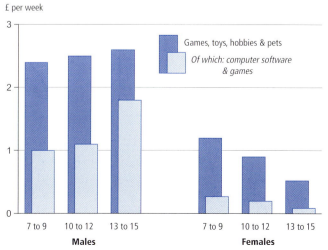

Figure **2.9**

Expenditure on clothing & footwear by age and gender, 2002-03 to 2003-04

£ per week

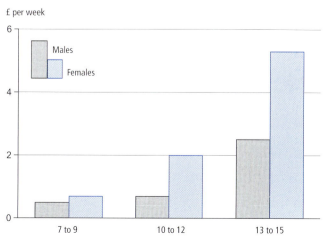

Table **2.3**

Percentage distribution of children's expenditure on sport and culture: by gender, age and type of purchase, 2002-03 to 2003-04 combined

United Kingdom   Per cent

	7 to 9		10 to 12		13 to 15		All	
	Males	Females	Males	Females	Males	Females	Males	Females
Musical instruments	0	1	1	2	6	0	4	1
Spectator sports	2	0	5	0	6	2	5	1
Partictpant sports	34	9	34	21	26	19	29	17
Sport club subscriptions	9	1	9	2	3	2	6	2
Fees for leisure classes	12	38	3	26	5	6	6	19
Cinema	7	7	9	9	18	22	14	15
Live entertainment	1	1	1	4	3	6	2	4
Entrance fee for theme parks, museums, zoos etc	0	1	0	2	1	1	1	1
Club or disco entrance fee	19	28	21	19	11	32	15	27
Social events eg youth club	4	2	3	2	2	1	2	2
Subscription fees for leisure activities eg scouts/brownies	6	7	1	5	0	0	1	3
Photography	0	1	0	4	0	4	0	3
Miscellaneous betting eg tombola, lucky dip	4	3	4	3	2	2	3	3
Bicycles and bicycle accessories	0	1	10	0	16	0	12	1
Other	2	0	0	0	0	0	0	0
All expenditure (=100%)	100	100	100	100	100	100	100	100
Total number of instances in sample	57761	71281	105138	113829	221470	169498	384369	354608

1 Children aged 7 to 15.

Equivalalised Income

Chapter 3

Background

This chapter introduces equivalisation into Family Spending. It describes the methodology used and its impact on EFS data. Equivalisation has been incorporated into Family Spending this year in response to requests from users of the data. Equivalisation is a standard methodology that adjusts the total annual income of a household to account for differing demands on resources, by considering the household size and composition. This is the only chapter of the current edition of Family Spending that presents equivalised income data; all other tables and figures in the publication use non-equivalised income data. This chapter presents a selection of tables and charts using equivalised income data, and other tables included within Family Spending are available on an equivalised income basis on request from ONS (see page xiii Introduction).

Equivalisation Methodology

An adjustment often made when seeking to establish the impact of costs on household budgets, is to equivalise household incomes by taking account of household size and composition. The McClements (1977) and the Modified OECD scales are typically used for such equivalisation.

The process reflects the common sense notion that a household of five will need a higher income than a single person living alone to enjoy a comparable standard of living. It takes into account both the greater income needs of larger households and the economies of scale achieved when people live together because household resources, especially housing, can be shared. By adjusting income in this way it is possible to make sensible income comparisons between households of different sizes and compositions.

There are several equivalisation scales, the most widely used being the McClements and the Modified OECD. Following consultation with a group of the main EFS users, it was decided to use the McClements (Before Housing Costs) Scale for this report as this is currently the most commonly used by ONS. However tables using the Modified OECD scale are also available on request.

The process of equivalisation utilises a scale which weights each household member, and compares the total income of that household against that of a childless cohabiting/married couple. The scale takes childless, two adult households as standard (that is, they are weighted by 1) and scales up the income of households with fewer people and scales down the income of households with more people. The weight applied to each additional adult has a decreasing value and children's weights are also applied on a sliding scale according to age.

The logic behind this is that the additional cost of adding another adult to the household decreases and that children have lower costs than adults dependent upon their age.

McClements Equivalence Scale (Before Housing Costs)

Position of household member	Equivalence value
Cohabiting head of household	0.61
Partner/Spouse	0.39
1st additional adult	0.42
Subsequent adults	0.36
Single head of household	0.61
1st additional adult	0.46
2nd additional adult	0.42
Subsequent adults	0.36
Child aged: 16-18	0.36
13-15	0.27
11-12	0.25
8-10	0.23
5-7	0.21
2-4	0.18
Under 2	0.09

Equivalised income is calculated by firstly assigning an equivalence value from the McClements Equivalence Scale to each household member. These individual values are then summed to give a total equivalence number for the household. The household disposable income is then divided by this total equivalence number to produce the equivalised disposable income.

Equivalisation increases relatively the incomes of single person households (since their incomes are divided by values less than 1) and reduces incomes of households with three or more persons (since their incomes are divided by values greater than 1).

For example, if a household consisting of a married couple with three children (aged three, nine and eleven) has an income of £20,000, their equivalised household size is 0.61 + 0.39 + 0.18 + 0.23 + 0.25 = 1.66. This implies they need 66 per cent more income than a couple with no children to have the same standard of living. Their equivalised income would therefore be £20,000/1.66 = £12,048.

A household consisting of one-person with an income of £20,000 has an equivalised household size of 0.61 and an equivalised income of £20,000/0.61=£32,787.

A further consequence of using equivalised income measures is that the amounts shown in the tables do not accord with the amounts that households actually receive, but are the amounts that they would need to have the same standard of living as a cohabiting/married couple with no children receiving that amount.

Results

Equivalised household incomes were calculated for each EFS household in 2003-04 using the McClements Equivalence Scale. Household equivalised incomes were then ranked in ascending order and divided into deciles, with households having the lowest equivalised income in the first decile. All individuals in the household were then allocated to the equivalised income decile to which their household had been allocated. Some tables (3.2E, 3.3E and 3.2, 3.3) show ten income groups (deciles) and some (3.4E to 3.10E and 3.4 to 3.10) show five income groups (quintiles), all have an equal number of households in each group.

In 2003-04 the income deciles shown in Tables 3.2 and 3.2E (household expenditure by gross income and gross equivalised income decile group in £ per week) were as follows:

Income decile	Gross weekly equivalised income	Gross weekly income
1	Up to £123	Up to £166
2	£124 to £192	£167 to £220
3	£193 to £262	£221 to £284
4	£263 to £350	£285 to £350
5	£351 to £444	£351 to £425
6	£445 to £557	£426 to £505
7	£558 to £672	£506 to £602
8	£672 to £827	£603 to £732
9	£828 to £1091	£733 to £970
10	£1092 and over	£971 and over

Household composition by income groups

To assess the impact that the scale has on the composition of households in the lowest and highest income groups, Table 3.1 shows the household composition in each income decile group by equivalised and gross (i.e. non-equivalised or recorded) income. Equivalisation slightly changed the distribution of income by household types, from that depicted by gross incomes.

The biggest change was among lone retired households which predominated in the lowest gross household income deciles but after equivalisation made up a much lower percentage. For example, over two fifths (45 per cent) of the lowest gross income decile group consisted of one-person retired households, whereas after equivalisation these retired households made up only 10 per cent of the decile. It can be

seen that these households moved up the income distribution by the process of equivalisation; one-person retired households were only 13 per cent of the fourth gross income decile but increased to 19 per cent of the fourth decile after income was equivalised and they accounted for 10 per cent of equivalised income in the fifth decile, compared to 5 per cent of gross income. This trend continued in the remaining deciles, there were twice as many one-person retired households in all other equivalised income deciles, compared to gross income deciles: 7 per cent in the sixth and seventh equivalised deciles, compared to 2 per cent in the gross income deciles; 4 per cent in the eighth equivalised income decile, 1 per cent in the eighth gross income decile and these households made up 3 per cent of both the ninth and final tenth decile when looking at equivalised income, there are none of these households in the corresponding ninth and tenth gross income deciles.

The overall spread of two adult households with one or more children also changed with equivalisation. These two adult households with children made up a lower proportion of deciles in the bottom half of the gross income distribution (i.e. in the five lowest deciles), than after equivalisation. Conversely, at the other end of the distribution, two adult households with children decreased as a proportion of each decile after equivalisation. For example, the percentage of two adult households with children increased from 2 per cent of the lowest gross income decile to 13 per cent of the lowest equivalised income decile, and in the top decile fell from 32 per cent to 18 per cent after equivalisation.

As discussed above, equivalisation tends to increase relatively the incomes of single person households and to reduce incomes of households with three or more persons and so these changes were expected.

Figures 3.1 and 3.2 (overleaf) show the distribution of households before and after income equivalisation by whether or not they have children. It can be seen that as gross income increased, the proportion of households with children increased: 15 per cent of the bottom gross income decile consisted of households with children increasing to 44 per cent of the top gross income decile (Figure 3.1). The pattern was somewhat different after equivalisation: the decile with the highest proportion of households with children was the first (40.1 per cent), they fell to 17 per cent of the second decile, and then slowly increased to 40 per cent of the fifth decile. As equivalised income continued to increase, the proportion of each decile made up of households with children fell (Figure 3.2). Two characteristics of low income families (who are likely to be found in the lowest income decile) are: lone parent (twice

Figure **3.1**

Percentage of household with children in each gross income decile group, 2003-04

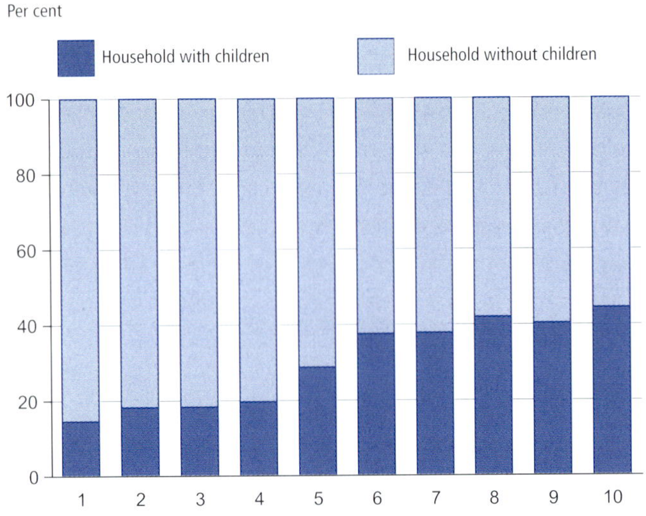

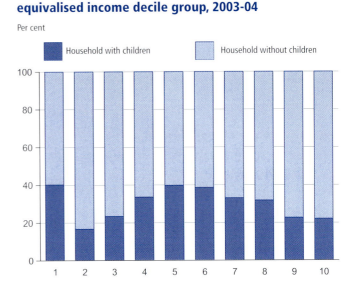

Figure **3.2**

Percentage of household with children in each equivalised income decile group, 2003-04

as likely as those in couples) and four or more children (twice as likely as other families with children). This is evident in the equivalised income data where households consisting of one adult and two children, make up only 2 per cent of the first decile when considering gross income and yet account for 12 per cent of the first equivalised income decile.

The average number of persons per household is also shown in Table 3.1 for each income group. As gross income increased, the average number of people in each household also increased: the highest income group had more than twice the average household size of the lowest income group (3.2 people compared with 1.3 people). After income was equivalised the average number of people in each household was very similar over the income deciles (increasing from 2.2 in the lowest group, to 2.7 in the sixth decile group and then falling again to 2.2 in the highest income group).

Household expenditure by income

Tables 3.2E, 3.2, 3.3E and 3.3 show household expenditure on commodities and services. The figures include information from the expenditure diaries kept by adults and by children aged 7 to 15. Differences in spending may be the result of other factors as well as income, for example, household size, and so the tables show both gross income deciles and equivalised income deciles.

Generally, although expenditure on different commodities and services increased as income increased using both the measures of income, the effect was less marked when equivalised income was used (see Figure 3.3). In the lowest gross income decile,

households spent £139.60 on average a week, rising to £905.00 in the highest decile (see Table 3.2). In comparison, households in the lowest equivalised income decile spent £199.20 a week, rising to £777.50 on average in the highest equivalised income decile (Table 3.2E).

A similar pattern is shown when individual items of expenditure are looked at, spending on food and non-alcoholic drinks is compared in Figure 3.4. In the lowest gross income decile, households spent £21.40 on average a week on food and non-alcoholic drinks, rising to £67.80 a week in the highest decile (Table 3.2). In comparison, households in the lowest equivalised income decile spent £30.30 a week on food and non-alcoholic

Figure **3.3**

Total expenditure by gross and equivalised income decile group, 2003-04

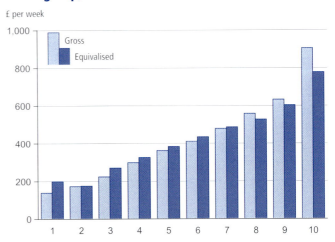

Figure **3.4**

Expenditure on food and non-alcoholic drink by gross and equivalised income decile group, 2003-04

£ per week

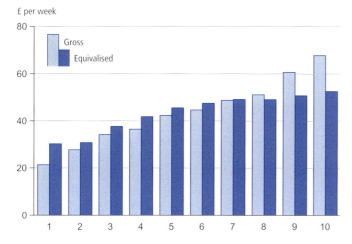

drink, rising to £52.50 on average in the highest equivalised income decile (Table 3.2E). The pattern is evident but less marked when expenditure on other individual items are considered.

There were also some notable differences in the expenditure patterns of households with different levels of equivalised income. Generally, overall total household expenditure increased as equivalised income increased, see Figure 3.3. However, expenditure in the lowest equivalised income decile was higher than that in the second decile: households in the lowest income decile spent, on average, £199.20 a week, compared with an average spend of £175.80 in the second decile and £270.60 in the third decile.

This difference may be explained by the large proportion of households with children found in the lowest equivalised income decile as described above. Alternatively this could be related to the tendency seen in gross income, where the lowest income decile appears to contain several households with a temporarily low income, where the household reference person has recently left work, either through redundancy or other reasons and they have a low income and maintain a high level of expenditure. It is also possible that this decile contains a number of households where the reference person is self-employed and reports a low income and high expenditure. Measurement of income for self-employed people is always difficult as their sources of income tend to be irregular and often unreported.

Table 3.3 shows that households in the bottom tenth of the equivalised income distribution spent nearly three tenths (29

per cent) of their expenditure on food and non-alcoholic drinks, and housing, fuel & power - a higher proportion than those households in the top decile of equivalised incomes (14 per cent of their total expenditure was on these items). Conversely, those with the highest equivalised incomes spent a greater proportion of their income on transport than those with lower equivalised incomes: 17 per cent of the expenditure of the highest decile of the equivalised income distribution was on transport compared with only 11 per cent of the expenditure of those respondents in the first decile group.

There was, however, very little difference in the distribution of the percentage of total expenditure spent on different goods and services when the two income distributions were considered (see Tables 3.3E and 3.3).

Household expenditure by household composition and income

Tables 3.4E to 3.9E and 3.4 to 3.9 show the expenditure of different household composition groups by equivalised income and gross income. It should be noted that the quintiles presented in these tables are calculated as described above and are the same for each household type. The figures are not shown for certain income composition groups, and others should be treated with caution as very few households fall into some of the categories.

Each of the tables shows a separate household type and presenting average expenditure on commodities and services by equivalised income quintiles has a different effect on these household types – having a larger effect among one-person non-retired households and two adult households with children than in other household types.

For example, the average amount spent on all expenditure items by one person non-retired households in the bottom fifth of the gross income distribution was £163.40 compared with an average £142.70 in the bottom fifth of the equivalised income distribution (see Tables 3.4E and 3.4). Similarly, among two adult households with children, the amount spent on all expenditure items was £253.60 on average in the bottom fifth of the gross income distribution compared with £305.60 in the bottom fifth of the equivalised income distribution (see Tables 3.5E and 3.5).

In contrast, the expenditure patterns of one person retired households mainly dependant on state pensions (Tables 3.6E and 3.6), two person non-retired households (Tables 3.7 and 3.7E), and two person retired households (Tables 3.8E, 3.8, 3.9E and 3.9) were not markedly different when using the two income measures.

Figure **3.5**

Sources of income by gross income quintile group, 2003-04

Per cent

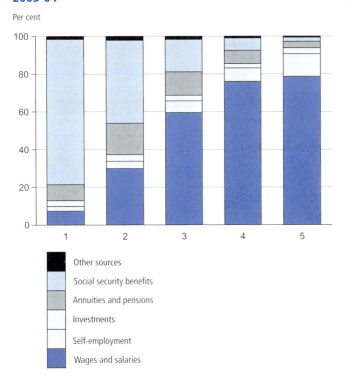

Other sources
Social security benefits
Annuities and pensions
Investments
Self-employment
Wages and salaries

Figure **3.6**

Sources of income by equivalised income quintile group, 2003-04

Per cent

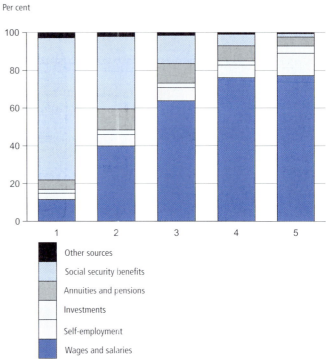

Other sources
Social security benefits
Annuities and pensions
Investments
Self-employment
Wages and salaries

Sources of income

Households receive income from a variety of sources, the main ones being earnings and self-employment, Social Security Benefits/Tax Credits, interest on investments and occupational pensions.

Tables 3.10E and 3.10 and Figures 3.5 and 3.6 show the distribution of gross income sources for each fifth, or quintile, of the population, ranked by gross household income and equivalised household income. The various sources of income are shown as a percentage of the total gross income of the quintile.

The principal source of income for about three quarters (77 per cent) of the lowest quintile gross income group was social security benefits. This did not change markedly when equivalised income was presented (75 per cent). The amount of income made up from wages and salaries was 7 per cent in the lowest gross income quintile, and 12 per cent in the lowest equivalised income quintile. Conversely, 9 per cent of income in the lowest gross income quintile was made up of annuities and pensions, compared with 5 per cent in the lowest equivalised income quintile. These differences largely reflect the fact that after equivalising income, the lowest quintile group contained fewer pensioner households.

Table **3.1**

Percentage of households by composition in each gross and equivalised income decile group, 2003-04

Per cent

	Income decile group									
	Lowest ten per cent		Second		Third		Fourth		Fifth	
	Gross	Equivalised	Gross	Equivalised	Gross	Equivalised	Gross	Equivalised	Gross	Equivalised
Lower boundary of group (£ per week)			124	167	193	221	263	285	351	351
Average size of household	1.3	2.2	1.6	1.9	1.9	2.2	1.9	2.4	2.4	2.6
One adult retired										
mainly dependent on state pensions[1]	26	6	15	23	2	10	0	3	0	1
One adult, other retired	18	4	28	20	18	16	13	15	5	9
One adult, non-retired	33	27	16	8	16	9	22	10	18	11
One adult, one child	10	11	3	2	3	3	6	4	3	4
One adult, two or more children	2	12	9	4	6	3	3	3	4	3
One man one woman										
mainly dependent on state pensions[1]	0	4	8	11	13	7	2	1	0	0
One man and one woman, other retired	0	2	3	7	14	16	22	15	18	15
One man and one woman, non-retired	6	11	8	8	11	10	16	11	18	14
One man and one woman, one child	1	5	2	2	3	2	3	6	7	9
One man and one woman, two children	1	4	2	3	3	6	3	11	9	13
One man and one woman, three children	0	3	0	1	2	3	1	4	2	4
Two adults, four or more children	0	1	0	1	0	2	1	1	0	1
Three adults	1	3	1	1	2	5	2	5	6	6
Three adults, one or more children	0	2	0	2	1	4	2	3	3	4
All other households without children	1	3	2	5	4	4	3	5	5	4
All other households with children	1	2	1	1	1	1	1	3	1	2

	Income decile group									
	Sixth		Seventh		Eighth		Ninth		Highest ten per cent	
	Gross	Equivalised	Gross	Equivalised	Gross	Equivalised	Gross	Equivalised	Gross	Equivalised
Lower boundary of group (£ per week)	445	426	558	506	673	603	828	733	1092	971
Average size of household	2.6	2.7	2.7	2.6	2.9	2.5	3	2.3	3.2	2.2
One adult retired										
mainly dependent on state pensions[1]	0	0	0	0	0	0	0	0	0	0
One adult, other retired	2	7	2	7	1	4	0	3	0	3
One adult, non-retired	15	13	11	13	9	15	7	18	3	26
One adult, one child	3	2	1	2	1	2	1	1	0	1
One adult, two or more children	2	1	1	1	0	0	1	0	0	0
One man one woman										
mainly dependent on state pensions[1]	0	0	0	0	0	0	0	0	0	0
One man and one woman, other retired	10	8	5	6	4	4	2	4	1	1
One man and one woman, non-retired	26	17	31	26	28	30	29	36	28	38
One man and one woman, one child	11	8	10	9	10	11	11	8	10	9
One man and one woman, two children	11	16	16	11	18	11	13	9	16	7
One man and one woman, three children	4	3	3	3	4	2	5	2	5	2
Two adults, four or more children	2	1	1	0	1	0	1	0	1	0
Three adults	4	10	10	10	10	9	14	9	13	6
Three adults, one or more children	3	5	4	4	5	4	7	2	8	2
All other households without children	5	5	3	5	6	6	7	7	10	4
All other households with children	1	2	1	2	3	1	3	1	4	1

1 Mainly dependent on state pension and not economically active - see Appendix B.

Table **3.2E**

Household expenditure by gross equivalised income decile group, 2003-04

based on weighted data and including children's expenditure

	Lowest ten per cent	Second decile group	Third decile group	Fourth decile group	Fifth decile group	Sixth decile group
Lower boundary of group (£ per week)		167	221	285	351	426
Grossed number of households (thousands)	2,467	2,468	2,467	2,466	2,468	2,467
Total number of households in sample	751	707	710	740	725	711
Total number of persons in sample	1,764	1,365	1,615	1,873	1,901	1,938
Total number of adults in sample	1,095	1,072	1,211	1,348	1,334	1,391
Weighted average number of persons per household	2.2	1.9	2.2	2.4	2.6	2.7
Commodity or service	Average weekly household expenditure (£)					
1 Food & non-alcoholic drinks	30.30	30.90	37.70	41.80	45.60	47.50
2 Alcoholic drinks, tobacco & narcotics	9.70	7.60	9.30	11.10	11.00	12.50
3 Clothing & footwear	12.40	8.70	13.90	17.10	21.80	24.90
4 Housing (net)[1], fuel & power	27.90	25.90	40.10	36.80	35.10	41.00
5 Household goods & services	15.30	11.10	19.10	21.80	28.70	30.80
6 Health	1.30	2.60	2.50	4.80	6.30	3.90
7 Transport	21.80	16.50	32.00	39.90	53.10	60.80
8 Communication	7.20	6.10	8.50	10.50	10.80	12.10
9 Recreation & culture	25.20	21.30	40.50	46.90	57.10	62.10
10 Education	3.60	1.40	0.90	2.70	2.90	2.20
11 Restaurants & hotels	15.30	11.80	19.40	27.40	32.00	36.70
12 Miscellaneous goods & services	13.70	15.30	17.40	25.40	31.30	35.90
1-12 All expenditure groups	183.80	159.20	241.20	286.00	335.70	370.40
13 Other expenditure items	15.40	16.60	29.40	39.50	47.00	64.50
Total expenditure	199.20	175.80	270.60	325.50	382.70	434.90
Average weekly expenditure per person (£)						
Total expenditure	88.80	94.90	120.90	133.00	148.70	163.50

Note: The commodity and service categories are not comparable to those in publications before 2001-02

1 Excluding mortgage interest payments, council tax and Northern Ireland rates

Table **3.2E** (cont.)

Household expenditure by gross equivalised income decile group, 2003-04

based on weighted data and including children's expenditure

Commodity or service	Seventh decile group	Eighth decile group	Ninth decile group	Highest ten per cent	All house-holds
Lower boundary of group (£ per week)	506	603	733	971	
Grossed number of households (thousands)	2,466	2,467	2,467	2,467	24,670
Total number of households in sample	698	681	668	657	7,048
Total number of persons in sample	1,792	1,704	1,571	1,442	16,965
Total number of adults in sample	1,373	1,326	1,288	1,179	12,617
Weighted average number of persons per household	2.6	2.5	2.3	2.2	2.4
	Average weekly household expenditure (£)				
1 Food & non-alcoholic drinks	49.10	49.10	50.70	52.50	43.50
2 Alcoholic drinks, tobacco & narcotics	13.30	13.20	15.70	13.60	11.70
3 Clothing & footwear	26.50	29.30	29.30	43.70	22.70
4 Housing (net)[1], fuel & power	42.60	39.60	47.30	53.40	39.00
5 Household goods & services	33.90	37.10	51.30	63.50	31.30
6 Health	5.00	5.50	9.20	9.30	5.00
7 Transport	76.10	83.30	92.20	131.70	60.70
8 Communication	12.50	13.70	15.50	15.20	11.20
9 Recreation & culture	69.40	72.10	83.90	94.50	57.30
10 Education	3.10	5.90	9.80	19.80	5.20
11 Restaurants & hotels	41.70	46.50	52.70	65.60	34.90
12 Miscellaneous goods & services	39.80	46.10	46.90	64.40	33.60
1-12 All expenditure groups	413.20	441.40	504.50	627.20	356.20
13 Other expenditure items	72.80	85.60	97.70	150.20	61.90
Total expenditure	486.00	526.90	602.20	777.50	418.10
Average weekly expenditure per person (£)					
Total expenditure	190.10	211.20	258.80	357.40	177.40

Note: The commodity and service categories are not comparable to those in publications before 2001-02

1 Excluding mortgage interest payments, council tax and Northern Ireland rates

Table 3.2

Household expenditure by gross income decile group, 2003-04

based on weighted data and including children's expenditure

Commodity or service	Lowest ten per cent	Second decile group	Third decile group	Fourth decile group	Fifth decile group	Sixth decile group
Lower boundary of group (£ per week)		124	193	263	351	445
Grossed number of households (thousands)	2,468	2,467	2,468	2,464	2,470	2,465
Total number of households in sample	703	720	729	729	715	719
Total number of persons in sample	930	1,212	1,457	1,461	1,730	1,899
Total number of adults in sample	781	924	1,142	1,169	1,296	1,354
Weighted average number of persons per household	1.3	1.6	1.9	1.9	2.4	2.6
Commodity or service			Average weekly household expenditure (£)			
1 Food & non-alcoholic drinks	21.40	27.80	34.20	36.50	42.40	44.70
2 Alcoholic drinks, tobacco & narcotics	6.80	7.00	7.90	10.50	12.10	12.30
3 Clothing & footwear	6.70	7.80	11.90	14.10	18.40	22.10
4 Housing (net)[1], fuel & power	22.80	28.30	31.90	34.90	42.00	43.60
5 Household goods & services	10.30	13.80	16.80	20.30	26.60	31.30
6 Health	1.60	1.80	3.10	4.60	5.10	4.50
7 Transport	13.00	16.90	23.30	40.70	48.00	55.30
8 Communication	5.40	5.70	7.20	9.00	10.70	11.20
9 Recreation & culture	17.10	24.00	30.00	42.80	52.10	56.00
10 Education	1.80	0.70	2.20	2.10	2.30	1.70
11 Restaurants & hotels	9.50	10.70	15.80	21.70	31.20	32.40
12 Miscellaneous goods & services	11.00	12.60	16.10	22.70	27.90	34.70
1-12 All expenditure groups	127.40	157.10	200.30	259.80	318.80	349.80
13 Other expenditure items	12.20	16.20	23.90	38.50	42.90	61.60
Total expenditure	139.60	173.30	224.20	298.30	361.70	411.40
Average weekly expenditure per person (£)						
Total expenditure	107.80	105.80	115.10	153.70	152.70	159.90

Note: The commodity and service categories are not comparable to those in publications before 2001-02

1 Excluding mortgage interest payments, council tax and Northern Ireland rates

Table **3.2** (cont.)

Household expenditure by gross income decile group, 2003-04

based on weighted data and including children's expenditure

	Seventh decile group	Eighth decile group	Ninth decile group	Highest ten per cent	All house-holds
Lower boundary of group (£ per week)	558	673	828	1,092	
Grossed number of households (thousands)	2,467	2,467	2,468	2,465	24,670
Total number of households in sample	712	687	681	653	7,048
Total number of persons in sample	1,997	2,062	2,093	2,124	16,965
Total number of adults in sample	1,440	1,452	1,522	1,537	12,617
Weighted average number of persons per household	2.7	2.9	3.0	3.2	2.4
Commodity or service	Average weekly household expenditure (£)				
1 Food & non-alcoholic drinks	48.80	51.10	60.60	67.80	43.50
2 Alcoholic drinks, tobacco & narcotics	13.70	14.10	16.60	16.20	11.70
3 Clothing & footwear	25.90	31.70	35.30	53.80	22.70
4 Housing (net)[1], fuel & power	41.50	44.00	42.80	58.00	39.00
5 Household goods & services	34.20	43.00	45.00	71.40	31.30
6 Health	4.90	5.50	8.30	11.00	5.00
7 Transport	67.60	88.20	104.00	150.10	60.70
8 Communication	12.70	14.50	15.60	20.20	11.20
9 Recreation & culture	68.60	77.80	88.40	116.20	57.30
10 Education	2.80	4.00	7.80	27.10	5.20
11 Restaurants & hotels	43.90	50.90	55.50	77.40	34.90
12 Miscellaneous goods & services	41.10	45.00	50.40	74.70	33.60
1-12 All expenditure groups	405.50	469.70	530.40	743.80	356.20
13 Other expenditure items	73.10	87.50	101.80	161.20	61.90
Total expenditure	478.60	557.20	632.30	905.00	418.10
Average weekly expenditure per person (£)					
Total expenditure	175.30	191.20	212.20	284.30	177.40

Note: The commodity and service categories are not comparable to those in publications before 2001-02

1 Excluding mortgage interest payments, council tax and Northern Ireland rates

Table **3.3E**

Household expenditure as a percentage of total expenditure by gross equivalised income decile group, 2003-04

based on weighted data and including children's expenditure

	Lowest ten per cent	Second decile group	Third decile group	Fourth decile group	Fifth decile group	Sixth decile group
Lower boundary of group (£ per week)		167	221	285	351	426
Grossed number of households (thousands)	2,467	2,468	2,467	2,466	2,468	2,467
Total number of households in sample	751	707	710	740	725	711
Total number of persons in sample	1,764	1,365	1,615	1,873	1,901	1,938
Total number of adults in sample	1,095	1,072	1,211	1,348	1,334	1,391
Weighted average number of persons per household	2.2	1.9	2.2	2.4	2.6	2.7
Commodity or service	Percentage of total expenditure					
1 Food & non-alcoholic drinks	15	18	14	13	12	11
2 Alcoholic drinks, tobacco & narcotics	5	4	3	3	3	3
3 Clothing & footwear	6	5	5	5	6	6
4 Housing (net)[1], fuel & power	14	15	15	11	9	9
5 Household goods & services	8	6	7	7	7	7
6 Health	1	1	1	1	2	1
7 Transport	11	9	12	12	14	14
8 Communication	4	3	3	3	3	3
9 Recreation & culture	13	12	15	14	15	14
10 Education	2	1	0	1	1	1
11 Restaurants & hotels	8	7	7	8	8	8
12 Miscellaneous goods & services	7	9	6	8	8	8
1-12 All expenditure groups	92	91	89	88	88	85
13 Other expenditure items	8	9	11	12	12	15
Total expenditure	100	100	100	100	100	100

Note: The commodity and service categories are not comparable to those in publications before 2001-02

1 Excluding mortgage interest payments, council tax and Northern Ireland rates

Table 3.3E (cont.)

Household expenditure as a percentage of total expenditure by gross equivalised income decile group, 2003-04

based on weighted data and including children's expenditure

	Seventh decile group	Eighth decile group	Ninth decile group	Highest ten per cent	All house-holds
Lower boundary of group (£ per week)	506	603	733	971	
Grossed number of households (thousands)	2,466	2,467	2,467	2,467	24,670
Total number of households in sample	698	681	668	657	7,048
Total number of persons in sample	1,792	1,704	1,571	1,442	16,965
Total number of adults in sample	1,373	1,326	1,288	1,179	12,617
Weighted average number of persons per household	2.6	2.5	2.3	2.2	2.4
Commodity or service	Percentage of total expenditure				
1 Food & non-alcoholic drinks	10	9	8	7	10
2 Alcoholic drinks, tobacco & narcotics	3	3	3	2	3
3 Clothing & footwear	5	6	5	6	5
4 Housing (net)[1], fuel & power	9	8	8	7	9
5 Household goods & services	7	7	9	8	7
6 Health	1	1	2	1	1
7 Transport	16	16	15	17	15
8 Communication	3	3	3	2	3
9 Recreation & culture	14	14	14	12	14
10 Education	1	1	2	3	1
11 Restaurants & hotels	9	9	9	8	8
12 Miscellaneous goods & services	8	9	8	8	8
1-12 All expenditure groups	85	84	84	81	85
13 Other expenditure items	15	16	16	19	15
Total expenditure	100	100	100	100	100

Note: The commodity and service categories are not comparable to those in publications before 2001-02

1 Excluding mortgage interest payments, council tax and Northern Ireland rates

Table **3.3**

Household expenditure as a percentage of total expenditure by gross income decile group, 2003-04

based on weighted data and including children's expenditure

	Lowest ten per cent	Second decile group	Third decile group	Fourth decile group	Fifth decile group	Sixth decile group
Lower boundary of group (£ per week)		124	193	263	351	445
Grossed number of households (thousands)	2,468	2,467	2,468	2,464	2,470	2,465
Total number of households in sample	703	720	729	729	715	719
Total number of persons in sample	930	1,212	1,457	1,461	1,730	1,899
Total number of adults in sample	781	924	1,142	1,169	1,296	1,354
Weighted average number of persons per household	1.3	1.6	1.9	1.9	2.4	2.6
Commodity or service	Percentage of total expenditure					
1 Food & non-alcoholic drinks	15	16	15	12	12	11
2 Alcoholic drinks, tobacco & narcotics	5	4	4	4	3	3
3 Clothing & footwear	5	4	5	5	5	5
4 Housing (net)[1], fuel & power	16	16	14	12	12	11
5 Household goods & services	7	8	7	7	7	8
6 Health	1	1	1	2	1	1
7 Transport	9	10	10	14	13	13
8 Communication	4	3	3	3	3	3
9 Recreation & culture	12	14	13	14	14	14
10 Education	1	0	1	1	1	0
11 Restaurants & hotels	7	6	7	7	9	8
12 Miscellaneous goods & services	8	7	7	8	8	8
1-12 All expenditure groups	91	91	89	87	88	85
13 Other expenditure items	9	9	11	13	12	15
Total expenditure	100	100	100	100	100	100

Note: The commodity and service categories are not comparable to those in publications before 2001-02

1 Excluding mortgage interest payments, council tax and Northern Ireland rates

Table **3.3** (cont.)

Household expenditure as a percentage of total expenditure by gross income decile group, 2003-04

based on weighted data and including children's expenditure

	Seventh decile group	Eighth decile group	Ninth decile group	Highest ten per cent	All house- holds
Lower boundary of group (£ per week)	558	673	828	1092	
Grossed number of households (thousands)	2,467	2,467	2,468	2,465	24,670
Total number of households in sample	712	687	681	653	7,048
Total number of persons in sample	1,997	2,062	2,093	2,124	16,965
Total number of adults in sample	1,440	1,452	1,522	1,537	12,617
Weighted average number of persons per household	2.7	2.9	3.0	3.2	2.4
Commodity or service	Percentage of total expenditure				
1 Food & non-alcoholic drinks	10	9	10	7	10
2 Alcoholic drinks, tobacco & narcotics	3	3	3	2	3
3 Clothing & footwear	5	6	6	6	5
4 Housing (net)[1], fuel & power	9	8	7	6	9
5 Household goods & services	7	8	7	8	7
6 Health	1	1	1	1	1
7 Transport	14	16	16	17	15
8 Communication	3	3	2	2	3
9 Recreation & culture	14	14	14	13	14
10 Education	1	1	1	3	1
11 Restaurants & hotels	9	9	9	9	8
12 Miscellaneous goods & services	9	8	8	8	8
1-12 All expenditure groups	85	84	84	82	85
13 Other expenditure items	15	16	16	18	15
Total expenditure	100	100	100	100	100

Note: The commodity and service categories are not comparable to those in publications before 2001-02

1 Excluding mortgage interest payments, council tax and Northern Ireland rates

Table **3.4E**

Expenditure of one person non-retired households by gross equivalised income quintile group, 2003-04

based on weighted data

	Lowest twenty per cent	Second quintile group	Third quintile group	Fourth quintile group	Highest twenty per cent	All house-holds
Lower boundary of group (£ per week)		221	351	506	733	
Average grossed number of households (thousands)	863	445	607	692	1084	3,691
Total number of households in sample	248	129	177	199	290	1,043
Total number of persons in sample	248	129	177	199	290	1,043
Total number of adults in sample	248	129	177	199	290	1,043
Weighted average number of persons per household	1.0	1.0	1.0	1.0	1.0	1.0
Commodity or service	Average weekly household expenditure (£)					
1 Food & non-alcoholic drinks	16.70	22.20	23.00	23.80	23.80	21.80
2 Alcoholic drinks, tobacco & narcotics	8.70	9.20	6.90	10.70	9.90	9.20
3 Clothing & footwear	4.00	7.70	8.80	12.60	19.20	11.30
4 Housing (net)[1], fuel & power	22.10	39.00	34.10	42.20	44.10	36.30
5 Household goods & services	10.90	13.30	16.50	17.40	33.20	19.90
6 Health	1.10	3.10	2.20	2.40	2.90	2.30
7 Transport	15.70	23.70	34.40	39.80	74.00	41.30
8 Communication	6.10	6.70	7.50	10.40	11.30	8.70
9 Recreation & culture	18.90	38.00	28.30	32.30	50.80	34.60
10 Education	1.70	1.90	1.40	0.50	4.10	2.20
11 Restaurants & hotels	10.00	16.30	16.60	25.80	40.70	23.80
12 Miscellaneous goods & services	9.50	11.90	18.80	19.80	31.80	19.80
1-12 All expenditure groups	125.30	193.10	198.30	237.60	345.80	231.30
13 Other expenditure items	17.40	20.20	37.80	49.50	95.60	50.10
Total expenditure	142.70	213.20	236.20	287.20	441.40	281.40
Average weekly expenditure per person (£) Total expenditure	142.70	213.20	236.20	287.20	441.40	281.40

Note: The commodity and service categories are not comparable to those in publications before 2001-02

1 Excluding mortgage interest payments, council tax and Northern Ireland rates

Table **3.4**

Expenditure of one person non-retired households by gross income quintile group, 2003-04

based on weighted data

	Lowest twenty per cent	Second quintile group	Third quintile group	Fourth quintile group	Highest twenty per cent	All house-holds
Lower boundary of group (£ per week)		193	351	558	828	
Average grossed number of households (thousands)	1,201	959	806	488	238	3,691
Total number of households in sample	345	278	226	132	62	1,043
Total number of persons in sample	345	278	226	132	62	1,043
Total number of adults in sample	345	278	226	132	62	1,043
Weighted average number of persons per household	1.0	1.0	1.0	1.0	1.0	1.0
Commodity or service	Average weekly household expenditure (£)					
1 Food & non-alcoholic drinks	18.10	23.50	22.40	23.90	27.80	21.80
2 Alcoholic drinks, tobacco & narcotics	9.20	7.60	10.50	8.70	11.90	9.20
3 Clothing & footwear	4.90	8.80	13.00	21.10	27.80	11.30
4 Housing (net)[1], fuel & power	27.30	36.00	41.80	41.40	54.20	36.30
5 Household goods & services	11.30	16.20	21.50	37.40	36.60	19.90
6 Health	1.30	2.70	2.70	2.40	4.00	2.30
7 Transport	18.30	33.10	46.40	81.50	91.40	41.30
8 Communication	6.10	8.50	9.90	11.70	13.00	8.70
9 Recreation & culture	25.60	27.70	41.20	45.50	63.50	34.60
10 Education	1.90	0.90	1.40	5.40	4.60	2.20
11 Restaurants & hotels	12.00	17.50	26.40	45.00	56.50	23.80
12 Miscellaneous goods & services	10.00	18.30	21.80	33.20	41.30	19.80
1-12 All expenditure groups	145.90	200.90	259.10	357.20	432.30	231.30
13 Other expenditure items	17.50	39.00	65.50	88.00	129.50	50.10
Total expenditure	163.40	239.90	324.50	445.20	561.90	281.40
Average weekly expenditure per person (£)						
Total expenditure	163.40	239.90	324.50	445.20	561.90	281.40

Note: The commodity and service categories are not comparable to those in publications before 2001-02

1 Excluding mortgage interest payments, council tax and Northern Ireland rates

Table **3.5E**

Expenditure of two adult households with children by gross equivalised income quintile group, 2003-04

based on weighted data and including children's expenditure

	Lowest twenty per cent	Second quintile group	Third quintile group	Fourth quintile group	Highest twenty per cent	All house- holds
Lower boundary of group (£ per week)		221	351	506	733	
Average grossed number of households (thousands)	545	888	1,396	1211	924	4,963
Total number of households in sample	176	288	439	375	282	1,560
Total number of persons in sample	731	1,202	1,717	1,411	1,047	6,108
Total number of adults in sample	352	576	878	750	564	3,120
Weighted average number of persons per household	4.1	4.1	3.8	3.7	3.7	3.9
Commodity or service	Average weekly household expenditure (£)					
1 Food & non-alcoholic drinks	50.20	54.00	57.90	63.80	73.80	60.80
2 Alcoholic drinks, tobacco & narcotics	14.50	13.10	13.40	14.50	13.20	13.70
3 Clothing & footwear	21.00	27.30	32.80	37.80	51.40	35.20
4 Housing (net)[1], fuel & power	33.40	48.60	42.70	42.20	50.30	44.00
5 Household goods & services	23.60	26.10	35.50	50.00	76.20	43.60
6 Health	2.00	3.20	4.30	4.90	8.70	4.80
7 Transport	34.60	55.00	75.30	90.00	139.70	82.80
8 Communication	9.40	14.60	13.80	14.30	15.80	14.00
9 Recreation & culture	36.30	62.70	78.20	93.40	122.00	82.70
10 Education	10.90	3.30	4.00	10.00	40.90	13.00
11 Restaurants & hotels	24.00	37.20	41.60	51.40	68.20	46.20
12 Miscellaneous goods & services	23.20	29.60	44.50	61.30	83.10	50.80
1-12 All expenditure groups	283.00	374.60	444.00	533.60	743.30	491.50
13 Other expenditure items	22.50	61.20	86.10	105.90	161.40	93.50
Total expenditure	305.60	435.70	530.10	639.50	904.70	585.00
Average weekly expenditure per person (£) Total expenditure	75.20	105.40	137.80	172.10	245.80	151.60

Note: The commodity and service categories are not comparable to those in publications before 2001-02

1 Excluding mortgage interest payments, council tax and Northern Ireland rates

Table **3.5**

Expenditure of two adult households with children by gross income quintile group, 2003-04

based on weighted data and including children's expenditure

	Lowest twenty per cent	Second quintile group	Third quintile group	Fourth quintile group	Highest twenty per cent	All house-holds
Lower boundary of group (£ per week)		193	351	558	828	
Average grossed number of households (thousands)	192	426	1,201	1,614	1,531	4,963
Total number of households in sample	58	140	376	509	477	1,560
Total number of persons in sample	211	557	1,471	1,999	1,870	6,108
Total number of adults in sample	116	280	752	1,018	954	3,120
Weighted average number of persons per household	3.6	3.9	3.9	3.9	3.9	3.9
Commodity or service			Average weekly household expenditure (£)			
1 Food & non-alcoholic drinks	41.20	50.60	51.90	61.00	72.70	60.80
2 Alcoholic drinks, tobacco & narcotics	12.80	12.30	13.80	14.30	13.50	13.70
3 Clothing & footwear	18.90	21.60	26.10	36.20	47.20	35.20
4 Housing (net)[1], fuel & power	34.10	39.00	47.30	41.80	46.40	44.00
5 Household goods & services	13.40	25.70	31.30	42.00	63.70	43.60
6 Health	3.00	1.50	3.10	4.20	7.90	4.80
7 Transport	30.10	37.90	57.10	82.40	122.50	82.80
8 Communication	7.40	11.90	12.90	14.40	15.70	14.00
9 Recreation & culture	29.70	38.30	59.70	88.70	113.40	82.70
10 Education	12.40	8.10	3.20	5.10	30.40	13.00
11 Restaurants & hotels	20.40	26.40	34.50	48.70	61.50	46.20
12 Miscellaneous goods & services	16.00	26.30	33.60	50.60	75.60	50.80
1-12 All expenditure groups	239.30	299.40	374.40	489.40	670.50	491.50
13 Other expenditure items	14.30	35.40	60.30	95.50	143.50	93.50
Total expenditure	253.60	334.80	434.70	584.90	814.00	585.00
Average weekly expenditure per person (£)						
Total expenditure	70.60	85.70	112.60	150.70	211.00	151.60

Note: The commodity and service categories are not comparable to those in publications before 2001-02

1 Excluding mortgage interest payments, council tax and Northern Ireland rates

Table **3.6E**

Expenditure of one person retired households mainly dependent on state pensions[1]

by gross equivalised income quintile group, 2003-04

based on weighted data

	Lowest twenty per cent	Second quintile group	Third quintile group	Fourth quintile group	Highest twenty per cent	All house-holds
Lower boundary of group (£ per week)		221	351	506	733	
Average grossed number of households (thousands)	736	321	29	9	0	1,095
Total number of households in sample	202	95	9	2	0	308
Total number of persons in sample	202	95	9	2	0	308
Total number of adults in sample	202	95	9	2	0	308
Weighted average number of persons per household	1.0	1.0	1.0	1.0	0	1.0
Commodity or service	Average weekly household expenditure (£)					
1 Food & non-alcoholic drinks	20.10	22.80	26.10	22.30	..	21.10
2 Alcoholic drinks, tobacco & narcotics	3.20	5.20	0.70	0.00	..	3.70
3 Clothing & footwear	4.20	4.40	7.70	8.80	..	4.40
4 Housing (net)[2], fuel & power	22.90	18.70	18.20	11.90	..	21.40
5 Household goods & services	6.20	8.70	16.80	13.50	..	7.30
6 Health	2.40	1.00	0.50	0.00	..	1.90
7 Transport	6.00	7.30	7.40	3.40	..	6.40
8 Communication	4.00	4.50	8.40	5.10	..	4.30
9 Recreation & culture	11.80	13.20	13.40	3.40	..	12.20
10 Education	0.00	0.00	0.00	0.00	..	0.00
11 Restaurants & hotels	4.30	6.00	6.90	1.90	..	4.80
12 Miscellaneous goods & services	13.80	9.40	18.90	7.00	..	12.60
1-12 All expenditure groups	99.10	101.20	124.90	77.20	..	100.20
13 Other expenditure items	10.60	12.00	11.80	40.30	..	11.30
Total expenditure	109.70	113.20	136.70	117.50	..	111.50
Average weekly expenditure per person (£)						
Total expenditure	109.70	113.20	136.70	117.50	..	111.50

Note: The commodity and service categories are not comparable to those in publications before 2001-02
1 Mainly dependent on state pension and not economically active - see appendix D.
2 Excluding mortgage interest payments, council tax and Northern Ireland rates

Table **3.6**

Expenditure of one person retired households mainly dependent on state pensions[1]

by gross income quintile group, 2003-04

based on weighted data

	Lowest twenty per cent	Second quintile group	Third quintile group	Fourth quintile group	Highest twenty per cent	All house-holds
Lower boundary of group (£ per week)		193	351	558	828	
Average grossed number of households (thousands)	1,023	68	4	0	0	1,095
Total number of households in sample	288	19	1	0	0	308
Total number of persons in sample	288	19	1	0	0	308
Total number of adults in sample	288	19	1	0	0	308
Weighted average number of persons per household	1.0	1.0	1.0	0	0	1.0
Commodity or service	Average weekly household expenditure (£)					
1 Food & non-alcoholic drinks	21.00	22.00	24.10	..	..	21.10
2 Alcoholic drinks, tobacco & narcotics	3.70	3.80	0.00	..	..	3.70
3 Clothing & footwear	4.20	7.20	14.00	..	..	4.40
4 Housing (net) [2], fuel & power	21.90	15.10	8.00	..	..	21.40
5 Household goods & services	6.90	11.90	20.80	..	..	7.30
6 Health	2.00	0.40	0.00	..	..	1.90
7 Transport	6.40	5.90	7.00	..	..	6.40
8 Communication	4.10	6.60	9.20	..	..	4.30
9 Recreation & culture	12.10	13.40	5.50	..	..	12.20
10 Education	0.00	0.00	0.00	..	..	0.00
11 Restaurants & hotels	4.60	8.20	3.90	..	..	4.80
12 Miscellaneous goods & services	12.60	12.60	7.80	..	..	12.60
1-12 All expenditure groups	99.80	106.90	100.30	..	..	100.20
13 Other expenditure items	10.90	13.90	66.60	..	..	11.30
Total expenditure	110.70	120.80	166.80	..	..	111.50
Average weekly expenditure per person (£)						
Total expenditure	110.70	120.80	166.80	..	..	111.50

Note: The commodity and service categories are not comparable to those in publications before 2001-02
1 Mainly dependent on state pension and not economically active - see appendix B.
2 Excluding mortgage interest payments, council tax and Northern Ireland rates

Table **3.7E**

Expenditure of one man one woman non-retired by gross equivalised income quintile group, 2003-04

based on weighted data

	Lowest twenty per cent	Second quintile group	Third quintile group	Fourth quintile group	Highest twenty per cent	All house-holds
Lower boundary of group (£ per week)		221	351	506	733	
Average grossed number of households (thousands)	472	537	769	1385	1824	4,988
Total number of households in sample	136	157	218	389	489	1,389
Total number of persons in sample	272	314	436	778	978	2,778
Total number of adults in sample	272	314	436	778	978	2,778
Weighted average number of persons per household	2.0	2.0	2.0	2.0	2.0	2.0
Commodity or service	Average weekly household expenditure (£)					
1 Food & non-alcoholic drinks	34.80	40.30	46.60	41.80	52.70	45.70
2 Alcoholic drinks, tobacco & narcotics	11.70	11.30	13.60	13.60	16.60	14.30
3 Clothing & footwear	12.70	12.50	18.80	20.70	36.60	24.60
4 Housing (net)[1], fuel & power	31.40	34.40	38.40	39.90	48.70	41.50
5 Household goods & services	17.10	24.10	36.10	34.90	56.00	40.00
6 Health	3.30	6.50	3.50	5.00	12.30	7.40
7 Transport	37.90	50.00	53.00	70.00	119.10	80.20
8 Communication	6.20	8.40	9.60	11.00	14.00	11.10
9 Recreation & culture	40.30	58.60	59.50	65.10	89.00	69.90
10 Education	1.80	0.30	1.70	1.60	5.10	2.70
11 Restaurants & hotels	19.70	28.20	32.20	40.70	58.70	42.60
12 Miscellaneous goods & services	19.30	20.60	31.00	34.60	52.70	37.70
1-12 All expenditure groups	236.40	295.10	344.00	379.00	561.50	417.80
13 Other expenditure items	23.70	38.20	48.00	74.50	131.80	82.60
Total expenditure	260.10	333.20	392.00	453.50	693.20	500.50
Average weekly expenditure per person (£)						
Total expenditure	130.00	166.60	196.00	226.70	346.60	250.20

Note: The commodity and service categories are not comparable to those in publications before 2001-02
1 Excluding mortgage interest payments, council tax and Northern Ireland rates

Table **3.7**

Expenditure of one man one woman non-retired by gross income quintile group, 2003-04

based on weighted data

	Lowest twenty per cent	Second quintile group	Third quintile group	Fourth quintile group	Highest twenty per cent	All house- holds
Lower boundary of group (£ per week)		193	351	558	828	
Average grossed number of households (thousands)	337	669	1,104	1,467	1,411	4,988
Total number of households in sample	96	196	316	406	375	1,389
Total number of persons in sample	192	392	632	812	750	2,778
Total number of adults in sample	192	392	632	812	750	2,778
Weighted average number of persons per household	2.0	2.0	2.0	2.0	2.0	2.0
Commodity or service	Average weekly household expenditure (£)					
1 Food & non-alcoholic drinks	34.60	39.40	44.70	43.40	54.50	45.70
2 Alcoholic drinks, tobacco & narcotics	13.10	10.70	13.40	13.50	17.70	14.30
3 Clothing & footwear	12.50	12.70	21.20	21.70	38.70	24.60
4 Housing (net) [1], fuel & power	33.60	32.50	38.20	41.20	50.50	41.50
5 Household goods & services	17.10	22.60	34.60	37.70	60.20	40.00
6 Health	3.30	5.80	3.60	6.50	13.20	7.40
7 Transport	43.00	45.20	56.90	79.90	124.10	80.20
8 Communication	6.10	8.10	9.70	11.60	14.40	11.10
9 Recreation & culture	45.40	52.50	61.10	69.60	91.30	69.90
10 Education	1.60	0.70	1.80	1.70	5.80	2.70
11 Restaurants & hotels	19.60	26.60	34.20	44.60	60.40	42.60
12 Miscellaneous goods & services	20.50	19.80	31.30	36.50	56.70	37.70
1-12 All expenditure groups	250.20	276.70	350.70	408.00	587.50	417.80
13 Other expenditure items	21.20	36.50	55.60	79.40	143.70	82.60
Total expenditure	271.40	313.20	406.30	487.40	731.20	500.50
Average weekly expenditure per person (£)						
Total expenditure	135.70	156.60	203.20	243.70	365.60	250.20

Note: The commodity and service categories are not comparable to those in publications before 2001-02
1 Excluding mortgage interest payments, council tax and Northern Ireland rates

Table **3.8E**

Expenditure of one man one woman retired households mainly dependent on state pensions[1]

by gross equivalised income quintile group, 2003-04

based on weighted data

Commodity or service	Lowest twenty per cent	Second quintile group	Third quintile group	Fourth quintile group	Highest twenty per cent	All house-holds
Lower boundary of group (£ per week)		221	351	506	733	
Average grossed number of households (thousands)	370	199	7	0	0	576
Total number of households in sample	106	54	3	0	0	163
Total number of persons in sample	212	108	6	0	0	326
Total number of adults in sample	212	108	6	0	0	326
Weighted average number of persons per household	2.0	2.0	2.0	0	0	2.0
Commodity or service	Average weekly household expenditure (£)					
1 Food & non-alcoholic drinks	38.90	39.20	51.00	..	..	39.10
2 Alcoholic drinks, tobacco & narcotics	5.80	8.10	1.10	..	..	6.60
3 Clothing & footwear	6.10	8.30	42.90	..	..	7.30
4 Housing (net)[2], fuel & power	23.30	37.30	17.40	..	..	28.00
5 Household goods & services	17.20	27.20	14.60	..	..	20.60
6 Health	3.30	4.40	1.60	..	..	3.70
7 Transport	18.60	19.20	8.90	..	..	18.70
8 Communication	4.50	5.00	5.70	..	..	4.70
9 Recreation & culture	27.70	32.90	22.20	..	..	29.40
10 Education	0.00	0.00	0.00	..	..	0.00
11 Restaurants & hotels	9.90	10.30	16.20	..	..	10.10
12 Miscellaneous goods & services	14.90	14.60	26.10	..	..	14.90
1-12 All expenditure groups	170.10	206.40	207.70	..	..	183.10
13 Other expenditure items	17.60	25.30	9.80	..	..	20.20
Total expenditure	187.70	231.70	217.50	..	..	203.30
Average weekly expenditure per person (£)						
Total expenditure	93.80	115.80	108.80	..	..	101.60

Note: The commodity and service categories are not comparable to those in publications before 2001-02
1 Mainly dependent on state pension and not economically active - see Appendix B.
2 Excluding mortgage interest payments, council tax and Northern Ireland rates

Table **3.8**

Expenditure of one man one woman retired households mainly dependent on state pensions[1]

by gross income quintile group, 2003-04

based on weighted data

Commodity or service	Lowest twenty per cent	Second quintile group	Third quintile group	Fourth quintile group	Highest twenty per cent	All house-holds
Lower boundary of group (£ per week)		193	351	558	828	
Average grossed number of households (thousands)	209	360	7	0	0	576
Total number of households in sample	60	100	3	0	0	163
Total number of persons in sample	120	200	6	0	0	326
Total number of adults in sample	120	200	6	0	0	326
Weighted average number of persons per household	2.0	2.0	2.0	0	0	2.0
Commodity or service	Average weekly household expenditure (£)					
1 Food & non-alcoholic drinks	37.80	39.70	51.00	..	..	39.10
2 Alcoholic drinks, tobacco & narcotics	4.70	7.70	1.10	..	..	6.60
3 Clothing & footwear	4.50	8.20	42.90	..	..	7.30
4 Housing (net)[2], fuel & power	23.10	31.10	17.40	..	..	28.00
5 Household goods & services	19.50	21.30	14.60	..	..	20.60
6 Health	1.70	4.90	1.60	..	..	3.70
7 Transport	15.00	21.00	8.90	..	..	18.70
8 Communication	4.90	4.50	5.70	..	..	4.70
9 Recreation & culture	27.30	30.70	22.20	..	..	29.40
10 Education	0.00	0.00	0.00	..	..	0.00
11 Restaurants & hotels	7.20	11.70	16.20	..	..	10.10
12 Miscellaneous goods & services	16.60	13.80	26.10	..	..	14.90
1-12 All expenditure groups	162.40	194.60	207.70	..	..	183.10
13 Other expenditure items	15.50	23.10	9.80	..	..	20.20
Total expenditure	177.90	217.70	217.50	..	..	203.30
Average weekly expenditure per person (£)						
Total expenditure	89.00	108.80	108.80	..	..	101.60

Note: The commodity and service categories are not comparable to those in publications before 2001-02
1 Mainly dependent on state pension and not economically active - see Appendix B.
2 Excluding mortgage interest payments, council tax and Northern Ireland rates

Table **3.9E**

Expenditure of one man one woman retired households not mainly dependent on state pensions[1]
by gross equivalised income quintile group, 2003-04

based on weighted data

Commodity or service	Lowest twenty per cent	Second quintile group	Third quintile group	Fourth quintile group	Highest twenty per cent	All house-holds
Lower boundary of group (£ per week)		221	351	506	733	
Average grossed number of households (thousands)	208	772	575	263	137	1,956
Total number of households in sample	61	224	158	76	37	556
Total number of persons in sample	122	448	316	152	74	1,112
Total number of adults in sample	122	448	316	152	74	1,112
Weighted average number of persons per household	2.0	2.0	2.0	2.0	2.0	2.0
Commodity or service	Average weekly household expenditure (£)					
1 Food & non-alcoholic drinks	39.70	43.30	47.80	50.40	52.90	45.90
2 Alcoholic drinks, tobacco & narcotics	9.40	9.60	11.20	10.50	14.20	10.50
3 Clothing & footwear	7.00	11.00	12.80	23.70	17.20	13.20
4 Housing (net)[2], fuel & power	25.50	28.70	28.50	31.80	42.90	29.70
5 Household goods & services	10.50	19.80	32.40	24.20	121.20	30.20
6 Health	1.60	5.80	12.20	11.20	23.60	9.20
7 Transport	25.40	37.70	57.60	57.60	104.70	49.60
8 Communication	5.70	5.80	7.80	9.20	11.50	7.20
9 Recreation & culture	21.10	47.90	57.60	79.50	128.30	57.80
10 Education	0.00	1.40	0.20	0.00	2.00	0.70
11 Restaurants & hotels	11.80	15.40	27.70	31.80	55.80	23.70
12 Miscellaneous goods & services	16.20	20.00	27.70	44.20	48.30	27.10
1-12 All expenditure groups	173.70	246.20	323.50	374.10	622.50	304.80
13 Other expenditure items	18.00	29.10	37.80	56.30	163.20	43.50
Total expenditure	191.70	275.30	361.30	430.40	785.70	348.30
Average weekly expenditure per person (£)						
Total expenditure	95.90	137.60	180.60	215.20	392.80	174.20

Note: The commodity and service categories are not comparable to those in publications before 2001-02
1 Mainly dependent on state pension and not economically active - see Appendix B.
2 Excluding mortgage interest payments, council tax and Northern Ireland rates

Table **3.9**

Expenditure of one man one woman retired households not mainly dependent on state pensions[1]
by gross income quintile group, 2003-04

based on weighted data

	Lowest twenty per cent	Second quintile group	Third quintile group	Fourth quintile group	Highest twenty per cent	All house-holds
Lower boundary of group (£ per week)		193	351	558	828	
Average grossed number of households (thousands)	80	889	680	223	85	1,956
Total number of households in sample	24	258	188	63	23	556
Total number of persons in sample	48	516	376	126	46	1,112
Total number of adults in sample	48	516	376	126	46	1,112
Weighted average number of persons per household	2.0	2.0	2.0	2.0	2.0	2.0
Commodity or service	Average weekly household expenditure (£)					
1 Food & non-alcoholic drinks	36.10	43.00	48.30	50.10	54.10	45.90
2 Alcoholic drinks, tobacco & narcotics	8.50	9.60	11.30	11.60	11.90	10.50
3 Clothing & footwear	5.40	10.60	12.30	27.00	19.70	13.20
4 Housing (net)[2], fuel & power	24.60	28.20	29.40	31.40	48.30	29.70
5 Household goods & services	10.80	18.60	30.50	61.90	85.10	30.20
6 Health	1.40	5.10	12.20	10.50	31.10	9.20
7 Transport	25.70	36.10	54.40	72.00	117.00	49.60
8 Communication	6.00	5.70	7.90	9.80	12.40	7.20
9 Recreation & culture	18.00	43.30	58.50	93.50	147.30	57.80
10 Education	0.00	1.20	0.10	0.00	3.20	0.70
11 Restaurants & hotels	9.00	15.10	26.90	39.00	61.00	23.70
12 Miscellaneous goods & services	10.50	19.90	31.60	39.10	50.60	27.10
1-12 All expenditure groups	156.00	236.50	323.40	445.90	641.80	304.80
13 Other expenditure items	16.30	27.70	37.70	66.40	221.80	43.50
Total expenditure	172.30	264.20	361.10	512.30	863.60	348.30
Average weekly expenditure per person (£)						
Total expenditure	86.20	132.10	180.50	256.20	431.80	174.20

Note: The commodity and service categories are not comparable to those in publications before 2001-02
1 Mainly dependent on state pension and not economically active - see Appendix B.
2 Excluding mortgage interest payments, council tax and Northern Ireland rates

Table **3.10E**

Income and source of income by gross equivalised income quintile group, 2003-04

based on weighted data

	Grossed number of house-holds	Number of house-holds in the sample	Weekly household income		Source of income					
			Dispo-sable	Gross	Wages and salaries	Self employ-ment	Invest-ments	Annuities and pensions[1]	Social security benefits[2]	Other sources
Gross income quintile group	(000s)	Number	£	£	Percentage of gross weekly household income					
Lowest twenty per cent	4,940	1,458	142	146	12	3	2	5	75	3
Second quintile group	4,930	1,450	277	303	40	6	2	11	38	2
Third quintile group	4,940	1,436	415	489	64	7	2	10	15	2
Fourth quintile group	4,930	1,379	553	686	76	7	2	8	6	1
Highest twenty per cent	4,930	1,325	933	1,228	77	12	4	5	2	1

1 Other than social security benefits.
2 Excluding housing benefit and council tax benefit (rates rebates in Northern Ireland) - see Appendix B.

Table **3.10**

Income and source of income by gross income quintile group, 2003-04

based on weighted data

	Grossed number of house-holds	Number of house-holds in the sample	Weekly household income		Source of income					
			Dispo-sable	Gross	Wages and salaries	Self employ-ment	Invest-ments	Annuities and pensions[1]	Social security benefits[2]	Other sources
Gross income quintile group	(000s)	Number	£	£	Percentage of gross weekly household income					
Lowest twenty per cent	4,940	1,423	121	124	7	2	3	8	77	2
Second quintile group	4,930	1,458	243	266	30	4	4	17	44	2
Third quintile group	4,930	1,434	384	450	59	6	3	12	17	2
Fourth quintile group	4,930	1,399	554	681	76	7	2	7	7	1
Highest twenty per cent	4,930	1,334	1018	1,330	79	12	3	3	2	1

1 Other than social security benefits.
2 Excluding housing benefit and council tax benefit (rates rebates in Northern Ireland) - see Appendix B.

Trends in household expenditure over time

Data in this chapter are presented solely for the purposes of historical comparisons.

In 2001-02, the Expenditure and Food Survey (EFS) introduced a new coding frame for expenditure items. This frame is known as COICOP (Classification of Individual Consumption by Purpose) and is the internationally agreed standard classification for reporting household consumption expenditure within National Accounts. As such, it is part of a wider framework which helps ensure consistency across UK economic statistics. Prior to 2001-02, the EFS's predecessor survey (the Family Expenditure Survey) used a different coding system ('FES classification'). In order to preserve a time series, data presented in this chapter for the years up to 2000-01 are based on the previous FES classification. Data from 2001-02 are presented under the same classification headings, having been mapped as closely as possible from the new COICOP codes.

Please note that it is not possible to directly compare data in this chapter with those elsewhere in the publication due to the differences in the definitions of the classification headings (for example, 'Motoring' in the FES classification includes vehicle insurance whereas the 'Transport' heading under COICOP excludes this expenditure item).

Table 4.1

Household expenditure 1980 to 2003-04 (at 2003-04 prices)

Year	1980	1982	1984	1986	1988	1990	1992	1994 -95	1995[1] -96
Total number of households in sample	6,944	7,428	7,081	7,178	7,265	7,046	7,418	6,853	7,418
Total number of persons	18,844	20,022	18,557	18,330	18,280	17,437	18,174	16,617	18,174
Average number of persons per household	2.7	2.7	2.6	2.6	2.5	2.5	2.5	2.4	2.5
Commodity or service	Average weekly household expenditure (£)								
1 Housing (Net)	44.40	49.10	48.30	54.80	61.10	64.30	62.40	58.20	58.60
2 Fuel and power	16.50	18.40	18.90	19.10	17.90	16.10	17.20	16.20	15.70
3 Food and non-alcoholic drinks	67.40	62.10	63.10	64.00	65.30	64.80	62.80	63.30	64.30
4 Alcoholic drink	14.30	13.50	14.60	15.00	15.70	14.50	14.60	15.50	13.90
5 Tobacco	8.90	8.50	8.80	8.30	7.60	7.00	7.10	7.00	7.10
6 Clothing and footwear	24.10	21.30	22.30	24.70	24.80	23.20	21.60	21.50	20.80
7 Household goods	22.80	21.70	23.00	25.00	25.60	28.90	28.90	28.40	28.50
8 Household services	10.60	10.70	11.20	15.60	16.70	17.80	17.70	18.90	18.40
9 Personal goods and services	10.50	9.60	10.50	11.90	13.90	13.70	13.40	13.50	14.00
10 Motoring	35.10	35.60	38.30	38.90	43.20	49.00	47.00	45.40	44.90
11 Fares and other travel costs	8.20	8.00	7.50	7.70	8.30	9.00	9.50	8.30	7.50
12 Leisure goods	12.90	14.00	15.40	15.60	16.50	16.30	17.50	17.40	16.70
13 Leisure services	19.40	20.40	20.30	24.10	30.90	31.20	36.30	39.10	38.90
14 Miscellaneous	1.40	1.20	1.30	1.40	1.30	2.00	2.30	2.90	2.90
1-14 All expenditure groups	296.60	294.20	303.40	326.20	348.80	357.70	358.20	355.80	352.20
Average weekly expenditure per person (£)									
All expenditure groups	109.20	109.40	116.40	127.70	138.60	144.50	146.20	146.70	144.30
	Average weekly household income (£)[4]								
Gross income (£)	376.40	370.50	375.70	404.90	457.30	459.10	451.80	463.30	462.80
Disposable income (£)	307.60	299.30	300.20	329.10	370.80	373.10	369.00	374.40	372.80

1 From 1980 to this version of 1995-96, figures shown are based on unweighted, adult only data.
2 From this version of 1995-96, figures are shown based on weighted data, including children's expenditure.
3 From 2001-02 onwards: commodities and services are based on COICOP codes broadly mapped to FES. Weighting is based on the population figures from the 2001 census
4 Does not include imputed income from owner-occupied and rent-free households

Table **4.1** (cont.)

Household expenditure 1980 to 2003-04 (at 2003-04 prices)

Year	1995[2] -96	1996 -97	1997 -98	1998 -99	1999 -2000	2000 -01	2001[3] -02	2002 -03	2003 -04
Grossed number of households (thousands)	24,130	24,310	24,560	24,660	25,330	25,030	24,450	24,350	24,670
Total number of households in sample	6,797	6,415	6,409	6,630	7,097	6,637	7,473	6,927	7,048
Total number of persons	16,586	15,732	15,430	16,218	16,786	15,925	18,122	16,586	16,965
Weighted average number of persons per household	2.4	2.5	2.4	2.4	2.3	2.4	2.4	2.4	2.4

Commodity or service	Average weekly household expenditure (£)								
1 Housing (Net)	59.10	58.10	59.10	63.70	62.50	68.10	69.10	68.60	69.90
2 Fuel and power	15.60	15.70	14.40	13.00	12.40	12.70	12.30	12.00	12.00
3 Food and non-alcoholic drinks	65.70	66.60	65.50	65.60	65.40	66.00	65.00	66.10	64.90
4 Alcoholic drink	14.90	15.60	16.30	15.60	16.80	16.00	15.00	15.20	14.70
5 Tobacco	7.20	7.40	7.20	6.50	6.60	6.50	5.70	5.60	5.50
6 Clothing and footwear	21.60	22.20	23.30	24.20	23.00	23.40	23.40	22.60	22.40
7 Household goods	29.00	31.60	31.00	33.00	33.70	34.80	34.70	34.80	35.10
8 Household services	18.40	19.20	20.30	21.10	20.70	23.40	24.80	24.00	24.90
9 Personal goods and services	14.30	14.00	14.50	14.80	15.20	15.70	15.70	15.70	16.20
10 Motoring	46.40	50.00	54.30	57.60	57.60	58.70	60.80	63.40	62.40
11 Fares and other travel costs	8.10	9.10	9.90	9.20	10.10	10.10	9.80	10.00	9.60
12 Leisure goods	17.60	18.70	19.90	19.80	20.30	21.00	20.60	21.10	21.40
13 Leisure services	39.80	41.50	45.30	46.70	48.20	53.90	54.50	55.10	55.00
14 Miscellaneous	1.50	1.20	1.20	1.40	1.60	0.80	1.90	2.00	1.90
1-14 All expenditure groups	359.10	370.80	382.30	392.20	394.10	410.80	413.30	416.00	415.80

Average weekly expenditure per person (£)									
All expenditure groups	150.00	148.30	159.30	163.40	171.30	174.50	174.70	173.90	176.40

	Average weekly household income (£)[4]								
Gross income (£)	473.50	479.10	492.80	508.90	526.20	535.20	567.30	567.60	570.30
Disposable income (£)	380.50	391.50	401.50	412.80	428.70	435.80	464.10	466.00	464.00

1 From 1980 to this version of 1995-96, figures shown are based on unweighted, adult only data.
2 From this version of 1995-96, figures are shown based on weighted data, including children's expenditure.
3 From 2001-02 onwards: commodities and services are based on COICOP codes broadly mapped to FES. Weighting is based on the population figures from the 2001 census
4 Does not include imputed income from owner-occupied and rent-free households

Table **4.2**

Household expenditure as a percentage of total expenditure 1980 to 2003-04

Year	1980	1982	1984	1986	1988	1990	1992	1994	1995[1] -97
Total number of households in sample	6,944	7,428	7,081	7,178	7,265	7,046	7,418	6,853	6,797
Total number of persons	18,844	20,022	18,557	18,330	18,280	17,437	18,174	16,617	16,586
Average number of persons per household	2.7	2.7	2.6	2.6	2.5	2.5	2.5	2.4	2.4
Commodity or service	Percentage of total expenditure								
1 Housing (Net)	15	17	16	17	18	18	17	16	17
2 Fuel and power	6	6	6	6	5	4	5	5	4
3 Food and non-alcoholic drinks	23	21	21	20	19	18	18	18	18
4 Alcoholic drink	5	5	5	5	4	4	4	4	4
5 Tobacco	3	3	3	3	2	2	2	2	2
6 Clothing and footwear	8	7	7	8	7	6	6	6	6
7 Household goods	8	7	8	8	7	8	8	8	8
8 Household services	4	4	4	5	5	5	5	5	5
9 Personal goods and services	4	3	3	4	4	4	4	4	4
10 Motoring	12	12	13	12	12	14	13	13	13
11 Fares and other travel costs	3	3	2	2	2	3	3	2	2
12 Leisure goods	4	5	5	5	5	5	5	5	5
13 Leisure services	7	7	7	7	9	9	10	11	11
14 Miscellaneous	0	0	0	0	0	1	1	1	1
1-14 All expenditure groups	100	100	100	100	100	100	100	100	100

1 From 1980 to this version of 1995-96, figures shown are based on unweighted, adult only data.
2 From this version of 1995-96, figures are shown based on weighted data, including children's expenditure.
3 From 2001-02 onwards: commodities and services are based on COICOP codes broadly mapped to FES. Weighting is based on the population figures from the 2001 census

Table **4.2** (cont.)

Household expenditure as a percentage of total expenditure 1980 to 2003-04

Year	1995[2] -96	1996 -97	1997 -98	1998 -99	1999 -2000	2000 -01	2001[3] -02	2002 -03	2003 -04
Grossed number of households (thousands)		24,310	24,560	24,660	25,330	25,030	24,900	24,350	24,670
Total number of households in sample	6,797	6,415	6,409	6,630	7,097	6,637	7,473	6,927	7,048
Total number of persons	16,586	15,732	15,430	16,218	16,786	15,925	18,122	16,586	16,965
Weighted average number of persons per household	2.4	2.5	2.4	2.4	2.3	2.4	2.4	2.4	2.4
Commodity or service					Percentage of total expenditure				
1 Housing (Net)	16	16	15	16	16	17	17	16	17
2 Fuel and power	4	4	4	3	3	3	3	3	3
3 Food and non-alcoholic drinks	18	18	17	17	17	16	16	16	16
4 Alcoholic drink	4	4	4	4	4	4	4	4	4
5 Tobacco	2	2	2	2	2	2	1	1	1
6 Clothing and footwear	6	6	6	6	6	6	6	5	5
7 Household goods	8	9	8	8	9	8	8	8	8
8 Household services	5	5	5	5	5	6	6	6	6
9 Personal goods and services	4	4	4	4	4	4	4	4	4
10 Motoring	13	13	14	15	15	14	15	15	15
11 Fares and other travel costs	2	2	3	2	3	2	2	2	2
12 Leisure goods	5	5	5	5	5	5	5	5	5
13 Leisure services	11	11	12	12	12	13	13	13	13
14 Miscellaneous	0	0	0	0	0	0	0	0	0
1-14 All expenditure groups	100	100	100	100	100	100	100	100	100

1   From 1980 to this version of 1995-96, figures shown are based on unweighted, adult only data.
2   From this version of 1995-96, figures are shown based on weighted data, including children's expenditure.
3   From 2001-02 onwards: commodities and services are based on COICOP codes broadly mapped to FES. Weighting is based on the population figures from the 2001 census

Most of the analysis in 'Family Spending' is done using quantiles. The quantiles of a distribution, e.g. of household expenditure or income, divide it into a number of equal parts; each of which contains the same number of households.

For example, the median of a distribution divides it into two equal parts, so that half the households in a distribution of household income will have income more than the median, and the other half will have income less than the median. Similarly, quartiles, quintiles and deciles divide the distribution into four, five and ten equal parts respectively.

The most common quantiles used in 'Family Spending' are quintile groups and decile groups. In the calculation of quantiles for this report, zero values are counted as part of the distribution.

From 2001-02, the Classification Of Individual COnsumption by Purpose (COICOP/HBS, referred to as COICOP in this volume) was introduced as a new coding frame for expenditure items (see definitions Page 195). COICOP is the internationally agreed classification system for reporting household consumption expenditure. Total expenditure is made up from the total of the COICOP expenditure groups (1-12) plus 'Other expenditure items (13)'. Other expenditure items are all items which are considered to be non-consumption expenditure and therefore are excluded from COICOP expenditure groups.

Table A1 provides the most detailed breakdown of household expenditure. Weekly expenditure is averaged over all households in the survey (including those reporting zero expenditure on a specific item) and is shown for over 160 items, many of which are further sub-divided. Details concerning other items that are not classified as expenditure in the context of Family Spending are also shown, under the heading 'Other items recorded'.

Appendix A

- Average weekly expenditure in 2003-04 was £418. It ranged from £140 a week in the lowest of the ten income decile groups to £905 a week in the highest. (Table A6)

- Average gross income was £570 a week in 2003-04. (Table A40)

- Spending was highest on transport at £61 a week. Next was recreation and culture at £57 a week, followed by food and non-alcoholic drinks at £44 a week. (Table A6)

- Spending on recreation and culture was £57 a week. Around 20 per cent of this was spent on package holidays, at £12 a week while £5 a week was spent on sports admissions, subscriptions and leisure class fees (eg aerobics, dancing), £2 a week on cinema, theatre and museums, and £4 a week on gambling (including the National Lottery). (Table A1)

- Of the £44 spent each week on food and non-alcoholic drinks, £36 was spent in large supermarket chains. Just under a third of the amount spent on petrol, diesel and other motor oils came from purchases in large supermarket chains. (Tables A3 & A4)

- Average weekly expenditure varied by age of household reference person. The highest level of expenditure, at £525 per week, was found in households where the reference person was aged 30 to 49 and the lowest level, at £183 each week, was found in households where the reference person was aged 75 or over. (Table A11)

- The proportion of spending on food and non-alcoholic drinks rose with age from eight per cent where the reference person was aged under 30 to 16 per cent for those aged 75 or over. The proportion spent on restaurants and hotels decreased with age from nine per cent of total spending where the reference person was aged under 50 to six per cent for those aged 75 or over. (Table A12)

- For households where the reference person was in employment, spending was greatest on transport and recreation and culture at £81 and £71 a week respectively. Where the household reference person was unemployed, most was spent on food and non-alcoholic drinks (£29 a week) and recreation and culture (£27 a week). For economically inactive households, the highest expenditure category was recreation and culture, at £38 a week. (Table A19)

- Average weekly household expenditure was highest for households consisting of three or more adults with children, at £686 a week. However, one person non-retired households spent the most per person at £281 a week. (Table A25)

- Average weekly expenditure by households with two adults and children increased from £531 for those with one child, to £611 for two children and £627 for three or more. (Table A25)

- Averaged over the last three years, total expenditure varied from £336 a week in the North East to £486 in London. The UK average was £406 per week and London, the South East and East of England were the only regions in which average expenditure was higher than the UK average. Spending in the North East was 17 per cent lower than the UK average. (Table A35)

● Households in Northern Ireland spent the most on cigarettes, at £8 a week, and households in the South East spent most on recreation and culture, at £64 a week. (Table A37)

● Rural areas spent more than other areas on transport, at £75 a week. They were also the highest spending households on food and non-alcoholic drinks (£47 a week), recreation and culture (£63 a week) and household goods and services (£37 a week). (Table A38)

● Averaged over the last three years, London, the South East and East of England were the only regions that recorded a gross weekly income above the UK average of £554 (£740, £658 and £594 a week respectively). The lowest average incomes were in the North East (£458 a week), Wales (£461 a week) and Northern Ireland (£461 a week). (Table A44)

● Sixty four per cent of all households consisted of one or two persons while only six per cent of households had five or more people in them. Around 30 per cent of households had children, half of which were households with two adults and one or two children. (Table A48)

● Ownership of mobile phones varied from 47 per cent in the lowest income group to 93 per cent in the highest. Other large differences between income groups were reported in the ownership of an internet connection (15 per cent in the lowest compared to 90 per cent in the highest). (Table A51)

● Seventy five per cent of all households owned a car or van, 31 per cent owning two or more. Ownership varied from 29 per cent in the lowest income group, to 97 per cent in the highest. (Table A52)

A1 Components of household expenditure 2003-04

based on weighted data and including children's expenditure

Commodity or service	Average weekly expenditure all house- holds (£)	Total weekly expenditure (£ million)	Recording house- holds in sample	Percentage standard error (full method)
Total number of households			7,048	
1 Food & non-alcoholic drinks	**43.50**	**1,074**	**7,007**	*0.8*
1.1 Food	39.70	980	7,006	*0.8*
1.1.1 Bread, rice and cereals	3.80	94	6,886	*0.9*
1.1.1.1 Rice	0.20	5	1,454	*4.4*
1.1.1.2 Bread	2.00	49	6,720	*1.0*
1.1.1.3 Other breads and cereals	1.60	40	5,568	*1.3*
1.1.2 Pasta products	0.30	8	2,800	*2.2*
1.1.3 Buns, cakes, biscuits etc.	2.70	68	6,213	*1.3*
1.1.3.1 Buns, crispbread and biscuits	1.50	36	5,663	*1.3*
1.1.3.2 Cakes and puddings	1.30	32	4,689	*1.9*
1.1.4 Pastry (savoury)	0.60	15	2,468	*2.0*
1.1.5 Beef (fresh, chilled or frozen)	1.40	35	3,395	*2.3*
1.1.6 Pork (fresh, chilled or frozen)	0.60	14	1,900	*2.6*
1.1.7 Lamb (fresh, chilled or frozen)	0.60	15	1,391	*3.7*
1.1.8 Poultry (fresh, chilled or frozen)	1.60	40	3,679	*1.9*
1.1.9 Bacon and ham	0.90	22	3,488	*1.8*
1.1.10 Other meats and meat preparations	4.90	122	6,340	*1.1*
1.1.10.1 Sausages	0.60	15	3,286	*2.1*
1.1.10.2 Offal, pate etc.	0.10	3	1,130	*4.8*
1.1.10.3 Other preserved or processed meat and meat preparations	4.20	104	6,131	*1.1*
1.1.10.4 Other fresh, chilled or frozen edible meat	0.00	0	26	*32.4*
1.1.11 Fish and fish products	1.80	45	4,496	*1.9*
1.1.11.1 Fish (fresh, chilled or frozen)	0.70	16	1,863	*3.1*
1.1.11.2 Seafood, dried, smoked or salted fish	0.40	9	1,300	*3.8*
1.1.11.3 Other preserved or processed fish and seafood	0.80	19	3,483	*2.2*
1.1.12 Milk	2.20	53	6,530	*1.2*
1.1.12.1 Whole milk	0.70	18	2,917	*2.5*
1.1.12.2 Low fat milk	1.30	32	4,967	*1.3*
1.1.12.3 Preserved milk	0.10	3	519	*6.5*
1.1.13 Cheese and curd	1.40	34	4,997	*1.5*
1.1.14 Eggs	0.40	10	4,123	*1.5*
1.1.15 Other milk products	1.50	37	5,222	*1.6*
1.1.15.1 Other milk products	0.80	19	3,969	*1.9*
1.1.15.2 Yoghurt	0.70	18	3,717	*2.2*
1.1.16 Butter	0.20	6	1,989	*2.6*
1.1.17 Margarine, other vegetable fats and peanut butter	0.40	11	3,661	*1.8*
1.1.18 Cooking oils and fats	0.20	5	1,637	*3.3*
1.1.18.1 Olive oil	0.10	2	459	*6.0*
1.1.18.2 Edible oils and other edible animal fats	0.10	2	1,264	*3.9*
1.1.19 Fresh fruit	2.50	62	5,866	*1.4*
1.1.19.1 Citrus fruits (fresh)	0.40	11	3,114	*2.2*
1.1.19.2 Bananas (fresh)	0.50	11	4,406	*1.5*
1.1.19.3 Apples (fresh)	0.50	13	3,654	*1.7*
1.1.19.4 Pears (fresh)	0.10	3	1,364	*3.4*
1.1.19.5 Stone fruits (fresh)	0.30	9	1,720	*3.4*
1.1.19.6 Berries (fresh)	0.60	15	2,819	*2.5*
1.1.20 Other fresh, chilled or frozen fruits	0.20	5	1,507	*3.5*
1.1.21 Dried fruit and nuts	0.30	9	1,903	*3.3*
1.1.22 Preserved fruit and fruit based products	0.10	4	1,466	*3.3*
1.1.23 Fresh vegetables	3.10	77	6,333	*1.2*
1.1.23.1 Leaf and stem vegetables (fresh or chilled)	0.70	16	4,193	*2.0*
1.1.23.2 Cabbages (fresh or chilled)	0.40	9	3,458	*1.8*
1.1.23.3 Vegetables grown for their fruit (fresh, chilled or frozen)	1.10	28	5,130	*1.5*
1.1.23.4 Root crops, non-starchy bulbs and mushrooms (fresh, chilled or frozen)	1.00	25	5,568	*1.4*

Note: The commodity and service categories are not comparable with those in publications before 2001-02
The numbering system is sequential, it does not use actual COICOP codes

A1 Components of household expenditure (cont.) 2003-04

based on weighted data and including children's expenditure

Commodity or service	Average weekly expenditure all house-holds (£)	Total weekly expenditure (£ million)	Recording house-holds in sample	Percentage standard error (full method)
1 Food & non-alcoholic drinks (continued)				
1.1.24 Dried vegetables and other preserved or processed vegetables	1.00	25	5,266	1.8
1.1.25 Potatoes	0.80	19	4,844	
1.1.26 Other tubers and products of tuber vegetables	1.20	30	4,907	1.3
1.1.27 Sugar and sugar products	0.30	6	2,709	2.5
1.1.28 1.1.28.1 Sugar	0.20	5	2,507	2.5
1.1.28.2 Other sugar products	0.00	1	455	5.8
1.1.29 Jams, marmalades	0.20	5	2,032	3.0
1.1.30 Chocolate	1.30	33	4,170	2.6
1.1.31 Confectionery products	0.60	14	3,512	2.2
1.1.32 Edible ices and ice cream	0.50	12	2,409	2.5
1.1.33 Other food products	1.80	45	5,715	1.6
1.1.33.1 Sauces, condiments	0.90	23	4,448	1.6
1.1.33.2 Baker's yeast, dessert preparations, soups	0.70	17	3,977	2.3
1.1.33.3 Salt, spices, culinary herbs and other food products	0.20	5	1,539	7.9
1.2 Non-alcoholic drinks	3.80	93	6,515	1.1
1.2.1 Coffee	0.50	12	2,130	2.4
1.2.2 Tea	0.40	10	2,651	2.1
1.2.3 Cocoa and powdered chocolate	0.10	2	666	4.9
1.2.4 Fruit and vegetable juices	0.90	23	4,192	1.8
1.2.5 Mineral or spring waters	0.20	5	1,462	3.7
1.2.5 Soft drinks	1.60	40	4,929	1.6
2 Alcoholic drink, tobacco & narcotics	**11.70**	**289**	**4,597**	**2.0**
2.1 Alcoholic drinks	6.20	154	3,696	2.3
2.1.1 Spirits and liqueurs (brought home)	1.30	31	990	4.5
2.1.2 Wines, fortified wines (brought home)	3.00	73	2,460	3.1
2.1.2.1 Wine from grape or other fruit (brought home)	2.60	64	2,211	3.4
2.1.2.2 Fortified wine (brought home)	0.20	5	355	7.0
2.1.2.3 Champagne and sparkling wines (brought home)	0.20	5	237	11.3
2.1.3 Beer, lager, ciders and Perry (brought home)	1.90	46	2,006	2.7
2.1.3.1 Beer and lager (brought home)	1.70	41	1,816	2.9
2.1.3.2 Ciders and Perry (brought home)	0.20	5	393	7.2
2.1.4 Alcopops (brought home)	0.10	4	295	9.2
2.2 Tobacco and narcotics	5.50	135	2,070	3.2
2.2.1 Cigarettes	4.90	120	1,918	3.0
2.2.2 Cigars, other tobacco products and narcotics	0.60	15	484	12.9
2.2.2.1 Cigars	0.10	3	83	16.6
2.2.2.2 Other tobacco	0.40	10	408	6.6
2.2.2.3 Narcotics	0.10	2	6	82.7
3 Clothing & footwear	**22.70**	**561**	**4,895**	**2.1**
3.1 Clothing	18.10	447	4,646	2.3
3.1.1 Men's outer garments	4.40	109	1,448	4.6
3.1.2 Men's under garments	0.40	10	570	5.8
3.1.3 Women's outer garments	8.00	198	2,607	3.3
3.1.4 Women's under garments	1.20	29	1,443	3.7
3.1.5 Boys' outer garments (5-15)	0.80	20	526	6.1
3.1.6 Girls' outer garments (5-15)	1.10	28	719	5.7
3.1.7 Infants' outer garments (under 5)	0.60	16	578	6.2
3.1.8 Children's under garments (under 16)	0.40	9	705	5.2

Note: The commodity and service categories are not comparable with those in publications before 2001-02
The numbering system is sequential, it does not use actual COICOP codes

A1 Components of household expenditure (cont.)   2003-04

based on weighted data and including children's expenditure

	Average weekly expenditure all house-holds (£)	Total weekly expenditure (£ million)	Recording house-holds in sample	Percentage standard error (full method)
Commodity or service				
3 Clothing & footwear (continued)				
3.1.9 Accessories	0.60	16	1,013	5.0
3.1.9.1 Men's accessories	0.30	6	378	7.7
3.1.9.2 Women's accessories	0.20	6	417	7.7
3.1.9.3 Children's accessories	0.10	3	336	8.0
3.1.9.4 Protective head gear (crash helmets)	0.00	1	22	34.0
3.1.10 Haberdashery, clothing materials and clothing hire	0.30	6	399	13.3
3.1.11 Dry cleaners, laundry and dyeing	0.30	6	291	8.4
3.1.11.1 Dry cleaners and dyeing	0.20	5	226	9.1
3.1.11.2 Laundry, launderettes	0.00	1	72	17.2
3.2 Footwear	4.60	114	1,949	3.2
3.2.1 Footwear for men	1.40	35	559	5.8
3.2.2 Footwear for women	2.20	55	1,080	4.5
3.2.3 Footwear for children (5 to 15 years) and infants (under 5)	0.90	22	612	5.1
3.2.4 Repair and hire of footwear	0.10	2	83	15.2
4 Housing (net)[1], fuel & power	**39.00**	**962**	**7,018**	**1.7**
4.1 Actual rentals for housing	23.50	580	2,016	2.5
4.1.1 Gross rent	23.50	579	2,011	2.5
4.1.2 *less* housing benefit, rebates and allowances received	10.20	252	1,386	3.4
4.1.3 Net rent	13.20	327	1,374	3.5
4.1.4 Second dwelling - rent	0.00	1	6	54.7
4.2 Maintenance and repair of dwelling	8.20	201	3,351	6.2
4.2.1 Central heating repairs	1.10	27	1,801	6.8
4.2.2 House maintenance etc.	4.20	104	1,611	9.4
4.2.3 Paint, wallpaper, timber	1.40	34	762	7.7
4.2.4 Equipment hire, small materials	1.50	36	657	18.2
4.3 Water supply and miscellaneous services relating to the dwelling	5.60	138	6,011	1.4
4.3.1 Water charges	4.80	118	5,808	0.2
4.3.2 Other regular housing payments including service charge for rent	0.70	17	843	7.8
4.3.3 Refuse collection, including skip hire	0.10	2	10	55.9
4.4 Electricity, gas and other fuels	12.00	295	6,681	0.8
4.4.1 Electricity	6.00	147	6,501	0.9
4.4.2 Gas	5.20	129	5,135	1.2
4.4.3 Other fuels	0.70	18	647	7.2
4.4.3.1 Coal and coke	0.20	5	185	14.6
4.4.3.2 Oil for central heating	0.50	13	456	8.2
4.4.3.3 Paraffin, wood, peat, hot water etc.	0.00	1	50	24.5
5 Household goods & services	**31.30**	**771**	**6,558**	**2.6**
5.1 Furniture and furnishings, carpets and other floor coverings	16.30	402	3,004	1.8
5.1.1 Furniture and furnishings	12.20	302	2,505	4.2
5.1.1.1 Furniture	10.80	266	1,676	4.6
5.1.1.2 Fancy, decorative goods	1.10	27	1,080	9.3
5.1.1.3 Garden furniture	0.40	9	90	23.2
5.1.2 Floor coverings	4.10	100	1,123	5.8
5.1.2.1 Soft floor coverings	3.40	85	1,043	6.1
5.1.2.2 Hard floor coverings	0.60	15	98	28.3
5.2 Household textiles	2.10	53	1,185	15.5
5.2.1 Bedroom textiles, including duvets and pillows	0.70	16	455	7.5
5.2.2 Other household textiles, including cushions, towels, curtains	1.50	36	867	21.9

Note: The commodity and service categories are not comparable with those in publications before 2001-02
The numbering system is sequential, it does not use actual COICOP codes
1 Excluding mortgage interest payments, council tax and Northern Ireland rates

A1 Components of household expenditure (cont.)

2003-04

based on weighted data and including children's expenditure

Commodity or service	Average weekly expenditure all house- holds (£)	Total weekly expenditure (£ million)	Recording house- holds in sample	Percentage standard error (full method)
5 Household goods & services (continued)				
5.3 Household appliances	3.60	88	817	7.9
5.3.1 Gas cookers	0.10	3	9	50.7
5.3.2 Electric cookers, combined gas/electric cookers	0.40	10	74	32.1
5.3.3 Clothes washing machines and drying machines	0.60	15	117	18.2
5.3.4 Refrigerators, freezers and fridge-freezers	0.40	9	91	21.8
5.3.5 Other major electrical appliances, dishwashers, micro-waves vacuum cleaners, heaters etc.	1.20	30	225	13.7
5.3.6 Fire extinguisher, water softener, safes etc	0.00	1	11	80.4
5.3.7 Small electric household appliances, excluding hairdryers	0.50	11	272	8.8
5.3.8 Repairs to gas and electrical appliances and spare parts	0.30	8	126	14.8
5.3.9 Rental/hire of major household appliances	0.00	1	24	30.6
5.4 Glassware, tableware and household utensils	1.60	40	2,003	7.8
5.4.1 Glassware, china, pottery, cutlery and silverware	0.70	17	848	17.1
5.4.2 Kitchen and domestic utensils	0.50	12	989	5.6
5.4.3 Repair of glassware, tableware and household utensils	0.00	0	2	79.6
5.4.4 Storage and other durable household articles	0.50	12	724	6.3
5.5 Tools and equipment for house and garden	2.80	69	2,482	5.8
5.5.1 Electrical tools	0.40	9	115	15.3
5.5.2 Garden tools, equipment and accessories e.g. lawn mowers etc.	0.50	11	348	11.9
5.5.3 Small tools	0.40	10	565	7.8
5.5.4 Door, electrical and other fittings	0.80	20	665	10.5
5.5.5 Electrical consumables	0.70	18	1,637	11.7
5.6 Goods and services for routine household maintenance	4.80	119	6,049	2.6
5.6.1 Cleaning materials	2.10	52	5,188	1.7
5.6.1.1 Detergents, washing-up liquid, washing powder	1.00	25	3,764	1.9
5.6.1.2 Disinfectants, polishes, other cleaning materials etc.	1.10	27	4,260	2.3
5.6.2 Household goods and hardware	1.20	28	4,417	2.4
5.6.2.1 Kitchen disposables	0.60	15	3,603	2.3
5.6.2.2 Household hardware and appliances, matches	0.30	7	1,121	5.0
5.6.2.3 Kitchen gloves, cloths etc.	0.10	3	1,180	4.1
5.6.2.4 Pins, needles, tape measures, nails, nuts and bolts etc.	0.10	4	521	9.4
5.6.3 Domestic services, carpet cleaning	1.60	39	1,141	7.3
5.6.3.1 Domestic services, including cleaners, gardeners, au pairs	1.10	27	382	10.1
5.6.3.2 Carpet cleaning, ironing service, window cleaner	0.40	10	856	7.7
5.6.3.3 Hire/repair of household furniture and furnishings	0.10	1	6	54.7
6 Health	**5.00**	**125**	**3,604**	**6.5**
6.1 Medical products, appliances and equipment	3.30	81	3,403	7.2
6.1.1 Medicines, prescriptions and healthcare products	1.60	39	3,230	2.8
6.1.1.1 NHS prescription charges and payments	0.30	7	344	8.5
6.1.1.2 Medicines and medical goods (not NHS)	1.20	29	2,952	3.1
6.1.1.3 Other medical products (e.g. plasters, condoms, hot water bottle etc.)	0.10	3	388	7.6
6.1.2 Spectacles, lenses, accessories and repairs	1.50	36	367	10.6
6.1.2.1 Purchase of spectacles, lenses, prescription sunglasses	1.40	35	314	10.8
6.1.2.2 Accessories/repairs to spectacles/lenses	0.00	1	65	17.5
6.1.3 Non-optical appliances and equipment (e.g. wheelchairs, batteries for hearing aids, shoe build-up)	0.30	6	30	64.8
6.2 Hospital services	1.70	43	522	12.8
6.2.1 Out patient services	1.50	36	514	7.0
6.2.1.1 NHS medical, optical, dental and medical auxiliary services	0.60	15	262	11.1
6.2.1.2 Private medical, optical, dental and medical auxiliary services	0.80	20	264	9.7
6.2.1.3 Other services	0.00	0	4	80.8
6.2.2 In-patient hospital services	0.30	7	11	68.0

Note: The commodity and service categories are not comparable with those in publications before 2001-02
The numbering system is sequential, it does not use actual COICOP codes

A1 Components of household expenditure (cont.)

2003-04

based on weighted data and including children's expenditure

	Average weekly expenditure all house-holds (£)	Total weekly expenditure (£ million)	Recording house-holds in sample	Percentage standard error (full method)
Commodity or service				
7 Transport	**60.70**	**1,498**	**6,200**	*2.6*
7.1 Purchase of vehicles	28.10	694	2,076	*4.8*
7.1.1 Purchase of new cars and vans	11.40	282	590	*8.1*
7.1.1.1 Outright purchases	6.80	167	246	*9.5*
7.1.1.2 Loan/Hire Purchase of new car/van	4.70	115	405	*12.0*
7.1.2 Purchase of second hand cars or vans	16.00	394	1,490	*6.1*
7.1.2.1 Outright purchases	9.50	235	896	*4.8*
7.1.2.2 Loan/Hire Purchase of second hand car/van	6.50	160	771	*13.2*
7.1.3 Purchase of motorcycles	0.70	18	114	*19.0*
7.1.3.1 Outright purchases of new or second hand motorcycles	0.30	8	42	*25.1*
7.1.3.2 Loan/Hire Purchase of new or second hand motorcycles	0.30	7	41	*38.8*
7.1.3.3 Purchase of bicycles and other vehicles	0.20	4	40	*20.8*
7.2 Operation of personal transport	23.80	587	5,133	*1.8*
7.2.1 Spares and accessories	2.00	49	589	*10.0*
7.2.1.1 Car/van accessories and fittings	0.20	5	149	*16.9*
7.2.1.2 Car/van spare parts	1.50	38	365	*12.0*
7.2.1.3 Motorcycle accessories and spare parts	0.10	3	30	*27.5*
7.2.1.4 Bicycle accessories, repairs and other costs	0.10	3	104	*17.6*
7.2.2 Petrol, diesel and other motor oils	15.00	369	4,564	*1.6*
7.2.2.1 Petrol	12.40	306	4,065	*1.8*
7.2.2.2 Diesel oil	2.50	61	858	*4.2*
7.2.2.3 Other motor oils	0.10	2	111	*12.5*
7.2.3 Repairs and servicing	5.00	122	2,155	*3.4*
7.2.3.1 Car or van repairs, servicing and other work	4.90	121	2,138	*3.4*
7.2.3.2 Motorcycle repairs and servicing	0.10	1	28	*28.5*
7.2.4 Other motoring costs	1.90	47	2,711	*3.7*
7.2.4.1 Motoring organisation subscription (e.g. AA and RAC)	0.40	10	1,122	*6.8*
7.2.4.2 Garage rent, other costs (excluding fines), car washing etc.	0.50	13	465	*7.8*
7.2.4.3 Parking fees, tolls, and permits (excluding motoring fines)	0.60	16	1,567	*6.2*
7.2.4.4 Driving lessons	0.20	6	92	*13.8*
7.2.4.5 Anti-freeze, battery water, cleaning materials	0.10	2	313	*9.7*
7.3 Transport services	8.80	217	3,248	*5.5*
7.3.1 Rail and tube fares	1.90	46	863	*5.5*
7.3.1.1 Season tickets	0.70	16	156	*11.2*
7.3.1.2 Other than season tickets	1.20	30	765	*5.9*
7.3.2 Bus and coach fares	1.40	36	1,859	*3.5*
7.3.2.1 Season tickets	0.40	9	269	*7.5*
7.3.2.2 Other than season tickets	1.10	27	1,732	*3.6*
7.3.3 Combined fares	0.70	17	234	*66.9*
7.3.3.1 Combined fares other than season tickets	0.10	4	130	*12.0*
7.3.3.2 Combined fares season tickets	0.50	14	124	*13.0*
7.3.4 Other travel and transport	4.80	118	1,710	*9.7*
7.3.4.1 Air fares (within UK)	0.20	5	24	*24.9*
7.3.4.2 Air fares (international)	1.70	43	63	*25.4*
7.3.4.3 School travel	0.10	1	100	*15.3*
7.3.4.4 Taxis and hired cars with drivers	1.30	33	1,193	*5.2*
7.3.4.5 Other personal travel and transport services	0.20	5	287	*8.5*
7.3.4.6 Hire of self-drive cars, vans, bicycles	0.20	5	44	*28.1*
7.3.4.7 Car leasing	0.90	22	137	*11.6*
7.3.4.8 Water travel, ferries and season tickets	0.20	4	78	*24.1*

Note: The commodity and service categories are not comparable with those in publications before 2001-02
The numbering system is sequential, it does not use actual COICOP codes

A1 Components of household expenditure (cont.) 2003-04
based on weighted data and including children's expenditure

Commodity or service	Average weekly expenditure all house-holds (£)	Total weekly expenditure (£ million)	Recording house-holds in sample	Percentage standard error (full method)
8 Communication	**11.20**	**277**	**6,763**	*1.8*
8.1 Postal services	0.50	12	1,563	*4.9*
8.2 Telephone and telefax equipment	0.60	15	232	*11.1*
8.2.1 Telephone purchase	0.10	3	62	*18.2*
8.2.2 Mobile phone purchase	0.50	12	165	*13.1*
8.2.3 Answering machine, fax machine, modem purchase	0.00	1	09	*42.7*
8.3 Telephone and telefax services	10.10	249	6,722	*1.7*
8.3.1 Telephone account	5.90	146	6,390	*1.1*
8.3.2 Telephone coin and other payments	0.10	2	246	*10.8*
8.3.3 Mobile phone account	2.70	68	1,757	*5.7*
8.3.4 Mobile phone - other payments	1.40	34	1,184	*3.3*
9 Recreation & culture	**57.30**	**1,413**	**6,988**	*1.9*
9.1 Audio-visual, photographic and information processing equipment	8.60	212	2,552	*5.4*
9.1.1 Audio equipment and accessories, CD players	2.10	52	1,327	*5.8*
9.1.1.1 Audio equipment, CD players including in car	0.70	17	191	*15.8*
9.1.1.2 Audio accessories e.g. tapes, headphones etc.	1.40	35	1,206	*3.6*
9.1.2 TV, video and computers	5.80	142	1,610	*7.3*
9.1.2.1 Purchase of TV and digital decoder	1.90	46	223	*17.3*
9.1.2.2 Satellite dish purchase and installation	0.00	1	9	*40.3*
9.1.2.3 Cable TV connection	0.00	0	1	*98.6*
9.1.2.4 Video recorder	0.40	10	108	*15.9*
9.1.2.5 DVD player/recorder	0.10	2	12	*37.8*
9.1.2.6 Blank, pre-recorded video cassettes, DVDs	1.30	33	1,058	*4.9*
9.1.2.7 Personal computers, printers and calculators	1.80	44	377	*13.4*
9.1.2.8 Spare parts for TV, video, audio	0.10	3	90	*21.4*
9.1.2.9 Repair of audio-visual, photographic and information processing	0.10	3	51	*19.2*
9.1.3 Photographic, cine and optical equipment	0.70	18	348	*13.6*
9.1.3.1 Photographic and cine equipment	0.60	15	191	*15.5*
9.1.3.2 Camera films	0.10	2	156	*11.2*
9.1.3.3 Optical instruments, binoculars, telescopes, microscopes	0.00	1	19	*27.4*
9.2 Other major durables for recreation and culture	2.30	56	192	*22.6*
9.2.1 Purchase of boats, trailers and horses	0.20	6	18	*45.4*
9.2.2 Purchase of caravans, mobile homes (including decoration)	1.40	34	43	*35.6*
9.2.3 Accessories for boats, horses, caravans and motor caravans	0.10	2	24	*46.2*
9.2.4 Musical instruments (purchase and hire)	0.20	4	62	*27.3*
9.2.5 Major durables for indoor recreation	0.00	0	13	*43.1*
9.2.6 Maintenance and repair of other major durables	0.20	6	38	*28.7*
9.2.7 Purchase of motor caravan (new and second-hand) - outright purchase	0.10	3	8	*41.7*
9.2.8 Purchase of motor caravan (new and second-hand) - loan/HP	0.00	1	5	*49.7*
9.3 Other recreational items and equipment, gardens and pets	10.30	254	4,975	*2.8*
9.3.1 Games, toys and hobbies	2.60	65	1,944	*6.0*
9.3.2 Computer software and games	1.10	27	430	*7.9*
9.3.2.1 Computer software and game cartridges	0.80	20	403	*7.0*
9.3.2.2 Computer games consoles	0.30	8	55	*19.2*
9.3.3 Equipment for sport, camping and open-air recreation	1.00	24	585	*9.5*
9.3.4 Horticultural goods, garden equipment and plants etc.	2.70	67	2,704	*3.7*
9.3.4.1 BBQ and swings	0.20	4	69	*32.9*
9.3.4.2 Plants, flowers, seeds, fertilisers, insecticides	2.40	59	2,596	*3.4*
9.3.4.3 Garden decorative	0.10	2	89	*20.2*
9.3.4.4 Artificial flowers, pot pourri	0.00	1	139	*11.9*
9.3.5 Pets and pet food	2.90	71	2,700	*5.2*
9.3.5.1 Pet food	1.50	38	2,578	*2.8*
9.3.5.2 Pet purchase and accessories	0.70	16	700	*16.8*
9.3.5.3 Veterinary and other services for pets identified separately	0.70	17	200	*10.9*

Note: The commodity and service categories are not comparable with those in publications before 2001-02
The numbering system is sequential, it does not use actual COICOP codes

A1 Components of household expenditure (cont.)

2003-04

based on weighted data and including children's expenditure

Commodity or service	Average weekly expenditure all house-holds (£)	Total weekly expenditure (£ million)	Recording house-holds in sample	Percentage standard error (full method)
9 Recreation & culture (continued)				
9.4 Recreational and cultural services	17.00	420	6,681	2.2
9.4.1 Sports admissions, subscriptions, leisure class fees and equipment hire	4.70	116	2,906	3.5
9.4.1.1 Spectator sports: admission charges	0.50	13	239	13.0
9.4.1.2 Participant sports (excluding subscriptions)	1.10	26	1,277	5.3
9.4.1.3 Subscriptions to sports and social clubs	1.40	36	1,238	7.5
9.4.1.4 Leisure class fees	1.70	41	1,378	4.4
9.4.1.5 Hire of equipment for sport and open air recreation	0.00	1	60	28.6
9.4.2 Cinema, theatre and museums etc.	1.70	42	1,202	5.2
9.4.2.1 Cinemas	0.50	12	698	4.7
9.4.2.2 Live entertainment: theatre, concerts, shows	0.80	19	357	8.1
9.4.2.3 Museums, zoological gardens, theme parks, houses and gardens	0.40	10	309	11.1
9.4.3 TV, video, satellite rental, cable subscriptions, TV licences and Internet	5.20	129	6,213	1.1
9.4.3.1 TV licences	1.90	46	5,998	0.7
9.4.3.2 Satellite subscriptions	1.90	47	1,788	2.4
9.4.3.3 Rent for TV/Satellite/VCR	0.30	7	366	6.0
9.4.3.4 Cable subscriptions	0.80	19	798	5.4
9.4.3.5 TV slot meter payments	0.00	1	25	37.9
9.4.3.6 Video, cassette and CD hire	0.10	4	405	7.0
9.4.3.7 Internet subscription fees	0.20	6	351	7.0
9.4.4 Miscellaneous entertainments	1.10	27	1,832	8.0
9.4.4.1 Admissions to clubs, dances, discos, bingo	0.50	14	982	5.2
9.4.4.2 Social events and gatherings	0.30	7	373	27.3
9.4.4.3 Subscriptions for leisure activities and other subscriptions	0.30	7	734	7.6
9.4.5 Development of film, deposit for film development, passport photos, holiday and school photos	0.70	16	535	23.6
9.4.6 Gambling payments	3.60	89	3,848	5.8
9.4.6.1 Football pools stakes	0.10	2	114	25.6
9.4.6.2 Bingo stakes excluding admission	0.40	10	316	9.0
9.4.6.3 Lottery	2.20	54	3,397	2.4
9.4.6.4 Bookmaker, tote, other betting stakes	1.00	24	1,027	19.3
9.5 Newspapers, books and stationery	6.70	166	6,462	2.2
9.5.1 Books, diaries, address books, cards etc.	3.60	90	4,525	3.4
9.5.1.1 Books	1.60	39	1,641	5.7
9.5.1.2 Stationery, diaries, address books, art materials	0.80	19	1,865	7.2
9.5.1.3 Cards, calendars, posters and other printed matter	1.30	32	3,503	2.9
9.5.2 Newspapers	2.00	50	5,096	1.7
9.5.3 Magazines and periodicals	1.10	26	3,543	2.6
9.6 Package holidays	12.40	306	1,221	4.0
9.6.1 Package holidays - UK	0.80	19	223	9.3
9.6.2 Package holidays - abroad	11.60	287	1,043	4.2
10 Education	**5.20**	**129**	**647**	**9.0**
10.1 Education fees	4.90	122	476	9.4
10.1.1 Nursery and primary education	1.00	25	80	15.7
10.1.2 Secondary education	1.30	31	74	21.7
10.1.3 Sixth form college/college education	0.40	10	62	27.9
10.1.4 University education	1.90	47	180	14.1
10.1.5 Other education	0.40	9	112	21.5
10.2 Payments for school trips, other ad-hoc expenditure	0.30	8	204	13.6
10.2.1 Nursery and primary education	0.10	2	98	16.7
10.2.2 Secondary education	0.10	3	82	18.9
10.2.3 Sixth form college/college education	0.00	1	16	61.9
10.2.4 University education	0.00	1	9	42.6
10.2.5 Other education	0.00	1	12	42.9

Note: The commodity and service categories are not comparable with those in publications before 2001-02
The numbering system is sequential, it does not use actual COICOP codes

A1 Components of household expenditure (cont.)

based on weighted data and including children's expenditure

2003-04

Commodity or service	Average weekly expenditure all house-holds (£)	Total weekly expenditure (£ million)	Recording house-holds in sample	Percentage standard error (full method)
11 **Restaurants & hotels**	**34.90**	**861**	**6,337**	*1.6*
11.1 Catering services	29.90	737	6,297	*1.5*
11.1.1 Restaurant and café meals	11.20	275	5,127	*2.1*
11.1.2 Alcoholic drinks (away from home)	8.50	210	3,538	*2.2*
11.1.3 Take away meals eaten at home	3.70	91	3,351	*2.2*
11.1.4 Other take-away and snack food	4.40	108	4,431	*2.0*
11.1.4.1 Hot and cold food	2.90	71	3,850	*2.3*
11.1.4.2 Confectionery	0.40	11	2,697	*2.2*
11.1.4.3 Ice cream	0.10	4	941	*4.7*
11.1.4.4 Soft drinks	0.90	22	3,047	*2.4*
11.1.5 Contract catering (food)	0.20	6	39	*37.7*
11.1.6 Canteens	1.90	47	2,506	*2.6*
11.1.6.1 School meals	0.60	15	940	*4.1*
11.1.6.2 Meals bought and eaten at the workplace	1.30	32	2,004	*3.1*
11.2 Accommodation services	5.00	124	1,205	*4.9*
11.2.1 Holiday in the UK	2.40	59	817	*5.4*
11.2.2 Holiday abroad	2.50	62	467	*7.7*
11.2.3 Room hire	0.10	3	19	*50.3*
12 **Miscellaneous goods and services**	**33.60**	**829**	**6,914**	*1.9*
12.1 Personal care	9.00	222	6,159	*1.8*
12.1.1 Hairdressing, beauty treatment	2.60	65	1,835	*3.4*
12.1.2 Toilet paper	0.70	17	3,542	*1.8*
12.1.3 Toiletries and soap	1.90	47	4,740	*1.9*
12.1.3.1 Toiletries (disposable including tampons, lipsyl, toothpaste etc.)	1.10	28	4,003	*2.0*
12.1.3.2 Bar of soap, liquid soap, shower gel etc.	0.30	8	1,828	*3.9*
12.1.3.3 Toilet requisites (durable including razors, hairbrushes, toothbrushes etc	0.50	12	1,724	*3.8*
12.1.4 Baby toiletries and accessories (disposable)	0.50	13	958	*4.1*
12.1.5 Hair products, cosmetics and electrical appliances for personal care	3.20	80	3,927	*2.9*
12.1.5.1 Hair products	0.70	17	2,414	*2.5*
12.1.5.2 Cosmetics and related accessories	2.20	54	2,898	*3.3*
12.1.5.3 Electrical appliances for personal care, including hairdryers, shavers etc.	0.30	9	191	*11.8*
12.2 Personal effects	3.40	84	1,794	*9.1*
12.2.1 Jewellery, clocks and watches and other personal effects	2.40	59	1,255	*12.1*
12.2.2 Leather and travel goods (excluding baby items)	0.70	16	664	*7.8*
12.2.3 Sunglasses (non-prescription)	0.10	2	96	*15.9*
12.2.4 Baby equipment (excluding prams and pushchairs)	0.10	2	50	*19.5*
12.2.5 Prams, pram accessories and pushchairs	0.10	3	25	*33.0*
12.2.6 Repairs to personal goods	0.10	3	50	*27.5*
12.3 Social protection	2.30	57	368	*9.8*
12.3.1 Residential homes	0.10	2	10	*60.1*
12.3.2 Home help	0.20	4	64	*19.8*
12.3.3 Nursery, crèche, playschools	0.60	15	110	*22.3*
12.3.4 Child care payments	1.40	35	200	*11.2*

Note: The commodity and service categories are not comparable with those in publications before 2001-02
The numbering system is sequential, it does not use actual COICOP codes

A1 Components of household expenditure (cont.)

2003-04

based on weighted data and including children's expenditure

	Average weekly expenditure all house-holds (£)	Total weekly expenditure (£ million)	Recording house-holds in sample	Percentage standard error (full method)
Commodity or service				
12 Miscellaneous goods and services (continued)				
12.4 Insurance	14.50	357	6,206	1.5
12.4.1 Household insurances	4.80	118	5,643	2.0
12.4.1.1 Structure insurance	2.30	56	4,476	2.3
12.4.1.2 Contents insurance	2.40	58	5,431	2.0
12.4.1.3 Insurance for household appliances	0.20	4	122	24.4
12.4.2 Medical insurance premiums	1.50	38	858	5.8
12.4.3 Vehicle insurance including boat insurance	7.90	196	5,076	1.7
12.4.3.1 Vehicle insurance	7.90	196	5,076	1.7
12.4.3.2 Boat insurance (not home)	0.00	0	5	47.7
12.4.4 Non-package holiday, other travel insurance	0.20	4	48	31.6
12.5 Other services	4.50	110	2,939	7.3
12.5.1 Moving house	2.30	56	563	8.1
12.5.1.1 Moving and storage of furniture	0.30	6	223	9.2
12.5.1.2 Property transaction - purchase and sale	0.90	22	129	14.5
12.5.1.3 Property transaction - sale only	0.50	12	75	16.8
12.5.1.4 Property transaction - purchase only	0.50	12	207	10.8
12.5.1.5 Property transaction - other payments	0.10	4	137	12.6
12.5.2 Bank, building society, post office, credit card charges	0.40	9	1,476	4.7
12.4.5.1 Bank and building society charges	0.30	6	956	6.2
12.4.5.2 Bank and Post Office counter charges	0.00	0	12	46.8
12.4.5.3 Annual standing charge for credit cards	0.00	1	483	8.1
12.4.5.4 Commission travellers' cheques and currency	0.10	1	184	10.4
12.5.3 Other services and professional fees	1.80	45	1587	15.9
12.5.3.1 Other professional fees including court fines	0.20	6	55	60.3
12.5.3.2 Legal fees	0.40	10	36	24.1
12.5.3.3 Funeral expenses	0.50	12	19	50.3
12.5.3.4 TU and professional organisations	0.60	14	1286	4.7
12.5.3.5 Other payments for services e.g. photocopying	0.10	3	292	16.3
1-12 All expenditure groups	**356.20**	**8,788**	**7,048**	*1.0*
13 Other expenditure items	**61.90**	**1,527**	**6,592**	*2.0*
13.1 Housing: mortgage interest payments, council tax etc.	41.00	1,012	6,015	1.5
13.1.1 Mortgage interest payments	24.20	596	2,852	2.0
13.1.2 Mortgage protection premiums	1.50	38	1,466	3.6
13.1.3 Council tax, domestic rates	14.70	361	5,947	0.8
13.1.4 Council tax, mortgage, insurance (secondary dwelling)	0.70	18	51	30.8
13.2 Licences, fines and transfers	2.90	72	4,986	3.8
13.2.1 Stamp duty, licences and fines (excluding motoring fines)	0.40	10	145	25.8
13.2.2 Motoring fines	0.10	1	18	25.8
13.2.3 Motor vehicle road taxation payments less refunds	2.50	61	4,962	1.2
13.3 Holiday spending	8.30	204	383	9.6
13.3.1 Money spent abroad	8.20	203	382	9.6
13.3.2 Duty free goods bought in UK	0.00	0	6	47.4

Note: The commodity and service categories are not comparable with those in publications before 2001-02
The numbering system is sequential, it does not use actual COICOP codes

A1   Components of household expenditure (cont.)

2003-04

based on weighted data and including children's expenditure

Commodity or service	Average weekly expenditure all house- holds (£)	Total weekly expenditure (£ million)	Recording house- holds in sample	Percentage standard error (full method)
13 Other expenditure items (continued)				
13.4 Money transfers and credit	9.70	238	4,139	4.4
13.4.1 Money, cash gifts given to children	0.10	3	202	11.0
13.4.1.1 Money given to children for specific purposes	0.10	3	192	11.5
13.4.1.2 Cash gifts to children (no specific purpose)	0.00	0	16	40.2
13.4.2 Cash gifts and donations	7.90	196	3,221	5.3
13.4.2.1 Money/presents given to those outside the household	3.30	80	1,372	9.4
13.4.2.2 Charitable donations and subscriptions	1.80	45	2,165	5.8
13.4.2.3 Money sent abroad	1.10	27	390	18.2
13.4.2.4 Maintenance allowance expenditure	1.70	43	194	9.5
13.4.3 Club instalment payments (child) and interest on credit cards	1.60	40	1,649	3.8
13.4.3.1 Club instalment payment	0.00	0	1	0.0
13.4.3.2 Interest on credit cards	1.60	40	1,649	3.8
Total expenditure	**418.10**	**10,315**	**7,048**	**1.0**
14 Other items recorded				
14.1 Life assurance, contributions to pension funds	19.90	490	4,268	2.4
14.1.1 Life assurance premiums eg mortgage endowment policies	7.00	173	3,285	3.3
14.1.2 Contributions to pension and superannuation funds etc.	8.70	214	2,222	2.6
14.1.3 Personal pensions	4.20	103	1,016	5.8
14.2 Other insurance including Friendly Societies	1.20	31	1,980	3.9
14.3 Income tax, payments less refunds	78.20	1,930	5,640	2.8
14.3.1 Income tax paid by employees under PAYE	59.40	1,465	3,802	2.9
14.3.2 Income tax paid direct eg by retired or unoccupied persons	2.10	52	267	20.7
14.3.3 Income tax paid direct by self-employed	6.60	162	407	8.6
14.3.4 Income tax deducted at source from income under covenant from investments or from annuities and pensions	8.30	205	3,704	3.5
14.3.5 Income tax on bonus earnings	3.00	75	1,231	17.1
14.3.6 Income tax refunds under PAYE	0.20	5	70	21.7
14.3.7 Income tax refunds other than PAYE	1.00	25	527	10.2
14.4 National insurance contribution	22.00	543	3,767	1.5
14.4.1 NI contributions paid by employees	21.80	539	3,729	1.5
14.4.2 NI contributions paid by non-employees	0.20	4	60	33.3
14.5 Purchase or alteration of dwellings (contracted out), mortgages	40.80	1,006	2,860	5.5
14.5.1 Outright purchase of houses, flats etc. including deposits	0.50	11	17	66.0
14.5.2 Capital repayment of mortgage	13.10	324	1,943	3.3
14.5.3 Central heating installation	1.20	29	169	10.7
14.5.4 DIY improvements: Double Glazing, Kitchen Units, Sheds etc.	3.00	75	157	22.1
14.5.5 Home improvements - contracted out	17.10	423	1,242	7.1
14.5.6 Bathroom fittings	0.70	18	116	
14.5.7 Purchase of materials for Capital Improvements	0.70	18	93	22.0
14.5.8 Purchase of second dwelling	4.30	107	68	38.3
14.6 Savings and investments	7.20	177	1,411	10.0
14.6.1 Savings, investments (excluding AVCs)	6.20	152	1,038	11.6
14.6.2 Additional Voluntary Contributions	0.80	19	222	9.7
14.6.3 Food stamps, other food related expenditure	0.20	5	339	9.8
14.7 Pay off loan to clear other debt	2.60	64	458	5.6
14.8 Windfall receipts from gambling etc.	1.90	47	767	11.8

Note: The commodity and service categories are not comparable with those in publications before 2001-02
The numbering system is sequential, it does not use actual COICOP codes

A2 Expenditure on alcoholic drink by type of premises

2003-04

based on weighted data and including children's expenditure

			Average weekly expenditure all households (£)	Total weekly expenditure (£ million)	Recording households in sample
By type of premises					
11	**Bought and consumed on licenced premises:**				
11.1.2	Alcoholic drinks (away from home)		8.50	210	3,538
	11.1.2.1 Spirits and liqueurs (away from home)		1.10	27	1,106
	11.1.2.2 Wine from grape or other fruit (away from home)		1.20	29	1,269
	11.1.2.3 Fortified wine (away from home)		0.00	1	85
	11.1.2.4 Champagne and sparkling wines (away from home)		0.10	3	125
	11.1.2.5 Ciders and Perry (away from home)		0.20	4	290
	11.1.2.6 Beer and lager (away from home)		5.10	126	2,936
	11.1.2.7 Alcopops (away from home)		0.40	10	468
	11.1.2.8 Round of drinks (away from home)		0.40	10	235
2	**Bought at off-licences (including large supermarket chains):**				
2.1	Alcoholic drinks		6.20	154	3,696
	2.1.1	Spirits and liqueurs (brought home)	1.30	31	990
	2.1.2	Wines, fortified wines (brought home)	3.00	73	2,460
		2.1.2.1 Wine from grape or other fruit (brought home)	2.60	64	2,211
		2.1.2.2 Fortified wine (brought home)	0.20	5	355
		2.1.2.3 Champagne and sparkling wines (brought home)	0.20	5	237
	2.1.3	Beer, lager, ciders and Perry (brought home)	1.90	46	2,006
		2.1.3.1 Beer and lager (brought home)	1.70	41	1,816
		2.1.3.2 Ciders and Perry (brought home)	0.20	5	393
	2.1.4	Alcopops (brought home)	0.10	4	295
2A	**Bought from large supermarket chains:**				
2.1A	Alcoholic drinks		4.50	112	3,141
	2.1.1A	Spirits and liqueurs (brought home)	1.00	24	807
	2.1.2A	Wines, fortified wines (brought home)	2.30	56	2,128
		2.1.2.1A Wine from grape or other fruit (brought home)	1.90	48	1,884
		2.1.2.2A Fortified wine (brought home)	0.20	4	319
		2.1.2.3A Champagne and sparkling wines (brought home)	0.20	4	215
	2.1.3A	Beer, lager, ciders and Perry (brought home)	1.20	30	1,536
		2.1.3.1A Beer and lager (brought home)	1.10	26	1,377
		2.1.3.2A Ciders and Perry (brought home)	0.10	3	299
	2.1.4A	Alcopops (brought home)	0.10	3	230
2B	**Bought from other off-licence outlets:**				
2.1B	Alcoholic drinks		1.70	42	1,371
	2.1.1B	Spirits and liqueurs (brought home)	0.30	7	260
	2.1.2B	Wines, fortified wines (brought home)	0.70	18	704
		2.1.2.1B Wine from grape or other fruit (brought home)	0.70	16	653
		2.1.2.2B Fortified wine (brought home)	0.00	1	46
		2.1.2.3B Champagne and sparkling wines (brought home)	0.00	1	27
	2.1.3B	Beer, lager, ciders and Perry (brought home)	0.70	16	755
		2.1.3.1B Beer and lager (brought home)	0.60	15	681
		2.1.3.2B Ciders and Perry (brought home)	0.10	1	122
	2.1.4B	Alcopops (brought home)	0.00	1	75

Note: The commodity and service categories are not comparable with those in publications before 2001-02
The numbering system is sequential, it does not use actual COICOP codes

A3 Expenditure on food and non-alcoholic drink by place of purchase 2003-04

based on weighted data and including children's expenditure

		Large supermarket chains			Other outlets		
		Average weekly expenditure all house-holds (£)	Total weekly expenditure (£ million)	Recording house-holds in sample	Average weekly expenditure all house-holds (£)	Total weekly expenditure (£ million)	Recording house-holds in sample
1	**Food and non-alcoholic drinks**	**35.50**	**877**	**6,802**	**8.00**	**197**	**6,356**
1.1	Food	32.40	800	6,797	7.30	181	6,284
1.1.1	Bread, rice and cereals	3.20	78	6,525	0.70	16	3,282
1.1.1.1	Rice	0.20	4	1,290	0.10	1	199
1.1.1.2	Bread	1.50	38	6,227	0.40	11	2,885
1.1.1.3	Other breads and cereals	1.40	36	5,175	0.20	4	1,190
1.1.2	Pasta products	0.30	7	2,604	0.00	1	316
1.1.3	Buns, cakes, biscuits etc.	2.30	58	5,827	0.40	10	2,154
1.1.3.1	Buns, crispbread and biscuits	1.30	31	5,251	0.20	5	1,524
1.1.3.2	Cakes and puddings	1.10	27	4,231	0.20	5	1,247
1.1.4	Pastry (savoury)	0.60	15	2,327	0.00	1	225
1.1.5	Beef (fresh, chilled or frozen)	1.00	25	2,791	0.40	10	893
1.1.6	Pork (fresh, chilled or frozen)	0.40	11	1,553	0.10	3	416
1.1.7	Lamb (fresh, chilled or frozen)	0.40	10	1,014	0.20	5	431
1.1.8	Poultry (fresh, chilled or frozen)	1.40	34	3,247	0.30	6	673
1.1.9	Bacon and ham	0.70	18	2,974	0.20	4	746
1.1.10	Other meats and meat preparations	4.30	107	5,962	0.60	15	2,088
1.1.10.1	Sausages	0.50	12	2,803	0.10	3	748
1.1.10.2	Offal, pate etc.	0.10	2	951	0.00	1	212
1.1.10.3	Other preserved or processed meat and meat preparations	3.70	92	5,765	0.50	12	1,763
1.1.10.4	Other fresh, chilled or frozen meat	0.00	0	10	0.00	0	16
1.1.11	Fish and fish products	1.50	38	4,177	0.30	7	726
1.1.11.1	Fish (fresh, chilled or frozen)	0.50	12	1,579	0.20	4	358
1.1.11.2	Seafood, dried, smoked or salted fish	0.30	8	1,152	0.10	2	195
1.1.11.3	Other preserved or processed fish and seafood	0.70	18	3,272	0.10	2	342
1.1.12	Milk	1.30	33	5,599	0.80	21	3,243
1.1.12.1	Whole milk	0.40	9	2,270	0.40	9	1,399
1.1.12.2	Low fat milk	0.80	21	4,241	0.50	11	2,180
1.1.12.3	Preserved milk	0.10	2	467	0.00	1	84
1.1.13	Cheese and curd	1.20	31	4,686	0.10	3	729
1.1.14	Eggs	0.30	8	3,220	0.10	3	1,156
1.1.15	Other milk products	1.40	34	4,939	0.10	3	863
1.1.15.1	Other milk products	0.70	17	3,734	0.10	2	554
1.1.15.2	Yoghurt	0.70	17	3,483	0.10	1	469
1.1.16	Butter	0.20	5	1,795	0.00	1	271
1.1.17	Margarine, other vegetable fats and peanut butter	0.40	10	3,474	0.00	1	436
1.1.18	Cooking oils and fats	0.20	4	1,479	0.00	1	195
1.1.18.1	Olive oil	0.10	2	417	0.00	0	44
1.1.18.2	Edible oils and other edible animal fats	0.10	2	1,139	0.00	0	153
1.1.19	Fresh fruit	2.10	52	5,352	0.40	10	1,739
1.1.19.1	Citrus fruits (fresh)	0.40	9	2,684	0.10	2	663
1.1.19.2	Bananas (fresh)	0.40	9	3,882	0.10	2	909
1.1.19.3	Apples (fresh)	0.40	11	3,176	0.10	2	772
1.1.19.4	Pears (fresh)	0.10	3	1,124	0.00	1	291
1.1.19.5	Stone fruits (fresh)	0.30	7	1,435	0.10	2	446
1.1.19.6	Berries (fresh)	0.50	13	2,481	0.10	2	571

Note: The commodity and service categories are not comparable with those in publications before 2001-02
The numbering system is sequential, it does not use actual COICOP codes

A3   Expenditure on food and non-alcoholic drink by place of purchase (cont.)   2003-04

based on weighted data and including children's expenditure

		Large supermarket chains			Other outlets		
		Average weekly expenditure all house-holds (£)	Total weekly expenditure (£ million)	Recording house-holds in sample	Average weekly expenditure all house-holds (£)	Total weekly expenditure (£ million)	Recording house-holds in sample
1	**Food and non-alcoholic drinks (continued)**						
1.1.20	Other fresh, chilled or frozen fruits	0.20	4	1,297	0.00	1	285
1.1.21	Dried fruit and nuts	0.30	7	1,596	0.10	2	434
1.1.22	Preserved fruit and fruit based products	0.10	3	1,355	0.00	0	149
1.1.23	Fresh vegetables	2.70	67	5,918	0.40	11	1,978
	1.1.23.1 Leaf and stem vegetables (fresh or chilled)	0.60	15	3,847	0.10	2	736
	1.1.23.2 Cabbages (fresh or chilled)	0.30	7	2,999	0.10	2	767
	1.1.23.3 Vegetables grown for their fruit (fresh, chilled or frozen)	1.00	24	4,685	0.10	4	1,127
	1.1.23.4 Root crops, non-starchy bulbs and mushrooms (fresh, chilled or frozen)	0.90	21	5,078	0.10	4	1,372
1.1.24	Dried vegetables	0.00	0	201	0.00	0	268
1.1.25	Other preserved or processed vegetables	0.00	12	4,179	0.50	12	3,089
1.1.26	Potatoes	0.60	15	4,124	0.10	4	1,238
1.1.27	Other tubers and products of tuber vegetables	1.10	26	4,537	0.10	4	1,295
1.1.28	Sugar and sugar products	0.20	6	2,430	0.00	1	407
	1.1.28.1 Sugar	0.20	5	2,248	0.00	1	364
	1.1.28.2 Other sugar products	0.00	1	404	0.00	0	54
1.1.29	Jams, marmalades	0.20	4	1,793	0.00	1	313
1.1.30	Chocolate	0.90	22	3,351	0.40	11	2,017
1.1.31	Confectionery products	0.30	8	2,552	0.20	6	1,831
1.1.32	Edible ices and ice cream	0.40	11	2,127	0.10	2	450
1.1.33	Other food products	1.60	38	5,352	0.30	7	1,176
	1.1.33.1 Sauces, condiments	0.80	21	4,181	0.10	2	578
	1.1.33.2 Baker's yeast, dessert preparations, soups	0.60	14	3,647	0.10	3	642
	1.1.33.3 Salt, spices, culinary herbs and other food products	0.10	3	1,312	0.10	2	281
1.2	**Non-alcoholic drinks**	3.10	77	6,060	0.70	17	2,725
1.2.1	Coffee	0.40	11	1,876	0.10	2	344
1.2.2	Tea	0.40	9	2,311	0.10	1	436
1.2.3	Cocoa and powdered chocolate	0.10	2	602	0.00	0	74
1.2.4	Fruit and vegetable juices, mineral waters	1.00	24	4,209	0.10	4	997
	1.2.4.1 Fruit and vegetable juices	0.80	20	3,846	0.10	3	723
	1.2.4.2 Mineral or spring waters	0.20	4	1,212	0.00	1	383
1.2.5	Soft drinks	1.30	31	4,343	0.40	10	2,009

Note: The commodity and service categories are not comparable with those in publications before 2001-02
The numbering system is sequential, it does not use actual COICOP codes

A4   Expenditure on selected items by place of purchase   2003-04
based on weighted data and including children's expenditure

		Large Supermarket chains			Other outlets		
		Average weekly expenditure all house-holds (£)	Total weekly expenditure (£ million)	Recording house-holds in sample	Average weekly expenditure all house-holds (£)	Total weekly expenditure (£ million)	Recording house-holds in sample
7.2.2	**Petrol, diesel & other motor oils**	**4.70**	**115**	**1,968**	**10.30**	**254**	**3,498**
10.5.1	Petrol	4.00	98	1,733	8.50	209	3,064
10.5.2	Diesel oil	0.70	17	298	1.80	44	673
10.5.3	Other motor oils	0.00	0	24	0.10	1	89
5	**Household goods and services**						
5.5.5	Electrical consumable	0.10	3	639	0.60	15	1,128
5.6.1	Cleaning materials	1.60	40	4,563	0.50	12	1,654
12	**Miscellaneous goods and services**						
12.1.2	Toilet paper	0.60	14	2,992	0.10	3	740
12.1.3.1 & 12.1.3.3	Toiletries and other toilet requisites - toothpaste, deodorant, tampons, razors, hairbrushes, toothbrushes	0.80	21	3,258	0.80	19	2,251
12.1.3.2	Bar of soap, liquid soap, shower gel etc	0.20	4	1,277	0.10	3	668
12.1.5.2	Cosmetics and related accessories	0.40	10	1,448	1.80	44	1,929
2.2	**Tobacco**	**1.70**	**41**	**1,072**	**3.70**	**92**	**1,801**
2.2.1	Cigarettes	1.50	37	980	3.40	83	1,675
2.2.2	Cigars and other tobacco products	0.20	4	186	0.40	9	389
2.2.2.1	Cigars	0.00	1	34	0.10	2	70
2.2.2.2	Other tobacco	0.10	3	154	0.30	7	327
9	**Recreation and culture**						
9.3.5.1	Pet food	0.90	22	1,975	0.60	16	1,242
9.5.2	Newspapers	0.20	6	2,237	1.80	44	4,693
9.5.3	Magazines and periodicals	0.30	7	1,658	0.80	19	2,669
9.5.1.2 & 9.5.1.3	Stationery, diaries, address books, art materials, cards, calendars, posters and other printed matter	0.40	9	1,511	1.70	43	3,568
8.1	Postal services	0.00	0	0	0.50	12	1,563

Note: The commodity and service categories are not comparable with those in publications before 2001-02
The numbering system is sequential, it does not use actual COICOP codes

A5 Expenditure on clothing and footwear by place of purchase

based on weighted data and including children's expenditure

2003-04

	Large supermarket chains			Clothing chains			Other outlets		
	Average weekly expenditure all households (£)	Total weekly expenditure (£ million)	Recording households in sample	Average weekly expenditure all households (£)	Total weekly expenditure (£ million)	Recording households in sample	Average weekly expenditure all households (£)	Total weekly expenditure (£ million)	Recording households in sample
3 Clothing and footwear	**3.50**	**87**	**1,942**	**6.70**	**166**	**2,016**	**12.10**	**299**	**4,177**
3.1 Clothing	3.20	78	1,827	6.00	147	1,932	8.70	215	3,853
3.1.1 Clothing materials	0.00	0	11	0.00	0	6	0.10	2	71
3.1.2 Men's outer garments	0.50	13	310	1.30	32	472	2.60	64	1,106
3.1.3 Men's under garments	0.10	4	204	0.20	5	183	0.10	1	373
3.1.4 Women's outer garments	1.40	35	699	3.10	77	1,128	3.50	85	1,986
3.1.5 Women's under garments	0.50	12	640	0.60	14	510	0.10	4	927
3.1.6 Boys' outer garments	0.10	3	143	0.10	3	104	0.60	14	405
3.1.7 Girls' outer garments	0.10	3	171	0.20	5	159	0.80	20	572
3.1.8 Infants' outer garments	0.10	3	179	0.10	4	130	0.40	9	394
3.1.9 Children's under garments	0.10	3	214	0.10	2	130	0.20	4	510
3.1.10 Accessories	0.10	3	222	0.20	5	229	0.30	8	754
3.1.10.1 Men's accessories	0.10	1	90	0.10	2	99	0.10	3	273
3.1.10.2 Women's accessories	0.00	1	87	0.10	2	103	0.10	3	297
3.1.10.3 Children's accessories	0.00	0	58	0.00	0	32	0.10	2	272
3.1.11 Haberdashery and clothing hire	0.00	0	28	0.00	0	21	0.20	4	308
3.2 Footwear	0.40	9	311	0.80	19	361	3.40	84	1,599
3.2.1 Men's	0.10	2	73	0.20	4	67	1.20	28	485
3.2.2 Women's	0.20	5	163	0.50	13	249	1.50	37	855
3.2.3 Children's	0.10	1	87	0.10	2	60	0.80	19	518

Note: The commodity and service categories are not comparable with those in publications before 2001-02
The numbering system is sequential, it does not use actual COICOP codes

A6 Household expenditure by gross income decile group 2003-04

based on weighted data and including children's expenditure

	Lowest ten per cent	Second decile group	Third decile group	Fourth decile group	Fifth decile group	Sixth decile group
Lower boundary of group (£ per week)		124	193	263	351	445
Grossed number of households (thousands)	2,470	2,470	2,470	2,460	2,470	2,460
Total number of households in sample	703	720	729	729	715	719
Total number of persons in sample	930	1,212	1,457	1,461	1,730	1,899
Total number of adults in sample	781	924	1,142	1,169	1,296	1,354
Weighted average number of persons per household	1.3	1.6	1.9	1.9	2.4	2.6
Commodity or service	**Average weekly household expenditure (£)**					
1 Food & non-alcoholic drinks	21.40	27.80	34.20	36.50	42.40	44.70
2 Alcoholic drinks, tobacco & narcotics	6.80	7.00	7.90	10.50	12.10	12.30
3 Clothing & footwear	6.70	7.80	11.90	14.10	18.40	22.10
4 Housing (net)[1], fuel & power	22.80	28.30	31.90	34.90	42.00	43.60
5 Household goods & services	10.30	13.80	16.80	20.30	26.60	31.30
6 Health	1.60	1.80	3.10	4.60	5.10	4.50
7 Transport	13.00	16.90	23.30	40.70	48.00	55.30
8 Communication	5.40	5.70	7.20	9.00	10.70	11.20
9 Recreation & culture	17.10	24.00	30.00	42.80	52.10	56.00
10 Education	[1.80]	0.70	2.20	2.10	2.30	1.70
11 Restaurants & hotels	9.50	10.70	15.80	21.70	31.20	32.40
12 Miscellaneous goods & services	11.00	12.60	16.10	22.70	27.90	34.70
1-12 All expenditure groups	127.40	157.10	200.30	259.80	318.80	349.80
13 Other expenditure items	12.20	16.20	23.90	38.50	42.90	61.60
Total expenditure	139.60	173.30	224.20	298.30	361.70	411.40
Average weekly expenditure per person (£)						
Total expenditure	107.80	105.80	115.10	153.70	152.70	159.90

Note: The commodity and service categories are not comparable with those in publications before 2001-02
1 Excluding mortgage interest payments, council tax and Northern Ireland rates

A6 Household expenditure by gross income decile group (cont.)   2003-04

based on weighted data and including children's expenditure

	Seventh decile group	Eighth decile group	Ninth decile group	Highest ten per cent	All house-holds
Lower boundary of group (£ per week)	558	673	828	1,092	
Grossed number of households (thousands)	2,470	2,470	2,470	2,460	24,670
Total number of households in sample	712	687	681	653	7,048
Total number of persons in sample	1,997	2,062	2,093	2,124	16,965
Total number of adults in sample	1,440	1,452	1,522	1,537	12,617
Weighted average number of persons per household	2.7	2.9	3.0	3.2	2.4

Commodity or service	Average weekly household expenditure (£)				
1 Food & non-alcoholic drinks	48.80	51.10	60.60	67.80	43.50
2 Alcoholic drinks, tobacco & narcotics	13.70	14.10	16.60	16.20	11.70
3 Clothing & footwear	25.90	31.70	35.30	53.80	22.70
4 Housing (net)[1], fuel & power	41.50	44.00	42.80	58.00	39.00
5 Household goods & services	34.20	43.00	45.00	71.40	31.30
6 Health	4.90	5.50	8.30	11.00	5.00
7 Transport	67.60	88.20	104.00	150.10	60.70
8 Communication	12.70	14.50	15.60	20.20	11.20
9 Recreation & culture	68.60	77.80	88.40	116.20	57.30
10 Education	2.80	4.00	7.80	27.10	5.20
11 Restaurants & hotels	43.90	50.90	55.50	77.40	34.90
12 Miscellaneous goods & services	41.10	45.00	50.40	74.70	33.60
1-12 All expenditure groups	405.50	469.70	530.40	743.80	356.20
13 Other expenditure items	73.10	87.50	101.80	161.20	61.90
Total expenditure	478.60	557.20	632.30	905.00	418.10
Average weekly expenditure per person (£)					
Total expenditure	175.30	191.20	212.20	284.30	177.40

Note: The commodity and service categories are not comparable with those in publications before 2001-02
1 Excluding mortgage interest payments, council tax and Northern Ireland rates

A7 Household expenditure as a percentage of total expenditure by gross income decile group

2003-04

based on weighted data and including children's expenditure

	Lowest ten per cent	Second decile group	Third decile group	Fourth decile group	Fifth decile group	Sixth decile group
Lower boundary of group (£ per week)		124	193	263	351	445
Grossed number of households (thousands)	2,470	2,470	2,470	2,460	2,470	2,460
Total number of households in sample	703	720	729	729	715	719
Total number of persons in sample	930	1,212	1,457	1,461	1,730	1,899
Total number of adults in sample	781	924	1,142	1,169	1,296	1,354
Weighted average number of persons per household	1.3	1.6	1.9	1.9	2.4	2.6
Commodity or service	**Percentage of total expenditure**					
1 Food & non-alcoholic drinks	15	16	15	12	12	11
2 Alcoholic drinks, tobacco & narcotics	5	4	4	4	3	3
3 Clothing & footwear	5	4	5	5	5	5
4 Housing (net)[1], fuel & power	16	16	14	12	12	11
5 Household goods & services	7	8	7	7	7	8
6 Health	1	1	1	2	1	1
7 Transport	9	10	10	14	13	13
8 Communication	4	3	3	3	3	3
9 Recreation & culture	12	14	13	14	14	14
10 Education	[1]	0	1	1	1	0
11 Restaurants & hotels	7	6	7	7	9	8
12 Miscellaneous goods & services	8	7	7	8	8	8
1-12 All expenditure groups	91	91	89	87	88	85
13 Other expenditure items	9	9	11	13	12	15
Total expenditure	100	100	100	100	100	100

Note: The commodity and service categories are not comparable with those in publications before 2001-02
1 Excluding mortgage interest payments, council tax and Northern Ireland rates

A7 Household expenditure as a percentage of total expenditure by gross income decile group (cont.)

2003-04

based on weighted data and including children's expenditure

	Seventh decile group	Eighth decile group	Ninth decile group	Highest ten per cent	All house-holds
Lower boundary of group (£ per week)	558	673	828	1092	
Grossed number of households (thousands)	2,470	2,470	2,470	2,460	24,670
Total number of households in sample	712	687	681	653	7,048
Total number of persons in sample	1,997	2,062	2,093	2,124	16,965
Total number of adults in sample	1,440	1,452	1,522	1,537	12,617
Weighted average number of persons per household	2.7	2.9	3.0	3.2	2.4
Commodity or service	Percentage of total expenditure				
1 Food & non-alcoholic drinks	10	9	10	7	10
2 Alcoholic drinks, tobacco & narcotics	3	3	3	2	3
3 Clothing & footwear	5	6	6	6	5
4 Housing (net)[1], fuel & power	9	8	7	6	9
5 Household goods & services	7	8	7	8	7
6 Health	1	1	1	1	1
7 Transport	14	16	16	17	15
8 Communication	3	3	2	2	3
9 Recreation & culture	14	14	14	13	14
10 Education	1	1	1	3	1
11 Restaurants & hotels	9	9	9	9	8
12 Miscellaneous goods & services	9	8	8	8	8
1-12 All expenditure groups	85	84	84	82	85
13 Other expenditure items	15	16	16	18	15
Total expenditure	100	100	100	100	100

Note: The commodity and service categories are not comparable with those in publications before 2001-02
1 Excluding mortgage interest payments, council tax and Northern Ireland rates

A8   Detailed household expenditure by gross income decile group   2003-04

based on weighted data and including children's expenditure

	Lowest ten per cent	Second decile group	Third decile group	Fourth decile group	Fifth decile group	Sixth decile group
Lower boundary of group (£ per week)		124	193	263	351	445
Grossed number of households (thousands)	2,470	2,470	2,470	2,460	2,470	2,460
Total number of households in sample	703	720	729	729	715	719
Total number of persons in sample	930	1,212	1,457	1,461	1,730	1,899
Total number of adults in sample	781	924	1,142	1,169	1,296	1,354
Weighted average number of persons per household	1.3	1.6	1.9	1.9	2.4	2.6

Commodity or service	Average weekly household expenditure (£)					
1 Food & non-alcoholic drinks	**21.40**	**27.80**	**34.20**	**36.50**	**42.40**	**44.70**
1.1 Food	19.70	25.60	31.50	33.60	38.70	40.70
1.1.1 Bread, rice and cereals	2.00	2.40	3.10	3.10	3.70	4.10
1.1.2 Pasta products	0.10	0.10	0.20	0.20	0.30	0.30
1.1.3 Buns, cakes, biscuits etc.	1.30	1.90	2.40	2.20	2.70	2.70
1.1.4 Pastry (savoury)	0.30	0.30	0.30	0.50	0.60	0.70
1.1.5 Beef (fresh, chilled or frozen)	0.60	0.80	1.10	1.20	1.60	1.40
1.1.6 Pork (fresh, chilled or frozen)	0.20	0.40	0.40	0.60	0.60	0.60
1.1.7 Lamb (fresh, chilled or frozen)	0.20	0.50	0.60	0.70	0.60	0.60
1.1.8 Poultry (fresh, chilled or frozen)	0.70	0.90	1.00	1.20	1.50	1.60
1.1.9 Bacon and ham	0.50	0.60	0.80	0.80	0.90	0.80
1.1.10 Other meat and meat preparations	2.70	3.40	3.80	4.00	4.70	5.20
1.1.11 Fish and fish products	0.90	1.20	1.50	1.70	1.80	1.70
1.1.12 Milk	1.40	1.70	2.20	2.00	2.30	2.30
1.1.13 Cheese and curd	0.70	0.80	0.90	1.00	1.30	1.50
1.1.14 Eggs	0.30	0.30	0.30	0.40	0.40	0.40
1.1.15 Other milk products	0.70	0.90	1.00	1.30	1.40	1.50
1.1.16 Butter	0.20	0.20	0.20	0.20	0.30	0.20
1.1.17 Margarine, other vegetable fats and peanut butter	0.30	0.30	0.40	0.40	0.50	0.50
1.1.18 Cooking oils and fats	0.10	0.10	0.20	0.20	0.10	0.20
1.1.19 Fresh fruit	1.20	1.50	2.00	2.20	2.30	2.60
1.1.20 Other fresh, chilled or frozen fruits	0.10	0.10	0.10	0.20	0.20	0.20
1.1.21 Dried fruit and nuts	0.20	0.20	0.30	0.30	0.30	0.30
1.1.22 Preserved fruit and fruit based products	0.10	0.10	0.20	0.20	0.10	0.20
1.1.23 Fresh vegetables	1.50	1.70	2.20	2.70	3.10	3.00
1.1.24 Dried vegetables	0.00	0.00	0.00	0.00	0.00	0.00
1.1.25 Other preserved or processed vegetables	0.50	0.50	0.60	0.70	0.90	1.00
1.1.26 Potatoes	0.40	0.50	0.70	0.70	0.80	0.80
1.1.27 Other tubers and products of tuber vegetables	0.50	0.80	0.90	0.90	1.20	1.40
1.1.28 Sugar and sugar products	0.20	0.30	0.30	0.20	0.30	0.30
1.1.29 Jams, marmalades	0.10	0.20	0.20	0.20	0.20	0.20
1.1.30 Chocolate	0.50	0.90	1.20	1.00	1.40	1.30
1.1.31 Confectionery products	0.30	0.40	0.50	0.50	0.50	0.70
1.1.32 Edible ices and ice cream	0.20	0.40	0.40	0.40	0.50	0.50
1.1.33 Other food products	0.90	1.10	1.20	1.40	1.70	1.80
1.2 Non-alcoholic drinks	1.70	2.20	2.70	2.90	3.70	4.00
1.2.1 Coffee	0.20	0.30	0.40	0.50	0.50	0.60
1.2.2 Tea	0.30	0.40	0.40	0.40	0.40	0.40
1.2.3 Cocoa and powdered chocolate	0.10	0.10	0.10	0.10	0.10	0.10
1.2.4 Fruit and vegetable juices	0.40	0.40	0.60	0.60	0.80	0.90
1.2.5 Mineral or spring waters	0.10	0.10	0.10	0.10	0.20	0.20
1.2.6 Soft drinks	0.60	0.90	1.10	1.20	1.60	1.80

Note: The commodity and service categories are not comparable with those in publications before 2001-02
The numbering system is sequential, it does not use actual COICOP codes

A8 Detailed household expenditure by gross income decile group (cont.)   2003-04
based on weighted data and including children's expenditure

	Seventh decile group	Eighth decile group	Ninth decile group	Highest ten per cent	All house- holds
Lower boundary of group (£ per week)	558	673	828	1092	
Grossed number of households (thousands)	2,470	2,470	2,470	2,460	24,670
Total number of households in sample	712	687	681	653	7,048
Total number of persons in sample	1,997	2,062	2,093	2,124	16,965
Total number of adults in sample	1,440	1,452	1,522	1,537	12,617
Weighted average number of persons per household	2.7	2.9	3.0	3.2	2.4

Commodity or service	Average weekly household expenditure (£)				
1 Food & non-alcoholic drinks	**48.80**	**51.10**	**60.60**	**67.80**	**43.50**
1.1 Food	44.40	46.40	55.10	61.70	39.70
1.1.1 Bread, rice and cereals	4.40	4.50	5.20	5.50	3.80
1.1.2 Pasta products	0.40	0.40	0.50	0.50	0.30
1.1.3 Buns, cakes, biscuits etc.	3.20	3.30	3.70	3.90	2.70
1.1.4 Pastry (savoury)	0.70	0.80	1.00	1.10	0.60
1.1.5 Beef (fresh, chilled or frozen)	1.60	1.50	2.00	2.40	1.40
1.1.6 Pork (fresh, chilled or frozen)	0.70	0.60	0.80	0.70	0.60
1.1.7 Lamb (fresh, chilled or frozen)	0.70	0.60	0.90	0.90	0.60
1.1.8 Poultry (fresh, chilled or frozen)	1.90	1.90	2.50	3.10	1.60
1.1.9 Bacon and ham	0.90	1.00	1.20	1.20	0.90
1.1.10 Other meat and meat preparations	5.60	5.90	6.90	7.20	4.90
1.1.11 Fish and fish products	1.80	2.10	2.50	3.00	1.80
1.1.12 Milk	2.40	2.40	2.40	2.50	2.20
1.1.13 Cheese and curd	1.40	1.70	2.10	2.50	1.40
1.1.14 Eggs	0.40	0.50	0.50	0.60	0.40
1.1.15 Other milk products	1.60	1.80	2.20	2.50	1.50
1.1.16 Butter	0.20	0.20	0.30	0.40	0.20
1.1.17 Margarine, other vegetable fats and peanut butter	0.50	0.50	0.50	0.50	0.40
1.1.18 Cooking oils and fats	0.10	0.20	0.20	0.30	0.20
1.1.19 Fresh fruit	2.60	2.80	3.30	4.50	2.50
1.1.20 Other fresh, chilled or frozen fruits	0.30	0.20	0.40	0.40	0.20
1.1.21 Dried fruit and nuts	0.30	0.30	0.50	0.60	0.30
1.1.22 Preserved fruit and fruit based products	0.10	0.10	0.20	0.20	0.10
1.1.23 Fresh vegetables	3.40	3.60	4.50	5.70	3.10
1.1.24 Dried vegetables	0.00	0.00	0.00	0.10	0.00
1.1.25 Other preserved or processed vegetables	1.10	1.30	1.40	1.70	1.00
1.1.26 Potatoes	0.80	0.80	1.00	1.00	0.80
1.1.27 Other tubers and products of tuber vegetables	1.60	1.60	1.70	1.60	1.20
1.1.28 Sugar and sugar products	0.30	0.20	0.30	0.30	0.30
1.1.29 Jams, marmalades	0.20	0.20	0.30	0.30	0.20
1.1.30 Chocolate	1.50	1.70	1.90	2.10	1.30
1.1.31 Confectionery products	0.70	0.70	0.70	0.70	0.60
1.1.32 Edible ices and ice cream	0.50	0.60	0.70	0.80	0.50
1.1.33 Other food products	2.30	2.40	2.60	3.00	1.80
1.2 Non-alcoholic drinks	4.40	4.70	5.50	6.10	3.80
1.2.1 Coffee	0.50	0.60	0.80	0.70	0.50
1.2.2 Tea	0.40	0.40	0.50	0.50	0.40
1.2.3 Cocoa and powdered chocolate	0.10	0.10	0.10	0.10	0.10
1.2.4 Fruit and vegetable juices, mineral waters	1.00	1.10	1.50	1.80	0.90
1.2.5 Mineral or spring waters	0.20	0.30	0.30	0.50	0.20
1.2.6 Soft drinks	2.10	2.20	2.30	2.50	1.60

Note: The commodity and service categories are not comparable with those in publications before 2001-02
The numbering system is sequential, it does not use actual COICOP codes

A8 Detailed household expenditure by gross income decile group (cont.) 2003-04

based on weighted data and including children's expenditure

		Lowest ten per cent	Second decile group	Third decile group	Fourth decile group	Fifth decile group	Sixth decile group
Commodity or service		Average weekly household expenditure (£)					
2	**Alcoholic drink, tobacco & narcotics**	**6.80**	**7.00**	**7.90**	**10.50**	**12.10**	**12.30**
2.1	Alcoholic drinks	2.40	2.60	3.50	4.80	6.10	6.70
2.1.1	Spirits and liqueurs (brought home)	0.70	0.70	1.00	1.20	1.30	1.30
2.1.2	Wines, fortified wines (brought home)	0.80	0.80	1.20	2.30	2.70	3.00
2.1.3	Beer, lager, ciders and Perry (brought home)	0.80	0.90	1.20	1.30	1.90	2.20
2.1.4	Alcopops (brought home)	[0.10]	[0.10]	[0.00]	0.10	0.10	0.20
2.2	Tobacco and narcotics	4.40	4.40	4.40	5.70	6.00	5.60
2.2.1	Cigarettes	3.70	3.80	3.70	5.10	5.20	5.20
2.2.2	Cigars, other tobacco products and narcotics	0.70	0.60	0.60	0.60	0.80	0.40
3	**Clothing & footwear**	**6.70**	**7.80**	**11.90**	**14.10**	**18.40**	**22.10**
3.1	Clothing	4.90	5.80	9.10	11.20	14.60	17.70
3.1.1	Men's outer garments	0.70	0.90	2.00	2.20	3.40	4.80
3.1.2	Men's under garments	0.10	0.20	0.20	0.30	0.40	0.30
3.1.3	Women's outer garments	2.40	2.70	4.00	5.50	6.60	7.60
3.1.4	Women's under garments	0.50	0.50	0.70	1.00	0.90	1.10
3.1.5	Boys' outer garments (5-15)	[0.20]	0.30	0.60	0.40	0.70	0.70
3.1.6	Girls' outer garments (5-15)	[0.30]	0.40	0.60	0.60	1.00	1.10
3.1.7	Infants' outer garments (under 5)	0.30	0.30	0.30	0.40	0.50	0.80
3.1.8	Children's under garments (under 16)	0.20	0.10	0.20	0.30	0.30	0.30
3.1.9	Accessories	0.10	0.20	0.20	0.30	0.60	0.70
3.1.10	Haberdashery and clothing hire	0.10	0.10	0.10	0.20	0.30	0.20
3.1.11	Dry cleaners, laundry and dyeing	[0.10]	[0.10]	0.20	[0.10]	0.10	0.10
3.2	Footwear	1.70	1.90	2.70	2.90	3.70	4.40
4	**Housing (net)[1], fuel & power**	**22.80**	**28.30**	**31.90**	**34.90**	**42.00**	**43.60**
4.1	Actual rentals for housing	50.10	40.00	31.90	24.50	22.70	17.80
4.1.1	Gross rent	50.10	40.00	31.90	24.50	22.70	17.80
4.1.2	*less* housing benefit, rebates & allowances rec'd	42.10	28.80	20.10	10.70	7.00	3.20
4.1.3	Net rent	8.00	11.20	11.80	13.80	15.70	14.60
4.1.4	Second dwelling rent	[0.00]	[0.00]	[0.00]	[0.00]	[0.00]	[0.00]
4.2	Maintenance and repair of dwelling	2.10	3.30	4.30	4.90	9.20	10.80
4.3	Water supply and miscellaneous services relating to the dwelling	4.90	4.90	5.20	5.60	5.50	6.10
4.4	Electricity, gas and other fuels	7.90	8.80	10.60	10.60	11.60	12.20
4.4.1	Electricity	4.30	4.50	5.50	5.40	5.70	5.90
4.4.2	Gas	3.20	3.70	4.60	4.70	5.30	5.40
4.4.3	Other fuels	0.40	0.60	0.50	0.50	0.60	0.90

Note: The commodity and service categories are not comparable with those in publications before 2001-02
The numbering system is sequential, it does not use actual COICOP codes
1 Excluding mortgage interest payments, council tax and Northern Ireland rates

A8 Detailed household expenditure by gross income decile group (cont.)   2003-04

based on weighted data and including children's expenditure

	Seventh decile group	Eighth decile group	Ninth decile group	Highest ten per cent	All house- holds
Commodity or service	Average weekly household expenditure (£)				
2 Alcoholic drink, tobacco & narcotics	**13.70**	**14.10**	**16.60**	**16.20**	**11.70**
2.1 Alcoholic drinks	7.40	8.10	9.30	11.50	6.20
2.1.1 Spirits and liqueurs (brought home)	1.30	1.60	1.80	1.60	1.30
2.1.2 Wines, fortified wines (brought home)	3.60	3.50	4.90	6.80	3.00
2.1.3 Beer, lager, ciders and Perry (brought home)	2.30	2.70	2.50	2.90	1.90
2.1.4 Alcopops (brought home)	0.10	0.30	0.20	0.20	0.10
2.2 Tobacco and narcotics	6.30	6.10	7.20	4.60	5.50
2.2.1 Cigarettes	5.70	5.60	6.00	4.50	4.90
2.2.2 Cigars, other tobacco products and narcotics	0.70	0.40	1.20	[0.20]	0.60
3 Clothing & footwear	**25.90**	**31.70**	**35.30**	**53.80**	**22.70**
3.1 Clothing	20.00	25.10	28.20	44.60	18.10
3.1.1 Men's outer garments	4.40	6.00	7.20	12.60	4.40
3.1.2 Men's under garments	0.30	0.60	0.60	1.00	0.40
3.1.3 Women's outer garments	9.10	11.00	12.20	19.30	8.00
3.1.4 Women's under garments	1.40	1.50	1.70	2.70	1.20
3.1.5 Boys' outer garments (5-15)	1.00	1.20	1.40	1.60	0.80
3.1.6 Girls' outer garments (5-15)	1.40	1.70	1.90	2.50	1.10
3.1.7 Infants' outer garments (under 5)	0.90	0.90	0.70	1.30	0.60
3.1.8 Children's under garments (under 16)	0.50	0.50	0.60	0.70	0.40
3.1.9 Accessories	0.60	0.80	1.20	1.70	0.60
3.1.10 Haberdashery and clothing hire	0.20	0.70	0.30	0.40	0.30
3.1.11 Dry cleaners, laundry and dyeing	0.20	0.30	0.40	0.90	0.30
3.2 Footwear	5.90	6.50	7.10	9.20	4.60
4 Housing (net)[1], fuel & power	**41.50**	**44.00**	**42.80**	**58.00**	**39.00**
4.1 Actual rentals for housing	16.30	15.20	12.70	18.50	25.00
4.1.1 Gross rent	16.20	15.20	12.30	18.40	24.90
4.1.2 *less* housing benefit, rebates & allowances rec'd	[2.00]	[1.00]	[0.80]	[1.20]	11.70
4.1.3 Net rent	14.30	14.20	11.50	17.30	13.20
4.1.4 Second dwelling rent	[0.00]	[0.00]	[0.40]	[0.00]	[0.00]
4.2 Maintenance and repair of dwelling	8.90	11.00	10.60	16.40	8.20
4.3 Water supply and miscellaneous services relating to the dwelling	5.50	5.60	5.60	6.90	5.60
4.4 Electricity, gas and other fuels	12.70	13.20	14.70	17.40	12.00
4.4.1 Electricity	6.50	6.40	7.30	8.30	6.00
4.4.2 Gas	5.50	6.00	6.20	7.90	5.20
4.4.3 Other fuels	0.70	0.80	1.20	1.20	0.70

Note: The commodity and service categories are not comparable with those in publications before 2001-02
The numbering system is sequential, it does not use actual COICOP codes
1 Excluding mortgage interest payments, council tax and Northern Ireland rates

A8 Detailed household expenditure by gross income decile group (cont.) 2003-04

based on weighted data and including children's expenditure

		Lowest ten per cent	Second decile group	Third decile group	Fourth decile group	Fifth decile group	Sixth decile group
Commodity or service		Average weekly household expenditure (£)					
5	**Household goods & services**	**10.30**	**13.80**	**16.80**	**20.30**	**26.60**	**31.30**
5.1	Furniture and furnishings, carpets and other floor coverings	5.80	5.40	8.00	9.80	14.70	14.30
	5.1.1 Furniture and furnishings	3.80	4.10	5.50	7.30	10.30	10.40
	5.1.2 Floor coverings	2.00	1.30	2.50	2.60	4.40	4.00
5.2	Household textiles	0.60	1.00	1.10	1.70	1.50	1.40
5.3	Household appliances	1.10	1.50	2.60	2.50	2.00	5.60
5.4	Glassware, tableware and household utensils	0.50	1.70	0.80	1.20	1.00	1.20
5.5	Tools and equipment for house and garden	0.40	1.10	1.20	1.60	3.40	3.70
5.6	Goods and services for routine household maintenance	1.90	3.10	3.10	3.60	3.90	5.00
	5.6.1 Cleaning materials	1.00	1.30	1.60	1.70	2.00	2.20
	5.6.2 Household goods and hardware	0.50	0.60	0.80	0.90	1.10	1.20
	5.6.3 Domestic services, carpet cleaning, repair of furniture	0.50	1.20	0.70	1.10	0.90	1.60
6	**Health**	**1.60**	**1.80**	**3.10**	**4.60**	**5.10**	**4.50**
6.1	Medical products, appliances and equipment	1.40	1.10	2.30	3.10	3.90	2.50
	6.1.1 Medicines, prescriptions, healthcare products etc.	0.70	0.70	1.20	1.50	3.10	1.60
	6.1.2 Spectacles, lenses, accessories and repairs	[0.80]	[0.50]	1.10	1.60	0.70	0.90
6.2	Hospital services	[0.20]	0.70	0.80	1.50	1.20	2.00
7	**Transport**	**13.00**	**16.90**	**23.30**	**40.70**	**48.00**	**55.30**
7.1	Purchase of vehicles	5.10	6.30	8.00	16.30	21.50	22.70
	7.1.1 Purchase of new cars and vans	[2.50]	[2.30]	[3.60]	8.10	10.50	7.60
	7.1.2 Purchase of second hand cars or vans	2.60	3.90	4.10	7.80	10.70	14.80
	7.1.3 Purchase of motorcycles and other vehicles	[0.10]	[0.10]	[0.30]	[0.40]	[0.40]	[0.30]
7.2	Operation of personal transport	5.30	6.60	10.50	16.40	21.10	26.90
	7.2.1 Spares and accessories	0.40	0.50	0.40	1.00	1.30	3.30
	7.2.2 Petrol, diesel and other motor oils	3.40	4.30	6.60	10.00	13.60	15.90
	7.2.3 Repairs and servicing	1.10	1.50	2.50	4.30	4.60	5.60
	7.2.4 Other motoring costs	0.40	0.40	1.00	1.20	1.60	2.00
7.3	Transport services	2.60	4.00	4.80	8.00	5.40	5.80
	7.3.1 Rail and tube fares	0.30	0.50	0.70	1.00	0.80	1.20
	7.3.2 Bus and coach fares	1.00	1.10	1.20	1.30	1.40	1.60
	7.3.3 Combined fares	[0.10]	[0.20]	[0.10]	[0.20]	[0.20]	[0.40]
	7.3.4 Other travel and transport	1.10	2.30	2.80	5.60	3.00	2.60

Note: The commodity and service categories are not comparable with those in publications before 2001-02
The numbering system is sequential, it does not use actual COICOP codes

A8 Detailed household expenditure by gross income decile group (cont.) 2003-04

based on weighted data and including children's expenditure

		Seventh decile group	Eighth decile group	Ninth decile group	Highest ten per cent	All house- holds
Commodity or service		Average weekly household expenditure (£)				
5	**Household goods & services**	**34.20**	**43.00**	**45.00**	**71.40**	**31.30**
5.1	Furniture and furnishings, carpets and other floor coverings	18.20	20.50	25.50	40.80	16.30
5.1.1	Furniture and furnishings	14.20	15.30	19.50	32.10	12.20
5.1.2	Floor coverings	3.90	5.20	6.00	8.70	4.10
5.2	Household textiles	1.70	5.40	2.90	4.00	2.10
5.3	Household appliances	4.50	5.10	4.60	6.10	3.60
5.4	Glassware, tableware and household utensils	2.10	2.00	2.10	3.60	1.60
5.5	Tools and equipment for house and garden	2.90	4.20	3.70	5.90	2.80
5.6	Goods and services for routine household maintenance	4.80	5.80	6.20	11.00	4.80
5.6.1	Cleaning materials	2.40	2.50	3.00	3.50	2.10
5.6.2	Household goods and hardware	1.30	1.60	1.70	1.90	1.20
5.6.3	Domestic services, carpet cleaning, repair of furniture	1.10	1.60	1.40	5.60	1.60
6	**Health**	**4.90**	**5.50**	**8.30**	**11.00**	**5.00**
6.1	Medical products, appliances and equipment	3.40	4.20	3.90	7.10	3.30
6.1.1	Medicines, prescriptions, healthcare products etc.	1.70	2.00	2.50	3.30	1.80
6.1.2	Spectacles, lenses, accessories and repairs	1.60	2.20	1.50	3.80	1.50
6.2	Hospital services	1.50	1.30	4.40	3.80	1.70
7	**Transport**	**67.60**	**88.20**	**104.00**	**150.10**	**60.70**
7.1	Purchase of vehicles	31.80	41.50	53.90	74.20	28.10
7.1.1	Purchase of new cars and vans	12.00	12.50	19.40	35.90	11.40
7.1.2	Purchase of second hand cars or vans	19.40	28.40	33.10	35.10	16.00
7.1.3	Purchase of motorcycles and other vehicles	[0.40]	[0.60]	1.50	3.30	0.70
7.2	Operation of personal transport	27.30	35.40	37.90	50.60	23.80
7.2.1	Spares and accessories	1.50	3.40	2.70	5.10	2.00
7.2.2	Petrol, diesel and other motor oils	18.20	21.50	24.90	31.20	15.00
7.2.3	Repairs and servicing	5.70	7.50	7.10	9.80	5.00
7.2.4	Other motoring costs	1.90	3.00	3.10	4.50	1.90
7.3	Transport services	8.50	11.30	12.20	25.30	8.80
7.3.1	Rail and tube fares	2.10	1.90	3.70	6.70	1.90
7.3.2	Bus and coach fares	1.60	2.10	1.80	1.50	1.40
7.3.3	Combined fares	[0.60]	1.10	1.30	2.80	0.70
7.3.4	Other travel and transport	4.40	6.20	5.50	14.30	4.80

Note: The commodity and service categories are not comparable with those in publications before 2001-02
The numbering system is sequential, it does not use actual COICOP codes

A8 Detailed household expenditure by gross income decile group (cont.) 2003-04
based on weighted data and including children's expenditure

Commodity or service	Lowest ten per cent	Second decile group	Third decile group	Fourth decile group	Fifth decile group	Sixth decile group
	Average weekly household expenditure (£)					
8 Communication	**5.40**	**5.70**	**7.20**	**9.00**	**10.70**	**11.20**
8.1 Postal services	0.20	0.30	0.40	0.50	0.50	0.50
8.2 Telephone and telefax equipment	[0.20]	[0.30]	[0.40]	[0.50]	0.40	[0.40]
8.3 Telephone and telefax services	5.00	5.10	6.40	8.00	9.70	10.40
9 Recreation & culture	**17.10**	**24.00**	**30.00**	**42.80**	**52.10**	**56.00**
9.1 Audio-visual, photographic and information processing equipment	1.60	5.00	3.10	5.70	7.10	9.30
9.1.1 Audio equipment and accessories, CD players	0.50	0.60	1.20	1.50	2.00	1.60
9.1.2 TV, video and computers	1.00	4.30	1.90	3.50	4.80	6.50
9.1.3 Photographic, cine and optical equipment	[0.00]	[0.20]	0.10	0.70	0.30	1.30
9.2 Other major durables for recreation and culture	[0.10]	[0.70]	[0.20]	[4.00]	[5.90]	[1.80]
9.3 Other recreational items and equipment, gardens and pets	3.00	4.10	6.00	6.40	10.60	10.10
9.3.1 Games, toys and hobbies	0.50	0.80	1.70	1.30	2.90	2.90
9.3.2 Computer software and games	[0.40]	[0.40]	0.30	0.60	1.00	1.20
9.3.3 Equipment for sport, camping and open-air recreation	[0.10]	[0.10]	0.30	0.50	0.70	0.30
9.3.4 Horticultural goods, garden equipment and plants	0.70	1.30	2.00	1.80	2.20	2.70
9.3.5 Pets and pet food	1.30	1.50	1.70	2.20	3.70	3.10
9.4 Recreational and cultural services	7.30	8.00	9.60	11.40	13.70	18.00
9.4.1 Sports admissions, subscriptions, leisure class fees and equipment hire	1.10	1.00	1.30	1.80	3.20	4.20
9.4.2 Cinema, theatre and museums etc.	0.30	0.40	0.70	1.30	1.10	1.30
9.4.3 TV, video, satellite rental, cable subscriptions, TV licences and the Internet	2.40	3.00	3.70	4.40	4.90	6.00
9.4.4 Miscellaneous entertainments	0.30	0.40	0.50	0.60	0.90	1.10
9.4.5 Development of film, deposit for film development, passport photos, holiday and school photos	[1.40]	[0.90]	0.20	0.10	0.30	0.40
9.4.6 Gambling payments	1.80	2.30	3.20	3.20	3.20	5.00
9.5 Newspapers, books and stationery	2.70	3.20	4.50	5.40	6.20	6.50
9.5.1 Books	0.30	0.30	0.60	0.90	1.40	1.40
9.5.2 Diaries, address books, cards etc.	0.70	0.80	1.20	1.60	1.80	2.00
9.5.3 Newspapers	1.30	1.60	2.10	2.10	2.00	2.10
9.5.4 Magazines and periodicals	0.40	0.50	0.70	0.90	1.00	1.00
9.6 Package holidays	2.30	3.00	6.50	9.80	8.70	10.30
9.6.1 Package holidays - UK	0.60	0.90	0.90	0.90	[0.50]	[0.70]
9.6.2 Package holidays - abroad	1.70	2.10	5.50	8.90	8.20	9.60
10 Education	**[1.80]**	**0.70**	**2.20**	**2.10**	**2.30**	**1.70**
10.1 Education fees	[1.70]	[0.60]	[2.10]	2.00	2.20	1.40
10.2 Payments for school trips, other ad-hoc expenditure	[0.00]	[0.10]	[0.10]	[0.10]	[0.20]	[0.30]

Note: The commodity and service categories are not comparable with those in publications before 2001-02
The numbering system is sequential, it does not use actual COICOP codes

A8   Detailed household expenditure by gross income decile group (cont.)   2003-04
based on weighted data and including children's expenditure

	Seventh decile group	Eighth decile group	Ninth decile group	Highest ten per cent	All house-holds
Commodity or service	Average weekly household expenditure (£)				
8 Communication	**12.70**	**14.50**	**15.60**	**20.20**	**11.20**
8.1 Postal services	0.50	0.50	0.70	0.70	0.50
8.2 Telephone and telefax equipment	0.90	1.20	1.00	0.90	0.60
8.3 Telephone and telefax services	11.30	12.80	13.90	18.50	10.10
9 Recreation & culture	**68.60**	**77.80**	**88.40**	**116.20**	**57.30**
9.1 Audio-visual, photographic and information processing equipment	12.70	10.20	15.10	15.90	8.60
9.1.1 Audio equipment and accessories, CD players	2.90	2.70	3.20	4.90	2.10
9.1.2 TV, video and computers	8.90	6.70	10.00	10.00	5.80
9.1.3 Photographic, cine and optical equipment	0.80	0.90	1.90	1.00	0.70
9.2 Other major durables for recreation and culture	[1.70]	[3.00]	2.20	3.40	2.30
9.3 Other recreational items and equipment, gardens and pets	11.00	15.40	16.80	19.50	10.30
9.3.1 Games, toys and hobbies	2.70	3.70	4.70	5.10	2.60
9.3.2 Computer software and games	1.40	1.80	1.70	2.30	1.10
9.3.3 Equipment for sport, camping and open-air recreation	0.70	2.70	2.10	1.90	1.00
9.3.4 Horticultural goods, garden equipment and plants	3.10	3.30	4.00	6.00	2.70
9.3.5 Pets and pet food	3.00	3.80	4.20	4.30	2.90
9.4 Recreational and cultural services	21.00	24.60	24.70	32.00	17.00
9.4.1 Sports admissions, subscriptions, leisure class fees and equipment hire	6.20	6.80	7.70	13.90	4.70
9.4.2 Cinema, theatre and museums etc.	2.30	3.00	2.40	4.20	1.70
9.4.3 TV, video, satellite rental, cable subscriptions, TV licences and the Internet	6.50	7.00	6.80	7.70	5.20
9.4.4 Miscellaneous entertainments	1.00	1.70	2.70	2.00	1.10
9.4.5 Development of film, deposit for film development, passport photos, holiday and school photos	1.10	0.60	0.40	1.10	0.70
9.4.6 Gambling payments	4.00	5.60	4.80	3.00	3.60
9.5 Newspapers, books and stationery	7.30	7.80	9.50	13.90	6.70
9.5.1 Books	1.60	1.90	2.70	4.60	1.60
9.5.2 Diaries, address books, cards etc.	2.30	2.60	3.00	4.70	2.10
9.5.3 Newspapers	2.10	2.00	2.20	2.70	2.00
9.5.4 Magazines and periodicals	1.20	1.30	1.60	1.90	1.10
9.6 Package holidays	15.00	16.80	20.10	31.60	12.40
9.6.1 Package holidays - UK	[1.00]	[0.80]	[0.70]	[0.80]	0.80
9.6.2 Package holidays - abroad	13.90	16.00	19.40	30.80	11.60
10 Education	**2.80**	**4.00**	**7.80**	**27.10**	**5.20**
10.1 Education fees	2.40	3.60	7.30	26.00	4.90
10.2 Payments for school trips, other ad-hoc expenditure	0.40	0.40	0.50	1.10	0.30

Note: The commodity and service categories are not comparable with those in publications before 2001-02
The numbering system is sequential, it does not use actual COICOP codes

A8   Detailed household expenditure by gross income decile group (cont.)   2003-04

based on weighted data and including children's expenditure

	Lowest ten per cent	Second decile group	Third decile group	Fourth decile group	Fifth decile group	Sixth decile group
Commodity or service	Average weekly household expenditure (£)					
11 Restaurants & hotels	**9.50**	**10.70**	**15.80**	**21.70**	**31.20**	**32.40**
11.1 Catering services	8.50	10.20	13.90	19.20	27.00	29.30
11.1.1 Restaurant and café meals	2.90	3.80	5.40	7.70	9.80	10.40
11.1.2 Alcoholic drinks (away from home)	2.40	2.90	3.60	5.20	8.20	8.10
11.1.3 Take away meals eaten at home	1.80	1.80	2.20	2.70	3.60	3.80
11.1.4 Other take-away and snack food	1.10	1.40	2.00	2.60	3.50	4.60
11.1.5 Contract catering (food) and canteens	0.20	0.30	0.70	1.00	1.90	2.40
11.2 Accommodation services	1.00	0.50	1.90	2.50	4.20	3.10
11.2.1 Holiday in the UK	0.50	0.40	1.40	1.40	2.70	1.80
11.2.2 Holiday abroad	[0.60]	[0.10]	[0.40]	1.10	1.50	1.20
11.2.3 Room hire	[0.00]	[0.00]	[0.10]	[0.00]	[0.00]	[0.10]
12 Miscellaneous goods & services	**11.00**	**12.60**	**16.10**	**22.70**	**27.90**	**34.70**
12.1 Personal care	3.10	4.20	5.30	6.30	7.40	8.90
12.1.1 Hairdressing, beauty treatment	0.80	1.30	1.80	2.00	2.20	2.60
12.1.2 Toilet paper	0.40	0.40	0.50	0.60	0.70	0.70
12.1.3 Toiletries and soap	0.60	0.90	1.10	1.40	1.60	1.90
12.1.4 Baby toiletries and accessories (disposable)	0.20	0.30	0.20	0.30	0.70	0.60
12.1.5 Hair products, cosmetics and related electrical appliances	1.10	1.20	1.60	2.00	2.30	3.10
12.2 Personal effects	0.70	1.50	1.10	2.10	2.10	3.60
12.3 Social protection	[0.10]	0.40	0.90	0.90	1.80	1.40
12.4 Insurance	4.20	5.20	7.30	11.50	12.70	15.70
12.4.1 Household insurances - structural, contents and appliances	1.80	2.10	3.00	4.10	4.10	5.20
12.4.2 Medical insurance premiums	[0.40]	[0.30]	0.30	1.00	1.00	1.40
12.4.3 Vehicle insurance including boat insurance	2.00	2.80	4.00	5.70	7.40	8.90
12.4.4 Non-package holiday, other travel insurance	[0.00]	[0.00]	[0.00]	[0.70]	[0.10]	[0.20]
12.5 Other services n.e.c	3.00	1.30	1.50	1.90	3.80	5.10
12.5.1 Moving house	0.90	0.60	1.10	1.00	2.60	3.10
12.5.2 Bank, building society, post office, credit card charges	0.10	0.10	0.20	0.20	0.30	0.30
12.5.3 Other services and professional fees	1.90	0.60	0.20	0.70	0.90	1.60
1-12 All expenditure groups	**127.40**	**157.10**	**200.30**	**259.80**	**318.80**	**349.80**

Note: The commodity and service categories are not comparable with those in publications before 2001-02
The numbering system is sequential, it does not use actual COICOP codes

A8 Detailed household expenditure by gross income decile group (cont.)

2003-04

based on weighted data and including children's expenditure

	Seventh decile group	Eighth decile group	Ninth decile group	Highest ten per cent	All house-holds
Commodity or service	Average weekly household expenditure (£)				
11 Restaurants & hotels	**43.90**	**50.90**	**55.50**	**77.40**	**34.90**
11.1 Catering services	37.30	43.90	47.70	61.80	29.90
11.1.1 Restaurant and café meals	13.50	15.30	17.00	25.80	11.20
11.1.2 Alcoholic drinks (away from home)	11.20	12.40	14.70	16.20	8.50
11.1.3 Take away meals eaten at home	4.60	5.50	5.20	5.80	3.70
11.1.4 Other take-away and snack food	5.50	6.50	7.40	9.10	4.40
11.1.5 Contract catering (food) and canteens	2.40	4.30	3.40	4.80	2.10
11.2 Accommodation services	6.60	7.00	7.80	15.60	5.00
11.2.1 Holiday in the UK	3.40	2.90	3.90	5.60	2.40
11.2.2 Holiday abroad	3.10	3.40	3.90	9.90	2.50
11.2.3 Room hire	[0.10]	[0.80]	[0.00]	[0.10]	[0.10]
12 Miscellaneous goods & services	**41.10**	**45.00**	**50.40**	**74.70**	**33.60**
12.1 Personal care	10.30	12.20	13.60	18.60	9.00
12.1.1 Hairdressing, beauty treatment	2.70	3.20	3.80	5.80	2.60
12.1.2 Toilet paper	0.80	0.80	0.90	0.90	0.70
12.1.3 Toiletries and soap	2.30	2.60	3.00	3.70	1.90
12.1.4 Baby toiletries and accessories (disposable)	0.70	0.80	0.60	0.90	0.50
12.1.5 Hair products, cosmetics and electrical personal appliances	3.70	4.90	5.40	7.30	3.20
12.2 Personal effects	3.60	3.80	4.60	10.90	3.40
12.3 Social protection	2.20	3.60	4.60	7.10	2.30
12.4 Insurance	17.60	19.80	21.10	29.60	14.50
12.4.1 Household insurances - structural, contents and appliances	6.10	6.50	6.60	8.50	4.80
12.4.2 Medical insurance premiums	1.90	1.90	1.80	5.50	1.50
12.4.3 Vehicle insurance including boat insurance	9.40	11.20	12.40	15.40	7.90
12.4.4 Non-package holiday, other travel insurance	[0.30]	[0.10]	[0.20]	[0.10]	[0.20]
12.5 Other services	7.30	5.60	6.50	8.60	4.50
12.5.1 Moving house	2.40	3.10	3.40	4.40	2.30
12.6.2 Bank, building society, post office, credit card charges	0.50	0.50	0.60	0.90	0.40
12.6.3 Other services and professional fees	4.40	1.90	2.50	3.40	1.80
1-12 All expenditure groups	**405.50**	**469.70**	**530.40**	**743.80**	**356.20**

Note: The commodity and service categories are not comparable with those in publications before 2001-02
The numbering system is sequential, it does not use actual COICOP codes

A8 Detailed household expenditure by gross income decile group (cont.) 2003-04

based on weighted data and including children's expenditure

	Lowest ten per cent	Second decile group	Third decile group	Fourth decile group	Fifth decile group	Sixth decile group
Commodity or service	**Average weekly household expenditure (£)**					
13 Other expenditure items	**12.20**	**16.20**	**23.90**	**38.50**	**42.90**	**61.60**
13.1 Housing: mortgage interest payments, council tax etc.	8.00	9.80	15.60	25.30	30.60	41.70
13.2 Licences, fines and transfers	0.70	1.00	1.40	2.10	2.70	3.00
13.3 Holiday spending	[0.80]	[1.80]	[2.60]	3.10	3.40	6.40
13.4 Money transfers and credit	2.60	3.60	4.30	8.00	6.20	10.40
13.4.1 Money, cash gifts given to children	[0.10]	[0.10]	[0.10]	[0.10]	[0.10]	0.10
13.4.2 Cash gifts and donations	2.20	3.30	3.60	7.10	4.60	8.20
13.4.3 Club instalment payments (child) and interest on credit cards	0.40	0.30	0.60	0.80	1.50	2.00
Total expenditure	**139.60**	**173.30**	**224.20**	**298.30**	**361.70**	**411.40**
14 Other items recorded						
14.1 Life assurance and contributions to pension funds	1.50	1.40	3.70	6.90	10.40	17.20
14.2 Other insurance inc. Friendly Societies	0.20	0.40	0.50	0.80	1.10	1.40
14.3 Income tax, payments less refunds	2.40	3.20	12.00	23.80	35.60	56.40
14.4 National insurance contributions	[0.10]	0.50	2.00	5.80	11.20	20.20
14.5 Purchase or alteration of dwellings, mortgages	4.20	7.90	12.80	20.20	23.60	36.60
14.6 Savings and investments	0.40	0.40	0.70	5.70	2.40	3.40
14.7 Pay off loan to clear other debt	[0.20]	[0.50]	0.90	1.60	1.80	4.40
14.8 Windfall receipts from gambling etc.	1.60	1.10	1.90	1.20	1.20	3.60

Note: The commodity and service categories are not comparable with those in publications before 2001-02
The numbering system is sequential, it does not use actual COICOP codes

A8 Detailed household expenditure by gross income decile group (cont.)   2003-04
based on weighted data and including children's expenditure

	Seventh decile group	Eighth decile group	Ninth decile group	Highest ten per cent	All house-holds
Commodity or service	Average weekly household expenditure (£)				
13 Other expenditure items	**73.10**	**87.50**	**101.80**	**161.20**	**61.90**
13.1 Housing: mortgage interest payments, council tax etc.	52.10	59.70	69.10	98.50	41.00
13.2 Licences, fines and transfers	3.60	4.70	4.80	5.20	2.90
13.3 Holiday spending	7.70	12.50	13.20	31.00	8.30
13.4 Money transfers and credit	9.70	10.60	14.70	26.50	9.70
13.4.1 Money, cash gifts given to children	0.20	0.10	[0.10]	0.20	0.10
13.4.2 Cash gifts and donations	7.30	7.80	12.00	23.30	7.90
13.4.3 Club instalment payments (child) and interest on credit cards	2.10	2.60	2.60	3.00	1.60
Total expenditure	**478.60**	**557.20**	**632.30**	**905.00**	**418.10**
14 Other items recorded					
14.1 Contributions to pension funds	21.40	27.50	38.90	69.90	19.90
14.2 Other insurance inc. Friendly Societies	1.40	1.60	2.00	3.00	1.20
14.3 Income tax, payments less refunds	75.50	97.90	142.20	333.70	78.20
14.4 National insurance contributions	28.20	37.80	49.10	65.10	22.00
14.5 Purchase or alteration of dwellings, mortgages	41.50	53.60	66.60	140.80	40.80
14.6 Savings and investments	11.20	8.30	15.80	23.20	7.20
14.7 Pay off loan to clear other debt	4.60	4.10	3.90	4.20	2.60
14.8 Windfall receipts from gambling etc.	1.90	3.20	2.20	1.30	1.90

Note: The commodity and service categories are not comparable with those in publications before 2001-02
The numbering system is sequential, it does not use actual COICOP codes

A9   Household expenditure by disposable income decile group   2003-04

based on weighted data and including children's expenditure

	Lowest ten per cent	Second decile group	Third decile group	Fourth decile group	Fifth decile group	Sixth decile group
Lower boundary of group (£ per week)		121	185	242	309	383
Grossed number of households (thousands)	2,470	2,470	2,470	2,470	2,470	2,460
Total number of households in sample	703	717	728	729	716	713
Total number of persons in sample	929	1,159	1,387	1,476	1,704	1,893
Total number of adults in sample	783	904	1,095	1,171	1,279	1,359
Weighted average number of persons per household	1.3	1.6	1.9	2.0	2.3	2.6

Commodity or service	Average weekly household expenditure (£)					
1 Food & non-alcoholic drinks	21.80	26.50	33.40	36.60	42.20	45.10
2 Alcoholic drinks, tobacco & narcotics	6.50	7.10	7.60	11.10	10.90	12.80
3 Clothing & footwear	7.10	7.40	12.20	14.20	17.10	21.40
4 Housing (net)[1], fuel & power	23.70	28.10	31.30	35.00	42.40	43.30
5 Household goods & services	10.50	13.50	16.30	21.70	27.50	30.90
6 Health	1.70	1.90	2.70	4.10	5.90	4.20
7 Transport	14.70	16.20	27.90	33.70	53.60	54.10
8 Communication	5.40	5.70	7.30	8.70	10.20	11.40
9 Recreation & culture	18.10	23.40	29.90	42.30	47.90	60.20
10 Education	[1.80]	0.50	2.40	1.20	2.50	2.40
11 Restaurants & hotels	9.70	11.50	15.50	21.40	30.50	33.90
12 Miscellaneous goods & services	11.70	12.60	17.30	21.10	28.30	34.40
1-12 All expenditure groups	132.80	154.50	203.90	251.20	319.00	354.10
13 Other expenditure items	13.50	16.70	25.70	36.40	47.90	61.10
Total expenditure	146.30	171.20	229.60	287.60	366.90	415.20
Average weekly expenditure per person (£)						
Total expenditure	112.80	108.50	123.50	145.40	158.40	160.40

Note: The commodity and service categories are not comparable with those in publications before 2001-02
1 Excluding mortgage interest payments, council tax and Northern Ireland rates

A9   Household expenditure by disposable income decile group (cont.)   2003-04

based on weighted data and including children's expenditure

	Seventh decile group	Eighth decile group	Ninth decile group	Highest ten per cent	All house-holds
Lower boundary of group (£ per week)	458	550	660	851	
Grossed number of households (thousands)	2,470	2,470	2,470	2,470	24,670
Total number of households in sample	714	694	677	657	7,048
Total number of persons in sample	2,030	2,059	2,168	2,160	16,965
Total number of adults in sample	1,430	1,475	1,549	1,572	12,617
Weighted average number of persons per household	2.8	2.9	3.1	3.2	2.4

Commodity or service	Average weekly household expenditure (£)				
1 Food & non-alcoholic drinks	48.50	52.50	60.80	67.80	43.50
2 Alcoholic drinks, tobacco & narcotics	13.50	14.70	16.10	16.90	11.70
3 Clothing & footwear	28.50	29.60	35.60	54.20	22.70
4 Housing (net)[1], fuel & power	39.00	44.90	45.40	56.90	39.00
5 Household goods & services	35.80	41.50	43.60	71.30	31.30
6 Health	5.00	5.10	8.70	11.20	5.00
7 Transport	70.10	81.60	105.00	150.40	60.70
8 Communication	12.80	14.50	16.80	19.20	11.20
9 Recreation & culture	67.60	74.00	90.20	119.30	57.30
10 Education	2.80	3.50	8.30	26.90	5.20
11 Restaurants & hotels	41.90	49.90	57.40	77.20	34.90
12 Miscellaneous goods & services	42.10	42.40	51.90	74.40	33.60
1-12 All expenditure groups	407.70	454.00	539.90	745.50	356.20
13 Other expenditure items	71.60	85.10	103.30	157.60	61.90
Total expenditure	479.30	539.10	643.20	903.10	418.10
Average weekly expenditure per person (£) Total expenditure	173.90	187.30	206.90	281.10	177.40

Note: The commodity and service categories are not comparable with those in publications before 2001-02
1 Excluding mortgage interest payments, council tax and Northern Ireland rates

A10 Household expenditure as a percentage of total expenditure by disposable income decile group

based on weighted data and including children's expenditure

2003-04

	Lowest ten per cent	Second decile group	Third decile group	Fourth decile group	Fifth decile group	Sixth decile group
Lower boundary of group (£ per week)		121	185	242	309	383
Grossed number of households (thousands)	2,470	2,470	2,470	2,470	2,470	2,460
Total number of households in sample	703	717	728	729	716	713
Total number of persons in sample	929	1,159	1,387	1,476	1,704	1,893
Total number of adults in sample	783	904	1,095	1,171	1,279	1,359
Weighted average number of persons per household	1.3	1.6	1.9	2.0	2.3	2.6

Commodity or service	Percentage of total expenditure					
1 Food & non-alcoholic drinks	15	15	15	13	12	11
2 Alcoholic drinks, tobacco & narcotics	4	4	3	4	3	3
3 Clothing & footwear	5	4	5	5	5	5
4 Housing (net)[1], fuel & power	16	16	14	12	12	10
5 Household goods & services	7	8	7	8	8	7
6 Health	1	1	1	1	2	1
7 Transport	10	9	12	12	15	13
8 Communication	4	3	3	3	3	3
9 Recreation & culture	12	14	13	15	13	15
10 Education	[1]	0	1	0	1	1
11 Restaurants & hotels	7	7	7	7	8	8
12 Miscellaneous goods & services	8	7	8	7	8	8
1-12 All expenditure groups	91	90	89	87	87	85
13 Other expenditure items	9	10	11	13	13	15
Total expenditure	100	100	100	100	100	100

Note: The commodity and service categories are not comparable with those in publications before 2001-02
1 Excluding mortgage interest payments, council tax and Northern Ireland rates

A10   Household expenditure as a percentage of total expenditure   2003-04
by disposable income decile group (cont.)
based on weighted data and including children's expenditure

	Seventh decile group	Eighth decile group	Ninth decile group	Highest ten per cent	All house- holds
Lower boundary of group (£ per week)	458	550	660	851	
Grossed number of households (thousands)	2,470	2,470	2,470	2,470	24,670
Total number of households in sample	714	694	677	657	7,048
Total number of persons in sample	2,030	2,059	2,168	2,160	16,965
Total number of adults in sample	1,430	1,475	1,549	1,572	12,617
Weighted average number of persons per household	2.8	2.9	3.1	3.2	2.4
Commodity or service	**Percentage of total expenditure**				
1 Food & non-alcoholic drinks	10	10	9	8	10
2 Alcoholic drinks, tobacco & narcotics	3	3	2	2	3
3 Clothing & footwear	6	5	6	6	5
4 Housing (net)[1], fuel & power	8	8	7	6	9
5 Household goods & services	7	8	7	8	7
6 Health	1	1	1	1	1
7 Transport	15	15	16	17	15
8 Communication	3	3	3	2	3
9 Recreation & culture	14	14	14	13	14
10 Education	1	1	1	3	1
11 Restaurants & hotels	9	9	9	9	8
12 Miscellaneous goods & services	9	8	8	8	8
1-12 All expenditure groups	85	84	84	83	85
13 Other expenditure items	15	16	16	17	15
Total expenditure	100	100	100	100	100

Note: The commodity and service categories are not comparable with those in publications before 2001-02
1 Excluding mortgage interest payments, council tax and Northern Ireland rates

A11 Household expenditure by age of household reference person

2003-04

based on weighted data and including children's expenditure

	Under 30	30 and under 50	50 and under 65	65 and under 75	75 or over	All house-holds
Grossed number of households (thousands)	2,540	9,640	6,120	3,280	3,090	24,670
Total number of households in sample	682	2,877	1,725	965	799	7,048
Total number of persons in sample	1,598	8,860	3,765	1,602	1,140	16,965
Total number of adults in sample	1,154	5,354	3,388	1,588	1,133	12,617
Weighted average number of persons per household	2.3	3.0	2.2	1.7	1.4	2.4

Commodity or service	Average weekly household expenditure (£)					
1 Food & non-alcoholic drinks	31.20	49.90	48.30	38.90	29.20	43.50
2 Alcoholic drinks, tobacco & narcotics	12.40	13.60	13.60	8.40	5.00	11.70
3 Clothing & footwear	23.10	31.30	23.20	11.60	6.60	22.70
4 Housing (net)[1], fuel & power	63.70	41.70	36.10	30.10	25.30	39.00
5 Household goods & services	29.90	37.60	33.00	26.80	14.10	31.30
6 Health	3.30	4.00	6.80	5.70	5.50	5.00
7 Transport	60.70	78.00	67.80	35.70	19.40	60.70
8 Communication	13.60	13.90	11.70	6.60	4.90	11.20
9 Recreation & culture	45.40	70.80	64.20	46.80	22.40	57.30
10 Education	4.70	8.10	6.10	[0.30]	[0.40]	5.20
11 Restaurants & hotels	38.50	45.40	36.90	20.40	10.60	34.90
12 Miscellaneous goods & services	32.60	42.40	33.80	22.60	18.40	33.60
1-12 All expenditure groups	359.00	436.60	381.50	253.90	161.60	356.20
13 Other expenditure items	49.40	88.20	59.80	35.70	21.70	61.90
Total expenditure	408.40	524.80	441.30	289.60	183.30	418.10
Average weekly expenditure per person (£)						
Total expenditure	178.00	175.90	198.30	173.00	127.40	177.40

Note: The commodity and service categories are not comparable with those in publications before 2001-02
1 Excluding mortgage interest payments, council tax and Northern Ireland rates

A12 Household expenditure as a percentage of total expenditure by age of household reference person

2003-04

based on weighted data and including children's expenditure

	Under 30	30 and under 50	50 and under 65	65 and under 75	75 or over	All house-holds
Grossed number of households (thousands)	2,540	9,640	6,120	3,280	3,090	24,670
Total number of households in sample	682	2,877	1,725	965	799	7,048
Total number of persons in sample	1,598	8,860	3,765	1,602	1,140	16,965
Total number of adults in sample	1,154	5,354	3,388	1,588	1,133	12,617
Weighted average number of persons per household	2.3	3.0	2.2	1.7	1.4	2.4

Commodity or service	Percentage of total expenditure					
1 Food & non-alcoholic drinks	8	10	11	13	16	10
2 Alcoholic drinks, tobacco & narcotics	3	3	3	3	3	3
3 Clothing & footwear	6	6	5	4	4	5
4 Housing (net)[1], fuel & power	16	8	8	10	14	9
5 Household goods & services	7	7	7	9	8	7
6 Health	1	1	2	2	3	1
7 Transport	15	15	15	12	11	15
8 Communication	3	3	3	2	3	3
9 Recreation & culture	11	13	15	16	12	14
10 Education	1	2	1	[0]	[0]	1
11 Restaurants & hotels	9	9	8	7	6	8
12 Miscellaneous goods & services	8	8	8	8	10	8
1-12 All expenditure groups	88	83	86	88	88	85
13 Other expenditure items	12	17	14	12	12	15
Total expenditure	100	100	100	100	100	100

Note: The commodity and service categories are not comparable with those in publications before 2001-02
1 Excluding mortgage interest payments, council tax and Northern Ireland rates

A13 Detailed household expenditure by age of household reference person   2003-04

based on weighted data and including children's expenditure

	Under 30	30 and under 50	50 and under 65	65 and under 75	75 or over	All house- holds
Grossed number of households (thousands)	2,540	9,640	6,120	3,280	3,090	24,670
Total number of households in sample	682	2,877	1,725	965	799	7,048
Total number of persons in sample	1,598	8,860	3,765	1,602	1,140	16,965
Total number of adults in sample	1,154	5,354	3,388	1,588	1,133	12,617
Weighted average number of persons per household	2.3	3.0	2.2	1.7	1.4	2.4

Commodity or service	Average weekly household expenditure (£)					
1 Food & non-alcoholic drinks	**31.20**	**49.90**	**48.30**	**38.90**	**29.20**	**43.50**
1.1 Food	28.00	45.20	44.30	36.10	27.20	39.70
1.1.1 Bread, rice and cereals	3.00	4.70	3.90	3.20	2.30	3.80
1.1.2 Pasta products	0.40	0.40	0.30	0.10	0.10	0.30
1.1.3 Buns, cakes, biscuits etc.	1.70	3.10	2.90	2.60	2.20	2.70
1.1.4 Pastry (savoury)	0.80	0.90	0.50	0.30	0.20	0.60
1.1.5 Beef (fresh, chilled or frozen)	0.70	1.50	1.80	1.40	1.00	1.40
1.1.6 Pork (fresh, chilled or frozen)	0.30	0.50	0.80	0.60	0.40	0.60
1.1.7 Lamb (fresh, chilled or frozen)	0.30	0.60	0.70	0.80	0.50	0.60
1.1.8 Poultry (fresh, chilled or frozen)	1.20	2.10	1.90	1.20	0.70	1.60
1.1.9 Bacon and ham	0.50	0.90	1.10	0.90	0.70	0.90
1.1.10 Other meat and meat preparations	3.40	5.90	5.40	4.10	3.30	4.90
1.1.11 Fish and fish products	0.90	1.70	2.20	2.20	1.80	1.80
1.1.12 Milk	1.70	2.40	2.20	2.10	1.80	2.20
1.1.13 Cheese and curd	1.10	1.60	1.60	1.10	0.80	1.40
1.1.14 Eggs	0.30	0.40	0.50	0.40	0.30	0.40
1.1.15 Other milk products	1.10	1.80	1.60	1.30	0.90	1.50
1.1.16 Butter	0.10	0.20	0.30	0.30	0.30	0.20
1.1.17 Margarine, other vegetable fats and peanut butter	0.30	0.40	0.50	0.50	0.40	0.40
1.1.18 Cooking oils and fats	0.20	0.20	0.20	0.20	0.10	0.20
1.1.19 Fresh fruit	1.30	2.50	3.00	2.80	2.10	2.50
1.1.20 Other fresh, chilled or frozen fruits	0.10	0.20	0.30	0.20	0.10	0.20
1.1.21 Dried fruit and nuts	0.10	0.30	0.40	0.40	0.30	0.30
1.1.22 Preserved fruit and fruit based products	0.10	0.10	0.20	0.20	0.20	0.10
1.1.23 Fresh vegetables	2.10	3.40	3.80	3.00	2.00	3.10
1.1.24 Dried vegetables	0.00	0.00	0.00	0.00	0.00	0.00
1.1.25 Other preserved or processed vegetables	0.80	1.20	1.10	0.70	0.40	1.00
1.1.26 Potatoes	0.50	0.80	0.90	0.80	0.60	0.80
1.1.27 Other tubers and products of tuber vegetables	1.10	1.70	1.20	0.70	0.50	1.20
1.1.28 Sugar and sugar products	0.20	0.30	0.30	0.30	0.30	0.30
1.1.29 Jams, marmalades	0.10	0.20	0.30	0.20	0.30	0.20
1.1.30 Chocolate	1.00	1.70	1.30	1.20	0.80	1.30
1.1.31 Confectionery products	0.40	0.70	0.50	0.50	0.40	0.60
1.1.32 Edible ices and ice cream	0.40	0.60	0.50	0.40	0.40	0.50
1.1.33 Other food products	2.00	2.20	1.90	1.30	1.00	1.80
1.2 Non-alcoholic drinks	3.20	4.60	4.10	2.80	2.00	3.80
1.2.1 Coffee	0.30	0.50	0.70	0.50	0.40	0.50
1.2.2 Tea	0.20	0.40	0.50	0.40	0.40	0.40
1.2.3 Cocoa and powdered chocolate	0.10	0.10	0.10	0.10	0.10	0.10
1.2.4 Fruit and vegetable juices	0.80	1.20	0.90	0.70	0.40	0.90
1.2.5 Mineral or spring waters	0.20	0.30	0.20	0.20	0.10	0.20
1.2.6 Soft drinks	1.60	2.20	1.60	0.90	0.60	1.60

Note: The commodity and service categories are not comparable with those in publications before 2001-02
The numbering system is sequential, it does not use actual COICOP codes

A13 Detailed household expenditure by age of household reference person (cont.)   2003-04

based on weighted data and including children's expenditure

	Under 30	30 and under 50	50 and under 65	65 and under 75	75 or over	All house-holds
Commodity or service	Average weekly household expenditure (£)					
2 Alcoholic drink, tobacco & narcotics	**12.40**	**13.60**	**13.60**	**8.40**	**5.00**	**11.70**
2.1 Alcoholic drinks	5.20	7.20	7.40	4.80	3.30	6.20
2.1.1 Spirits and liqueurs (brought home)	1.00	1.10	1.60	1.60	1.20	1.30
2.1.2 Wines, fortified wines (brought home)	2.00	3.40	3.80	2.30	1.50	3.00
2.1.3 Beer, lager, ciders and Perry (brought home)	2.00	2.50	2.00	0.80	0.60	1.90
2.1.4 Alcopops (brought home)	0.30	0.20	0.10	[0.00]	[0.00]	0.10
2.2 Tobacco and narcotics	7.20	6.40	6.20	3.60	1.70	5.50
2.2.1 Cigarettes	6.00	5.80	5.40	3.30	1.50	4.90
2.2.2 Cigars, other tobacco products and narcotics	1.20	0.60	0.80	0.40	0.20	0.60
3 Clothing & footwear	**23.10**	**31.30**	**23.20**	**11.60**	**6.60**	**22.70**
3.1 Clothing	17.80	24.80	19.00	9.30	5.20	18.10
3.1.1 Men's outer garments	5.20	5.90	5.00	2.00	0.70	4.40
3.1.2 Men's under garments	0.30	0.40	0.60	0.20	0.20	0.40
3.1.3 Women's outer garments	7.40	10.20	9.20	4.80	2.70	8.00
3.1.4 Women's under garments	1.10	1.30	1.40	0.90	0.70	1.20
3.1.5 Boys' outer garments (5-15)	0.60	1.70	0.30	0.20	[0.00]	0.80
3.1.6 Girls' outer garments (5-15)	0.40	2.40	0.40	0.30	[0.20]	1.10
3.1.7 Infants' outer garments (under 5)	1.30	0.90	0.50	0.10	[0.10]	0.60
3.1.8 Children's under garments (under 16)	0.30	0.70	0.20	0.10	[0.00]	0.40
3.1.9 Accessories	0.70	0.90	0.60	0.30	0.10	0.60
3.1.10 Haberdashery, clothing materials and clothing hire	[0.30]	0.20	0.40	0.20	0.10	0.30
3.1.11 Dry cleaners, laundry and dyeing	0.20	0.30	0.30	0.10	0.30	0.30
3.2 Footwear	5.30	6.50	4.20	2.30	1.50	4.60
4 Housing (net)[1], fuel & power	**63.70**	**41.70**	**36.10**	**30.10**	**25.30**	**39.00**
4.1 Actual rentals for housing	60.50	24.10	16.10	17.50	24.00	25.00
4.1.1 Gross rent	60.50	24.00	16.10	17.40	24.00	24.90
4.1.2 *less* housing benefit, rebates & allowances rec'd	16.00	9.90	9.60	11.60	17.70	11.70
4.1.3 Net rent	44.50	14.10	6.40	5.80	6.30	13.20
4.1.4 Second dwelling rent	[0.00]	[0.10]	[0.00]	[0.10]	[0.00]	[0.00]
4.2 Maintenance and repair of dwelling	4.10	9.50	10.30	7.50	3.70	8.20
4.3 Water supply and miscellaneous services relating to the dwelling	5.80	5.50	5.70	5.30	5.70	5.60
4.4 Electricity, gas and other fuels	9.30	12.60	13.60	11.40	9.60	12.00
4.4.1 Electricity	4.80	6.40	6.70	5.50	4.90	6.00
4.4.2 Gas	4.20	5.40	5.80	5.40	4.20	5.20
4.4.3 Other fuels	0.30	0.80	1.10	0.60	0.50	0.70

Note: The commodity and service categories are not comparable with those in publications before 2001-02
The numbering system is sequential, it does not use actual COICOP codes
1 Excluding mortgage interest payments, council tax and Northern Ireland rates

A13 Detailed household expenditure by age of household reference person (cont.) 2003-04

based on weighted data and including children's expenditure

	Under 30	30 and under 50	50 and under 65	65 and under 75	75 or over	All house- holds
Commodity or service	Average weekly household expenditure (£)					
5 Household goods & services	**29.90**	**37.60**	**33.00**	**26.80**	**14.10**	**31.30**
5.1 Furniture and furnishings, carpets and other floor coverings	18.30	21.20	16.60	11.60	3.60	16.30
5.1.1 Furniture and furnishings	14.50	16.40	12.00	7.60	2.70	12.20
5.1.2 Floor coverings	3.80	4.80	4.60	4.00	0.90	4.10
5.2 Household textiles	1.20	2.10	1.90	4.20	1.00	2.10
5.3 Household appliances	4.00	3.90	3.90	2.90	2.00	3.60
5.4 Glassware, tableware and household utensils	1.50	1.90	1.60	1.20	1.40	1.60
5.5 Tools and equipment for house and garden	1.80	3.40	3.40	1.90	1.60	2.80
5.6 Goods and services for routine household maintenance	3.00	5.00	5.60	4.90	4.40	4.80
5.6.1 Cleaning materials	1.50	2.50	2.40	1.80	1.20	2.10
5.6.2 Household goods and hardware	0.80	1.30	1.40	1.10	0.70	1.20
5.6.3 Domestic services, carpet cleaning & repair of furniture	0.70	1.20	1.90	1.90	2.60	1.60
6 Health	**3.30**	**4.00**	**6.80**	**5.70**	**5.50**	**5.00**
6.1 Medical products, appliances and equipment	2.70	2.60	4.10	3.80	3.80	3.30
6.1.1 Medicines, prescriptions and healthcare products	1.00	1.60	2.20	1.80	2.70	1.80
6.1.2 Spectacles, lenses, accessories and repairs	1.70	1.00	2.00	2.00	[1.20]	1.50
6.2 Hospital services	0.60	1.50	2.70	1.90	1.60	1.70
7 Transport	**60.70**	**78.00**	**67.80**	**35.70**	**19.40**	**60.70**
7.1 Purchase of vehicles	27.40	37.00	31.50	16.60	6.60	28.10
7.1.1 Purchase of new cars and vans	9.00	13.00	14.60	10.30	3.00	11.40
7.1.2 Purchase of second hand cars or vans	17.20	22.70	16.50	6.30	3.40	16.00
7.1.3 Purchase of motorcycles and other vehicles	[1.10]	1.30	[0.40]	[0.00]	[0.00]	0.70
7.2 Operation of personal transport	20.50	30.40	27.80	15.20	7.10	23.80
7.2.1 Spares and accessories	2.20	2.90	1.90	0.80	[0.30]	2.00
7.2.2 Petrol, diesel and other motor oils	13.30	19.40	17.50	9.00	3.70	15.00
7.2.3 Repairs and servicing	3.70	5.80	5.90	4.20	2.40	5.00
7.2.4 Other motoring costs	1.30	2.40	2.40	1.20	0.70	1.90
7.3 Transport services	12.80	10.50	8.50	3.90	5.70	8.80
7.3.1 Rail and tube fares	2.60	2.40	2.10	0.70	0.40	1.90
7.3.2 Bus and coach fares	1.80	1.70	1.70	0.60	0.60	1.40
7.3.4 Combined fares	1.70	0.90	0.50	[0.10]	[0.10]	0.70
7.3.5 Other travel and transport	6.70	5.50	4.10	2.50	4.50	4.80

Note: The commodity and service categories are not comparable with those in publications before 2001-02
The numbering system is sequential, it does not use actual COICOP codes

A13 Detailed household expenditure by age of household reference person (cont.)   2003-04
based on weighted data and including children's expenditure

	Under 30	30 and under 50	50 and under 65	65 and under 75	75 or over	All house- holds
Commodity or service	Average weekly household expenditure (£)					
8 Communication	**13.60**	**13.90**	**11.70**	**6.60**	**4.90**	**11.20**
8.1 Postal services	0.30	0.40	0.60	0.60	0.60	0.50
8.2 Telephone and telefax equipment	[0.70]	0.80	0.80	[0.10]	[0.10]	0.60
8.3 Telephone and telefax services	12.50	12.60	10.40	5.90	4.20	10.10
9 Recreation & culture	**45.40**	**70.80**	**64.20**	**46.80**	**22.40**	**57.30**
9.1 Audio-visual, photographic and information processing equipment	9.10	12.00	8.60	4.10	2.10	8.60
9.1.1 Audio equipment and accessories, CD players	3.20	2.90	1.90	0.80	0.40	2.10
9.1.2 TV, video and computers	5.30	8.00	6.00	3.00	1.40	5.80
9.1.3 Photographic, cine and optical equipment	0.50	1.00	0.70	0.30	[0.30]	0.70
9.2 Other major durables for recreation and culture	[0.30]	2.00	4.00	[1.20]	[2.40]	2.30
9.3 Other recreational items and equipment, gardens and pets	8.60	13.60	11.10	7.20	2.90	10.30
9.3.1 Games, toys and hobbies	2.70	4.00	2.00	1.70	0.40	2.60
9.3.2 Computer software and games	1.50	1.90	0.80	[0.10]	[0.10]	1.10
9.3.3 Equipment for sport, camping and open-air recreation	1.00	1.40	1.20	0.20	[0.00]	1.00
9.3.4 Horticultural goods, garden equipment and plants	1.50	2.70	3.80	3.10	1.40	2.70
9.3.5 Pets and pet food	1.80	3.70	3.40	2.00	1.00	2.90
9.4 Recreational and cultural services	15.40	21.60	18.40	12.90	5.80	17.00
9.4.1 Sports admissions, subscriptions, leisure class fees and equipment hire	4.50	7.00	4.40	2.20	1.10	4.70
9.4.2 Cinema, theatre and museums etc.	2.10	2.30	1.50	1.20	0.40	1.70
9.4.3 TV, video, satellite rental, cable subscriptions, TV licences and the Internet	5.60	6.40	5.90	4.20	1.10	5.20
9.4.4 Miscellaneous entertainments	1.20	1.30	1.10	1.30	0.40	1.10
9.4.5 Development of film, deposit for film development, passport photos, holiday and school photos	0.40	1.00	0.70	0.30	[0.10]	0.70
9.4.6 Gambling payments	1.60	3.60	4.90	3.70	2.70	3.60
9.5 Newspapers, books and stationery	4.60	7.30	7.90	6.30	4.60	6.70
9.5.1 Books	1.30	1.80	2.00	1.00	0.60	1.60
9.5.2 Diaries, address books, cards etc.	1.60	2.60	2.30	1.80	1.00	2.10
9.5.3 Newspapers	0.80	1.60	2.50	2.90	2.40	2.00
9.5.4 Magazines and periodicals	0.90	1.30	1.10	0.70	0.60	1.10
9.6 Package holidays	7.40	14.20	14.10	15.10	4.50	12.40
9.6.1 Package holidays - UK	[0.20]	0.40	0.60	2.00	1.30	0.80
9.6.2 Package holidays - abroad	7.20	13.80	13.50	13.10	3.10	11.60
10 Education	**4.70**	**8.10**	**6.10**	**[0.30]**	**[0.40]**	**5.20**
10.1 Education fees	4.70	7.40	5.90	[0.30]	[0.40]	4.90
10.2 Payments for school trips, other ad-hoc expenditure	[0.00]	0.60	[0.20]	[0.00]	[0.00]	0.30

Note: The commodity and service categories are not comparable with those in publications before 2001-02
The numbering system is sequential, it does not use actual COICOP codes

A13 Detailed household expenditure by age of household reference person (cont.) 2003-04

based on weighted data and including children's expenditure

	Under 30	30 and under 50	50 and under 65	65 and under 75	75 or over	All house-holds
Commodity or service	Average weekly household expenditure (£)					
11 Restaurants & hotels	**38.50**	**45.40**	**36.90**	**20.40**	**10.60**	**34.90**
11.1 Catering services	35.30	39.70	30.80	15.50	8.40	29.90
11.1.1 Restaurant and café meals	10.10	13.30	12.40	8.90	5.40	11.20
11.1.2 Alcoholic drinks (away from home)	11.80	10.40	9.90	4.20	1.70	8.50
11.1.3 Take away meals eaten at home	5.70	5.30	3.10	1.30	0.90	3.70
11.1.4 Other take-away and snack food	5.30	7.10	3.70	0.80	0.40	4.40
11.1.5 Contract catering (food) and canteens	2.50	3.60	1.70	0.30	0.10	2.10
11.2 Accommodation services	3.20	5.70	6.10	4.90	2.20	5.00
11.2.1 Holiday in the UK	1.10	2.50	2.80	3.00	1.60	2.40
11.2.2 Holiday abroad	2.00	3.20	2.90	1.80	0.60	2.50
11.2.3 Room hire	[0.00]	[0.00]	[0.40]	[0.10]	[0.00]	[0.10]
12 Miscellaneous goods & services	**32.60**	**42.40**	**33.80**	**22.60**	**18.40**	**33.60**
12.1 Personal care	8.90	10.70	10.10	6.00	4.60	9.00
12.1.1 Hairdressing, beauty treatment	2.20	2.70	3.10	2.40	2.10	2.60
12.1.2 Toilet paper	0.50	0.80	0.70	0.60	0.40	0.70
12.1.3 Toiletries and soap	1.80	2.30	2.10	1.30	0.90	1.90
12.1.4 Baby toiletries and accessories (disposable)	1.10	0.90	0.20	0.10	0.10	0.50
12.1.5 Hair products, cosmetics and related electrical appliances	3.20	4.10	3.80	1.70	1.10	3.20
12.2 Personal effects	3.20	4.60	3.80	1.80	0.60	3.40
12.3 Social protection	2.80	4.40	[0.20]	[0.20]	1.70	2.30
12.4 Insurance	13.70	16.70	16.30	11.30	7.90	14.50
12.4.1 Household insurances - structural, contents and appliances	3.10	5.40	5.70	4.40	3.00	4.80
12.4.2 Medical insurance premiums	0.40	1.30	2.10	2.10	1.40	1.50
12.4.3 Vehicle insurance including boat insurance	9.90	9.80	8.40	4.60	3.00	7.90
12.4.4 Non-package holiday, other travel insurance	[0.20]	[0.10]	[0.10]	[0.20]	[0.50]	[0.20]
12.5 Other services	4.10	5.90	3.50	3.30	3.50	4.50
12.5.1 Moving house	2.50	3.30	1.60	1.90	[0.60]	2.30
12.5.2 Bank, building society, post office, credit card charges	0.30	0.50	0.40	0.20	0.10	0.40
12.5.3 Other services and professional fees	1.20	2.00	1.60	1.20	2.90	1.80
1-12 All expenditure groups	**359.00**	**436.60**	**381.50**	**253.90**	**161.60**	**356.20**

Note: The commodity and service categories are not comparable with those in publications before 2001-02
The numbering system is sequential, it does not use actual COICOP codes

A13 Detailed household expenditure by age of household reference person (cont.)   2003-04

based on weighted data and including children's expenditure

	Under 30	30 and under 50	50 and under 65	65 and under 75	75 or over	All house-holds
Commodity or service	Average weekly household expenditure (£)					
13 Other expenditure items	**49.40**	**88.20**	**59.80**	**35.70**	**21.70**	**61.90**
13.1 Housing: mortgage interest payments, council tax etc.	33.00	61.70	38.40	18.50	12.30	41.00
13.2 Licences, fines and transfers	2.20	3.50	3.40	2.30	1.20	2.90
13.3 Holiday spending	6.40	12.00	7.60	5.70	[2.00]	8.30
13.4 Money transfers and credit	7.70	10.90	10.40	9.30	6.20	9.70
13.4.1 Money, cash gifts given to children	[0.10]	0.20	[0.10]	[0.00]	[0.00]	0.10
13.4.2 Cash gifts and donations	6.00	8.30	8.70	8.70	6.10	7.90
13.4.3 Club instalment payments (child) and interest on credit cards	1.70	2.40	1.60	0.60	[0.00]	1.60
Total expenditure	**408.40**	**524.80**	**441.30**	**289.60**	**183.30**	**418.10**
14 Other items recorded						
14.1 Life assurance & contributions to pension funds	10.10	29.70	26.20	3.80	1.70	19.90
14.2 Other insurance inc. Friendly Societies	0.70	1.70	1.40	0.80	0.40	1.20
14.3 Income tax, payments less refunds	69.10	110.20	88.00	32.30	15.60	78.20
14.4 National insurance contributions	25.80	33.40	23.90	1.60	[1.10]	22.00
14.5 Purchase or alteration of dwellings, mortgages	26.10	67.40	33.10	16.40	10.70	40.80
14.6 Savings and investments	3.60	8.40	10.90	5.30	0.80	7.20
14.7 Pay off loan to clear other debt	4.30	4.00	1.90	[080]	[0.20]	2.60
14.8 Windfall receipts from gambling etc.	1.40	1.90	2.30	2.00	1.40	1.90

Note: The commodity and service categories are not comparable with those in publications before 2001-02
The numbering system is sequential, it does not use actual COICOP codes

A14 Household expenditure by gross income quintile group where the household reference person is aged under 30

2001-02 — 2003-04

based on weighted data and including children's expenditure

	Lowest twenty per cent	Second quintile group	Third quintile group	Fourth quintile group	Highest twenty per cent	All house-holds
Lower boundary of group (£ per week)[1]		193	351	558	828	
Average number of grossed households (thousands)	500	450	610	580	430	2,560
Total number of households in sample (over 3 years)	468	405	517	460	288	2,138
Total number of persons in sample (over 3 years)	1,016	975	1,260	1,117	713	5,081
Total number of adults in sample (over 3 years)	557	627	914	929	640	3,667
Weighted average number of persons per household	2.1	2.3	2.4	2.3	2.6	2.3

Commodity or service	Average weekly household expenditure (£)					
1 Food & non-alcoholic drinks	24.10	26.60	30.50	33.30	42.30	31.10
2 Alcoholic drinks, tobacco & narcotics	8.30	10.10	10.80	12.10	15.90	11.30
3 Clothing & footwear	13.60	15.90	21.90	28.90	39.00	23.70
4 Housing (net)[2], fuel & power	33.70	50.20	59.80	58.50	100.40	59.50
5 Household goods & services	14.40	18.40	23.10	32.90	44.50	26.20
6 Health	0.50	1.70	2.00	2.90	6.90	2.60
7 Transport	18.10	35.00	53.70	78.70	118.70	60.00
8 Communication	7.30	11.10	13.00	15.00	22.00	13.60
9 Recreation & culture	21.40	32.80	38.90	62.60	82.70	46.90
10 Education	5.10	4.00	4.30	2.90	5.10	4.20
11 Restaurants & hotels	15.60	26.80	36.70	50.50	78.70	41.00
12 Miscellaneous goods & services	11.40	21.50	32.60	38.30	54.10	31.40
1-12 All expenditure groups	173.60	254.10	327.20	416.70	610.20	351.60
13 Other expenditure items	8.80	27.30	48.80	67.10	98.90	49.70
Total expenditure	182.30	281.40	376.10	483.80	709.10	401.30
Average weekly expenditure per person (£)						
Total expenditure	85.30	121.80	159.30	206.40	278.10	171.80

Note: The commodity and service categories are not comparable with those in publications before 2001-02
1 Lower boundary of 2003-04 gross income quintile groups (£ per week)
2 Excluding mortgage interest payments, council tax and Northern Ireland rates

A15 Household expenditure by gross income quintile group where the household reference person is aged 30 to 49

2001-02 — 2003-04

based on weighted data and including children's expenditure

	Lowest twenty per cent	Second quintile group	Third quintile group	Fourth quintile group	Highest twenty per cent	All house-holds
Lower boundary of group (£ per week)[1]		193	351	558	828	
Average number of grossed households (thousands)	1,020	1,210	2,030	2,520	2,790	9,550
Total number of households in sample (over 3 years)	942	1,156	1,898	2,257	2,385	8,638
Total number of persons in sample (over 3 years)	2,016	3,204	5,731	7,450	8,180	26,581
Total number of adults in sample (over 3 years)	1,157	1,742	3,313	4,544	5,264	16,020
Weighted average number of persons per household	2.1	2.7	2.9	3.2	3.3	3.0

Commodity or service	Average weekly household expenditure (£)					
1 Food & non-alcoholic drinks	27.40	36.00	42.90	51.30	63.10	48.50
2 Alcoholic drinks, tobacco & narcotics	9.50	11.30	12.70	14.30	15.30	13.30
3 Clothing & footwear	12.00	18.60	21.80	31.30	47.20	30.30
4 Housing (net)[2], fuel & power	26.40	35.10	39.20	38.20	47.50	39.50
5 Household goods & services	14.40	19.40	27.90	34.70	60.00	36.50
6 Health	1.20	1.70	3.00	4.60	6.60	4.10
7 Transport	19.60	34.20	51.70	79.10	123.30	74.20
8 Communication	7.20	10.40	11.80	13.50	16.70	13.00
9 Recreation & culture	27.00	34.90	50.90	72.90	106.20	68.20
10 Education	2.60	2.70	3.00	4.80	19.00	8.10
11 Restaurants & hotels	14.90	23.50	32.00	46.20	68.70	43.50
12 Miscellaneous goods & services	13.60	20.00	29.90	42.40	64.90	40.40
1-12 All expenditure groups	175.70	247.80	326.80	433.20	638.50	419.70
13 Other expenditure items	17.40	37.90	59.60	86.10	146.00	84.60
Total expenditure	193.10	285.70	386.40	519.40	784.50	504.30
Average weekly expenditure per person (£)						
Total expenditure	94.00	107.00	132.30	162.20	235.70	168.70

Note: The commodity and service categories are not comparable with those in publications before 2001-02
1 Lower boundary of 2003-04 gross income quintile groups (£ per week)
2 Excluding mortgage interest payments, council tax and Northern Ireland rates

A16 Household expenditure by gross income quintile group where the household reference person is aged 50 to 64

2001-02 — 2003-04

based on weighted data and including children's expenditure

	Lowest twenty per cent	Second quintile group	Third quintile group	Fourth quintile group	Highest twenty per cent	All house- holds
Lower boundary of group (£ per week)[1]		193	351	558	828	
Average number of grossed households (thousands)	950	1,080	1,250	1,360	1,470	6,100
Total number of households in sample (over 3 years)	879	1,002	1,100	1,165	1,155	5,301
Total number of persons in sample (over 3 years)	1,210	1,796	2,358	2,893	3,294	11,551
Total number of adults in sample (over 3 years)	1,146	1,640	2,148	2,569	2,948	10,451
Weighted average number of persons per household	1.4	1.8	2.2	2.5	2.9	2.2

Commodity or service	Average weekly household expenditure (£)					
1 Food & non-alcoholic drinks	26.60	37.10	44.30	53.40	66.10	47.50
2 Alcoholic drinks, tobacco & narcotics	9.40	10.60	12.70	14.70	18.20	13.60
3 Clothing & footwear	6.50	13.50	20.50	25.90	41.00	23.20
4 Housing (net)[2], fuel & power	23.00	30.50	35.90	35.00	43.80	34.60
5 Household goods & services	14.00	23.50	27.60	39.00	55.30	34.00
6 Health	1.90	4.60	4.70	7.30	13.10	6.90
7 Transport	23.20	35.80	56.40	75.20	127.00	68.70
8 Communication	5.70	7.90	9.40	12.00	16.50	10.80
9 Recreation & culture	21.60	39.90	57.30	76.10	102.60	63.70
10 Education	[0.20]	0.70	2.50	4.90	19.60	6.50
11 Restaurants & hotels	12.80	19.10	29.20	43.00	67.00	37.00
12 Miscellaneous goods & services	11.50	19.30	26.80	37.10	59.90	33.30
1-12 All expenditure groups	156.30	242.50	327.40	423.80	630.00	379.80
13 Other expenditure items	15.50	31.70	49.40	67.30	109.70	59.40
Total expenditure	171.80	274.20	376.80	491.10	739.70	439.20
Average weekly expenditure per person (£)						
Total expenditure	124.90	153.60	173.50	198.00	255.00	197.60

Note: The commodity and service categories are not comparable with those in publications before 2001-02
1 Lower boundary of 2003-04 gross income quintile groups (£ per week)
2 Excluding mortgage interest payments, council tax and Northern Ireland rates

A17 Household expenditure by gross income quintile group where the household reference person is aged 65 to 74

2001-02 — 2003-04

based on weighted data and including children's expenditure

	Lowest twenty per cent	Second quintile group	Third quintile group	Fourth quintile group	Highest twenty per cent	All house-holds
Lower boundary of group (£ per week)[1]		193	351	558	828	
Average number of grossed households (thousands)	970	1,190	630	320	160	3,270
Total number of households in sample (over 3 years)	900	1,083	569	265	134	2,951
Total number of persons in sample (over 3 years)	1,084	1,871	1,136	576	315	4,982
Total number of adults in sample (over 3 years)	1,075	1,850	1,117	563	306	4,911
Weighted average number of persons per household	1.2	1.7	2.0	2.2	2.4	1.7

Commodity or service	Average weekly household expenditure (£)					
1 Food & non-alcoholic drinks	25.30	37.40	45.70	52.80	63.70	38.30
2 Alcoholic drinks, tobacco & narcotics	4.80	7.90	10.00	12.50	11.50	8.10
3 Clothing & footwear	5.80	10.50	15.70	22.50	26.50	12.00
4 Housing (net)[2], fuel & power	23.10	28.90	30.60	37.30	49.40	29.40
5 Household goods & services	10.80	20.90	29.70	40.80	50.40	22.90
6 Health	1.90	5.20	8.30	8.30	12.60	5.40
7 Transport	11.10	27.70	51.50	66.70	99.10	34.70
8 Communication	4.90	6.20	7.40	9.60	12.10	6.70
9 Recreation & culture	18.70	39.50	54.90	73.60	105.80	42.90
10 Education	[0.00]	[0.20]	[0.40]	[0.70]	[7.10]	0.60
11 Restaurants & hotels	7.20	15.30	27.10	40.50	53.10	19.50
12 Miscellaneous goods & services	10.30	18.10	30.90	35.80	54.20	21.80
1-12 All expenditure groups	124.00	217.80	312.20	401.20	545.50	242.20
13 Other expenditure items	13.00	26.40	36.10	49.70	107.20	30.40
Total expenditure	137.00	244.20	348.30	450.90	652.70	272.60
Average weekly expenditure per person (£)						
Total expenditure	113.90	141.40	174.60	203.70	272.10	160.10

Note: The commodity and service categories are not comparable with those in publications before 2001-02
1 Lower boundary of 2003-04 gross income quintile groups (£ per week)
2 Excluding mortgage interest payments, council tax and Northern Ireland rates

A18 Household expenditure by gross income quintile group where the household reference person is aged 75 or over

2001-02 — 2003-04

based on weighted data and including children's expenditure

	Lowest twenty per cent	Second quintile group	Third quintile group	Fourth quintile group	Highest twenty per cent	All house-holds
Lower boundary of group (£ per week)[1]		193	351	558	828	
Average number of grossed households (thousands)	1,470	970	380	130	60	3,010
Total number of households in sample (over 3 years)	1,186	794	298	102	40	2,420
Total number of persons in sample (over 3 years)	1,366	1,286	545	195	86	3,478
Total number of adults in sample (over 3 years)	1,365	1,283	538	194	84	3,464
Weighted average number of persons per household	1.1	1.6	1.8	1.9	2.3	1.4

Commodity or service	Average weekly household expenditure (£)					
1 Food & non-alcoholic drinks	21.50	32.20	39.60	44.00	52.60	28.80
2 Alcoholic drinks, tobacco & narcotics	2.80	5.40	6.90	12.10	14.00	4.80
3 Clothing & footwear	4.10	7.60	13.60	12.20	[30.10]	7.30
4 Housing (net)[2], fuel & power	22.80	26.30	30.50	36.40	31.60	25.60
5 Household goods & services	9.90	17.80	21.10	33.80	30.30	15.30
6 Health	2.10	3.20	10.50	8.20	[8.40]	3.90
7 Transport	5.70	21.60	31.80	41.00	66.10	16.80
8 Communication	4.10	5.00	6.50	7.20	10.70	5.00
9 Recreation & culture	12.20	23.70	35.30	46.90	74.30	21.60
10 Education	[0.00]	[0.40]	[0.10]	[1.90]	[8.30]	[0.40]
11 Restaurants & hotels	5.60	10.60	18.20	29.00	[41.80]	10.50
12 Miscellaneous goods & services	10.00	16.10	26.90	55.10	107.70	17.70
1-12 All expenditure groups	100.80	169.90	240.80	327.70	475.80	157.80
13 Other expenditure items	11.20	20.40	30.30	38.40	91.20	19.20
Total expenditure	112.00	190.40	271.10	366.20	567.00	177.00
Average weekly expenditure per person (£)						
Total expenditure	98.10	118.60	147.60	189.70	244.20	123.20

Note: The commodity and service categories are not comparable with those in publications before 2001-02
1 Lower boundary of 2003-04 gross income quintile groups (£ per week)
2 Excluding mortgage interest payments, council tax and Northern Ireland rates

A19 Household expenditure by economic activity status of the household reference person

2003-04

based on weighted data and including children's expenditure

	Employees			Self-employed	All in employ-ment[1]
	Full-time	Part-time	All		
Grossed number of households (thousands)	10,980	1,840	12,820	1,890	14,720
Total number of households in sample	3,098	562	3,660	548	4,212
Total number of persons in sample	8,549	1,452	10,001	1,606	11,614
Total number of adults in sample	6,081	954	7,035	1,131	8,171
Weighted average number of persons per household	2.7	2.5	2.7	2.8	2.7

Commodity or service	Average weekly household expenditure (£)				
1 Food & non-alcoholic drinks	49.50	43.90	48.70	53.70	49.30
2 Alcoholic drinks, tobacco & narcotics	13.20	11.70	13.00	17.20	13.50
3 Clothing & footwear	30.40	23.50	29.40	35.80	30.20
4 Housing (net)[2], fuel & power	45.10	54.20	46.40	45.40	46.30
5 Household goods & services	39.00	28.80	37.50	42.90	38.20
6 Health	5.10	4.10	5.00	5.80	5.10
7 Transport	85.10	55.70	80.90	80.40	80.80
8 Communication	14.10	11.40	13.70	16.20	14.00
9 Recreation & culture	72.20	54.60	69.70	79.60	70.90
10 Education	7.10	4.30	6.70	13.70	7.60
11 Restaurants & hotels	47.20	30.30	44.70	55.00	46.00
12 Miscellaneous goods & services	43.60	31.60	41.90	46.40	42.40
1-12 All expenditure groups	451.50	354.20	437.50	492.10	444.20
13 Other expenditure items	90.50	46.60	84.20	95.90	85.60
Total expenditure	542.00	400.80	521.70	588.00	529.90
Average weekly expenditure per person (£)					
Total expenditure	200.50	157.90	194.70	207.70	196.40

Note: The commodity and service categories are not comparable with those in publications before 2001-02
1 Includes households where the head was on a government- supported training scheme
2 Excluding mortgage interest payments, council tax and Northern Ireland rates

A19 Household expenditure by economic activity status of the household reference person (cont.)

2003-04

based on weighted data and including children's expenditure

| | Unem-ployed | All economi-cally active[1] | Economically inactive | | | All house-holds |
			Retired	Other	All	
Grossed number of households (thousands)	450	15,180	6,300	3,190	9,490	24,670
Total number of households in sample	132	4,344	1,747	957	2,704	7,048
Total number of persons in sample	306	11,920	2,675	2,370	5,045	16,965
Total number of adults in sample	204	8,375	2,652	1,590	4,242	12,617
Weighted average number of persons per household	2.2	2.7	1.5	2.4	1.8	2.4

Commodity or service	Average weekly household expenditure (£)					
1 Food & non-alcoholic drinks	28.90	48.70	33.60	38.40	35.20	43.50
2 Alcoholic drinks, tobacco & narcotics	10.90	13.50	7.00	12.70	8.90	11.70
3 Clothing & footwear	13.60	29.70	9.30	16.20	11.60	22.70
4 Housing (net)[2], fuel & power	26.30	45.70	27.10	30.60	28.30	39.00
5 Household goods & services	24.30	37.80	20.00	22.50	20.90	31.30
6 Health	0.80	4.90	5.40	4.90	5.20	5.00
7 Transport	26.40	79.20	27.00	39.60	31.30	60.70
8 Communication	7.70	13.80	5.70	9.50	7.00	11.20
9 Recreation & culture	26.70	69.60	34.10	44.80	37.70	57.30
10 Education	[6.60]	7.50	[0.30]	4.00	1.60	5.20
11 Restaurants & hotels	20.70	45.30	14.70	25.50	18.30	34.90
12 Miscellaneous goods & services	14.70	41.60	20.20	22.20	20.90	33.60
1-12 All expenditure groups	207.70	437.20	204.40	271.00	226.80	356.20
13 Other expenditure items	24.00	83.80	27.80	24.90	26.80	61.90
Total expenditure	231.70	521.00	232.30	295.80	253.70	418.10

Average weekly expenditure per person (£)						
Total expenditure	105.70	194.20	150.80	122.20	138.10	177.40

Note: The commodity and service categories are not comparable with those in publications before 2001-02
1 Includes households where the head was on a government- supported training scheme
2 Excluding mortgage interest payments, council tax and Northern Ireland rates

A20 Household expenditure by gross income: the household reference person is a full-time employee

2003-04

based on weighted data and including children's expenditure

	Lowest twenty per cent	Second quintile group	Third quintile group	Fourth quintile group	Highest twenty per cent	All house-holds
Lower boundary of group (£ per week)		193	351	558	828	
Grossed number of households (thousands)	160	960	2,470	3,540	3,860	10,980
Total number of households in sample	48	280	723	1,006	1,041	3,098
Total number of persons in sample	76	433	1,767	2,978	3,295	8,549
Total number of adults in sample	63	360	1,236	2,049	2,373	6,081
Weighted average number of persons per household	1.6	1.5	2.4	2.9	3.1	2.7
Commodity or service	**Average weekly household expenditure (£)**					
1 Food & non-alcoholic drinks	22.30	28.20	39.20	48.90	63.10	49.50
2 Alcoholic drinks, tobacco & narcotics	11.30	8.90	11.70	13.20	15.40	13.20
3 Clothing & footwear	[9.60]	11.50	20.80	28.50	43.70	30.40
4 Housing (net)[1], fuel & power	49.50	41.70	41.80	43.40	49.50	45.10
5 Household goods & services	[11.70]	15.90	29.90	35.80	54.50	39.00
6 Health	[0.60]	3.60	2.60	4.20	8.10	5.10
7 Transport	24.40	33.30	50.50	78.70	128.30	85.10
8 Communication	8.40	9.00	11.30	13.80	17.70	14.10
9 Recreation & culture	26.20	30.30	49.70	69.60	101.10	72.20
10 Education	[2.70]	[1.30]	1.90	3.80	15.00	7.10
11 Restaurants & hotels	[15.10]	19.60	32.00	45.50	66.40	47.20
12 Miscellaneous goods & services	10.20	20.20	30.50	41.00	61.50	43.60
1-12 All expenditure groups	192.00	223.30	321.70	426.60	624.40	451.50
13 Other expenditure items	28.60	43.50	60.70	85.40	128.50	90.50
Total expenditure	220.60	266.90	382.40	512.00	752.90	542.00
Average weekly expenditure per person (£)						
Total expenditure	139.20	174.10	159.40	178.50	244.30	200.50

Note: The commodity and service categories are not comparable with those in publications before 2001-02
1 Excluding mortgage interest payments, council tax and Northern Ireland rates

A21 Household expenditure by gross income: the household reference person is self-employed

2001-02 — 2003-04

based on weighted data and including children's expenditure

	Lowest twenty per cent	Second quintile group	Third quintile group	Fourth quintile group	Highest twenty per cent	All house-holds
Lower boundary of group (£ per week)[1]		193	351	558	828	
Average number of grossed households (thousands)	180	300	430	420	530	1,860
Total number of households in sample (over 3 years)	155	274	390	376	442	1,637
Total number of persons in sample (over 3 years)	278	664	1,143	1,172	1,404	4,661
Total number of adults in sample (over 3 years)	212	499	779	811	1,006	3,307
Weighted average number of persons per household	1.6	2.3	2.8	3.0	3.1	2.8

Commodity or service	Average weekly household expenditure (£)					
1 Food & non-alcoholic drinks	31.40	39.90	48.90	58.70	64.10	52.40
2 Alcoholic drinks, tobacco & narcotics	10.90	10.10	13.00	15.30	19.40	14.70
3 Clothing & footwear	13.20	20.10	22.90	32.90	47.20	30.80
4 Housing (net)[2], fuel & power	35.80	35.50	40.00	40.40	54.80	43.20
5 Household goods & services	23.50	24.70	29.90	44.40	65.50	42.10
6 Health	3.50	4.00	3.70	7.20	6.80	5.40
7 Transport	49.30	54.40	62.50	87.90	121.70	82.60
8 Communication	9.60	11.40	14.40	15.60	19.50	15.20
9 Recreation & culture	40.80	57.90	58.60	70.00	103.40	72.10
10 Education	[4.30]	1.80	3.70	9.10	33.10	13.00
11 Restaurants & hotels	22.80	31.20	37.40	52.20	74.70	49.00
12 Miscellaneous goods & services	26.00	27.50	31.50	46.30	62.60	42.60
1-12 All expenditure groups	271.20	318.40	366.50	479.90	672.80	463.10
13 Other expenditure items	45.50	53.00	66.70	87.00	163.70	94.40
Total expenditure	316.70	371.30	433.20	566.90	836.50	557.50
Average weekly expenditure per person (£)						
Total expenditure	192.80	159.30	152.20	187.70	269.20	201.50

Note: The commodity and service categories are not comparable with those in publications before 2001-02

1 Lower boundary of 2003-04 gross income quintile groups (£ per week)

2 Excluding mortgage interest payments, council tax and Northern Ireland rates

A22 Household expenditure by number of persons working — 2003-04

based on weighted data and including children's expenditure

	Number of persons working					All house-holds
	None	One	Two	Three	Four or more	
Grossed number of households (thousands)	8,640	6,910	7,130	1,570	420	24,670
Total number of households in sample	2,486	2,018	2,047	388	109	7,048
Total number of persons in sample	4,314	4,440	6,176	1,517	518	16,965
Total number of adults in sample	3,623	3,145	4,301	1,127	421	12,617
Weighted average number of persons per household	1.7	2.1	2.9	3.8	4.6	2.4
Weighted average age of head of household	65	45	42	47	48	51
Employment status of head[1]:						
- % working full-time or self-employed	0	68	89	90	94	52
- % working part-time	0	17	9	8	6	8
- % not working	100	15	2	3	1	40
Commodity or service	Average weekly household expenditure (£)					
1 Food & non-alcoholic drinks	32.30	39.50	54.50	64.90	74.10	43.50
2 Alcoholic drinks, tobacco & narcotics	8.00	11.00	15.10	17.30	22.50	11.70
3 Clothing & footwear	9.90	21.10	32.70	44.80	61.60	22.70
4 Housing (net)[2], fuel & power	26.70	44.80	44.70	52.20	50.50	39.00
5 Household goods & services	19.10	31.40	43.20	42.60	34.40	31.30
6 Health	4.70	4.50	5.50	6.90	6.70	5.00
7 Transport	25.90	57.70	89.40	102.90	182.30	60.70
8 Communication	6.20	11.50	13.90	21.30	25.90	11.20
9 Recreation & culture	33.20	54.60	79.10	85.90	119.80	57.30
10 Education	1.30	5.00	8.60	10.50	14.40	5.20
11 Restaurants & hotels	14.90	32.60	50.30	68.70	96.10	34.90
12 Miscellaneous goods & services	18.20	32.10	48.10	52.40	60.50	33.60
1-12 All expenditure groups	200.40	345.60	485.20	570.50	748.90	356.20
13 Other expenditure items	23.40	65.30	96.50	92.00	98.00	61.90
Total expenditure	223.80	410.80	581.80	662.50	846.90	418.10
Average weekly expenditure per person (£)						
Total expenditure	132.10	192.60	198.20	175.40	186.00	177.40

Note: The commodity and service categories are not comparable with those in publications before 2001-02
1 Excludes households where the head was on a government- supported training scheme
2 Excluding mortgage interest payments, council tax and Northern Ireland rates

A23 Household expenditure by age at which the household reference person completed continuous full-time education   2003-04

based on weighted data and including children's expenditure

	Aged 14 and under	Aged 15	Aged 16	Aged 17 and under 19	Aged 19 and under 22	Aged 22 or over
Grossed number of households (thousands)	3,280	5,320	7,420	4,010	2,290	2,170
Total number of households in sample	921	1,491	2,166	1,182	634	606
Total number of persons in sample	1,533	3,282	5,952	2,959	1,562	1,540
Total number of adults in sample	1,445	2,790	3,931	2,048	1,155	1,122
Weighted average number of persons per household	1.7	2.2	2.7	2.4	2.4	2.5
Weighted average age of head of household	74	57	46	46	44	44

Commodity or service	Average weekly household expenditure (£)					
1 Food & non-alcoholic drinks	32.70	42.20	44.80	45.00	48.60	51.60
2 Alcoholic drinks, tobacco & narcotics	7.20	12.70	12.80	11.70	12.70	11.50
3 Clothing & footwear	8.20	17.80	25.10	27.30	28.70	33.60
4 Housing (net)[1], fuel & power	28.70	29.90	35.90	43.30	53.90	57.30
5 Household goods & services	16.80	25.10	32.30	37.10	42.30	43.90
6 Health	3.40	4.00	4.00	6.20	7.10	9.20
7 Transport	20.80	49.70	64.80	68.70	90.40	87.10
8 Communication	5.50	9.30	11.60	13.10	15.80	14.10
9 Recreation & culture	27.70	49.10	59.60	67.00	74.10	79.50
10 Education	[0.10]	0.80	2.50	7.70	12.80	19.10
11 Restaurants & hotels	12.10	28.70	37.40	40.90	47.00	51.00
12 Miscellaneous goods & services	16.50	24.80	34.60	39.40	47.70	52.70
1-12 All expenditure groups	179.60	294.10	365.50	407.20	481.00	510.30
13 Other expenditure items	23.20	45.50	61.40	73.00	94.10	111.00
Total expenditure	202.80	339.50	426.90	480.20	575.10	621.40

Average weekly expenditure per person (£)

Total expenditure	121.30	154.10	160.00	197.50	238.30	251.00

Note: The commodity and service categories are not comparable with those in publications before 2001-02
1 Excluding mortgage interest payments, council tax and Northern Ireland rates

A24 Household expenditure by socio-economic class of the household reference person

2003-04

based on weighted data and including children's expenditure

	Large employers & higher manag-erial	Higher profess-ional	Lower manag-erial & profess-ional	Inter-mediate	Small employ-ers	Lower super-visory
Grossed number of households (thousands)	1,210	1,590	4,920	1,680	1,580	1,980
Total number of households in sample	337	451	1,398	496	461	563
Total number of persons in sample	948	1,223	3,688	1,205	1,330	1,578
Total number of adults in sample	672	857	2,663	846	939	1,099
Weighted average number of persons per household	2.7	2.6	2.6	2.4	2.8	2.7

Commodity or service	Average weekly household expenditure (£)					
1 Food & non-alcoholic drinks	59.00	56.20	50.10	41.10	50.40	45.00
2 Alcoholic drinks, tobacco & narcotics	14.10	12.20	14.10	10.60	15.70	14.20
3 Clothing & footwear	39.30	35.40	31.70	25.30	31.80	23.00
4 Housing (net)[3], fuel & power	48.30	51.00	48.60	43.00	37.10	35.70
5 Household goods & services	61.20	52.00	42.00	27.70	38.20	29.90
6 Health	11.40	9.20	5.80	4.50	4.60	3.10
7 Transport	113.50	102.90	88.00	62.20	70.60	65.80
8 Communication	14.60	14.60	14.80	12.60	14.60	11.40
9 Recreation & culture	100.30	88.20	80.40	53.70	62.80	62.90
10 Education	14.00	17.00	9.20	5.30	4.30	2.70
11 Restaurants & hotels	63.10	54.30	48.10	32.80	49.80	39.90
12 Miscellaneous goods & services	60.90	54.80	46.10	35.80	39.80	33.70
1-12 All expenditure groups	599.80	547.90	478.90	354.60	419.80	367.50
13 Other expenditure items	121.70	115.40	91.20	66.10	83.50	66.10
Total expenditure	721.50	663.20	570.00	420.80	503.30	433.60
Average weekly expenditure per person (£)						
Total expenditure	264.30	254.00	219.90	174.20	180.90	157.80

Note: The commodity and service categories are not comparable with those in publications before 2001-02
1 Includes those who have never worked
2 Includes those who are economically inactive
3 Excluding mortgage interest payments, council tax and Northern Ireland rates

A24 Household expenditure by socio-economic class of the household reference person (cont.)

2003-04

based on weighted data and including children's expenditure

	Semi-routine	Routine	Long-term unem-ployed[1]	Students	Occupation not stated[2]	All house-holds
Grossed number of households (thousands)	2,500	2,330	490	310	6,090	24,670
Total number of households in sample	730	690	157	83	1,682	7,048
Total number of persons in sample	1,908	1,852	460	205	2,568	16,965
Total number of adults in sample	1,295	1,280	251	169	2,546	12,617
Weighted average number of persons per household	2.6	2.6	2.8	2.4	1.5	2.4

Commodity or service

		Semi-routine	Routine	Long-term unem-ployed[1]	Students	Occupation not stated[2]	All house-holds
1	Food & non-alcoholic drinks	41.10	41.50	34.90	30.00	33.30	43.50
2	Alcoholic drinks, tobacco & narcotics	13.30	13.40	10.80	7.90	6.70	11.70
3	Clothing & footwear	19.70	19.50	15.90	22.10	8.80	22.70
4	Housing (net)[3], fuel & power	37.40	36.20	26.10	84.90	27.10	39.00
5	Household goods & services	21.40	26.50	14.40	14.20	19.00	31.30
6	Health	3.20	2.10	1.50	3.80	5.20	5.00
7	Transport	51.60	43.80	17.10	57.50	26.50	60.70
8	Communication	11.00	10.60	9.00	15.20	5.70	11.20
9	Recreation & culture	46.60	41.80	27.40	34.40	33.60	57.30
10	Education	1.90	0.60	[0.70]	[34.30]	[0.30]	5.20
11	Restaurants & hotels	29.80	27.90	22.10	34.10	14.40	34.90
12	Miscellaneous goods & services	24.20	23.50	13.50	24.50	20.10	33.60
1-12	All expenditure groups	301.30	287.50	193.40	362.70	200.70	356.20
13	Other expenditure items	39.40	42.10	10.40	16.60	27.40	61.90
	Total expenditure	340.70	329.60	203.70	379.30	228.10	418.10

Average weekly expenditure per person (£)

	Semi-routine	Routine	Long-term unem-ployed[1]	Students	Occupation not stated[2]	All house-holds
Total expenditure	131.70	125.60	72.00	159.10	148.60	177.40

Note: The commodity and service categories are not comparable with those in publications before 2001-02
1 Includes those who have never worked
2 Includes those who are economically inactive
3 Excluding mortgage interest payments, council tax and Northern Ireland rates

A25 Expenditure by household composition

2003-04

based on weighted data and including children's expenditure

	Retired households				Non-retired	
	State pension[1]		Other retired		One person	One man and one woman
	One person	One man and one woman	One person	One man and one woman		
Grossed number of households (thousands)	1,090	580	2,190	1,960	3,690	4,990
Total number of households in sample	308	163	601	556	1,043	1,389
Total number of persons in sample	308	326	601	1,112	1,043	2,778
Total number of adults in sample	308	326	601	1,112	1,043	2,778
Weighted average number of persons per household	1.0	2.0	1.0	2.0	1.0	2.0
Commodity or service	Average weekly household expenditure (£)					
1 Food & non-alcoholic drinks	21.10	39.10	22.90	45.90	21.80	45.70
2 Alcoholic drinks, tobacco & narcotics	3.70	6.60	4.30	10.50	9.20	14.30
3 Clothing & footwear	4.40	7.30	7.00	13.20	11.30	24.60
4 Housing (net)[2], fuel & power	21.40	28.00	26.10	29.70	36.30	41.50
5 Household goods & services	7.30	20.60	14.40	30.20	19.90	40.00
6 Health	1.90	3.70	3.90	9.20	2.30	7.40
7 Transport	6.40	18.70	14.50	49.60	41.30	80.20
8 Communication	4.30	4.70	5.00	7.20	8.70	11.10
9 Recreation & culture	12.20	29.40	22.10	57.80	34.60	69.90
10 Education	[0.00]	[0.00]	[0.20]	[0.70]	2.20	2.70
11 Restaurants & hotels	4.80	10.10	9.80	23.70	23.80	42.60
12 Miscellaneous goods & services	12.60	14.90	17.10	27.10	19.80	37.70
1-12 All expenditure groups	100.20	183.10	147.20	304.80	231.30	417.80
13 Other expenditure items	11.30	20.20	21.90	43.50	50.10	82.60
Total expenditure	111.50	203.30	169.10	348.30	281.40	500.50
Average weekly expenditure per person (£)						
Total expenditure	111.50	101.60	169.10	174.20	281.40	250.20

Note: The commodity and service categories are not comparable with those in publications before 2001-02
1 Mainly dependent on state pension and not economically active - see definitions in Appendix B
2 Excluding mortgage interest payments, council tax and Northern Ireland rates

A25 Expenditure by household composition (cont.) 2003-04
based on weighted data and including children's expenditure

| | Retired and non-retired households | | | | | | |
| | One adult | | Two adults | | | Three or more adults | |
	with one child	with two or more children	with one child	with two children	with three or more children	without children	with children
Grossed number of households (thousands)	770	680	1,790	2,300	870	2,110	1,020
Total number of households in sample	248	249	530	721	309	457	301
Total number of persons in sample	496	876	1,590	2,884	1,634	1,503	1,468
Total number of adults in sample	248	249	1,060	1,442	618	1,503	983
Weighted average number of persons per household	2.0	3.5	3.0	4.0	5.3	3.3	4.8

Commodity or service	Average weekly household expenditure (£)						
1 Food & non-alcoholic drinks	30.80	43.00	50.60	64.00	73.30	60.50	71.50
2 Alcoholic drinks, tobacco & narcotics	8.30	8.30	13.70	13.10	15.40	18.40	18.90
3 Clothing & footwear	21.90	24.60	33.40	34.80	39.90	34.80	50.40
4 Housing (net)[2], fuel & power	35.00	35.40	43.70	41.00	52.70	57.80	43.40
5 Household goods & services	24.00	25.50	41.70	46.30	40.50	32.60	44.50
6 Health	2.30	1.30	4.20	5.60	4.00	6.60	5.60
7 Transport	27.40	26.90	80.30	85.00	82.20	100.30	102.20
8 Communication	10.30	12.00	12.70	14.50	15.10	18.70	23.20
9 Recreation & culture	31.80	37.20	70.70	91.00	85.40	73.10	99.20
10 Education	1.50	4.80	7.30	17.10	13.80	8.90	14.20
11 Restaurants & hotels	20.10	23.50	42.10	47.90	50.00	57.80	71.30
12 Miscellaneous goods & services	23.10	26.90	47.80	52.00	53.60	44.10	54.00
1-12 All expenditure groups	236.80	269.50	448.20	512.20	525.90	513.60	598.50
13 Other expenditure items	32.30	28.70	83.10	98.90	100.70	68.20	87.60
Total expenditure	269.10	298.20	531.30	611.10	626.60	581.80	686.10

Average weekly expenditure per person (£)

| Total expenditure | 134.50 | 85.20 | 177.10 | 152.80 | 119.20 | 177.40 | 143.70 |

Note: The commodity and service categories are not comparable with those in publications before 2001-02
1 Mainly dependent on state pension and not economically active - see definitions in Appendix B
2 Excluding mortgage interest payments, council tax and Northern Ireland rates

A26 Expenditure of one adult retired households mainly dependent on state pension[1] by gross income quintile group   2001-02 — 2003-04
based on weighted data

	Lowest twenty per cent	Second quintile group	Third quintile group	Fourth quintile group	Highest twenty per cent	All house-holds
Lower boundary of group (£ per week)[2]		193	351	558	828	
Average grossed number of households (thousands)	1,350	100	0	0	0	1,450
Total number of households in sample (over 3 years)	1,157	80	1	0	0	1,238
Total number of persons in sample (over 3 years)	1,157	80	1	0	0	1,238
Total number of adults in sample (over 3 years)	1,157	80	1	0	0	1,238
Weighted average number of persons per household	1.0	1.0	1.0	0	0	1.0

Commodity or service	Average weekly household expenditure (£)					
1 Food & non-alcoholic drinks	20.40	21.50	[8.00]	..	..	20.50
2 Alcoholic drinks, tobacco & narcotics	3.50	3.30	[0.00]	..	..	3.50
3 Clothing & footwear	4.50	9.00	[4.70]	..	..	4.90
4 Housing (net) [3], fuel & power	20.40	17.30	[2.70]	..	..	20.20
5 Household goods & services	8.20	15.60	[6.90]	..	..	8.80
6 Health	1.90	0.80	[0.00]	..	..	1.90
7 Transport	5.20	7.30	[2.30]	..	..	5.40
8 Communication	4.30	5.30	[3.10]	..	..	4.30
9 Recreation & culture	12.10	15.10	[1.80]	..	..	12.30
10 Education	[0.00]	[0.00]	[0.00]	..	..	[0.00]
11 Restaurants & hotels	5.00	7.10	[1.30]	..	..	5.10
12 Miscellaneous goods & services	9.60	12.10	[2.60]	..	..	9.80
1-12 All expenditure groups	95.20	114.40	[33.40]	..	..	96.50
13 Other expenditure items	8.80	10.30	[22.20]	..	..	9.00
Total expenditure	104.00	124.70	[55.60]	..	..	105.50
Average weekly expenditure per person (£)						
Total expenditure	104.00	124.70	[55.60]	..	..	105.50

Note: The commodity and service categories are not comparable with those in publications before 2001-02
1 Mainly dependent on state pension and not economically active - see definitions in Appendix B
2 Lower boundary of 2003-04 gross income quintile groups (£ per week)
3 Excluding mortgage interest payments, council tax and Northern Ireland rates

A27   Expenditure of one adult retired households   2001-02 — 2003-04
not mainly dependent on state pensions[1] by gross income quintile group
based on weighted data

	Lowest twenty per cent	Second quintile group	Third quintile group	Fourth quintile group	Highest twenty per cent	All house-holds
Lower boundary of group (£ per week)[2]		193	351	558	828	
Average grossed number of households (thousands)	630	690	170	60	30	1,580
Total number of households in sample (over 3 years)	538	587	142	49	20	1,336
Total number of persons in sample (over 3 years)	538	587	142	49	20	1,336
Total number of adults in sample (over 3 years)	538	587	142	49	20	1,336
Weighted average number of persons per household	1.0	1.0	1.0	1.0	1.0	1.0

Commodity or service	Average weekly household expenditure (£)					
1 Food & non-alcoholic drinks	20.90	24.60	26.00	33.40	[30.80]	23.80
2 Alcoholic drinks, tobacco & narcotics	3.30	5.00	4.90	5.80	[3.80]	4.40
3 Clothing & footwear	5.10	7.20	11.30	19.70	[12.80]	7.40
4 Housing (net)[3], fuel & power	27.50	27.80	31.20	31.60	[56.90]	28.80
5 Household goods & services	14.80	17.70	19.20	40.70	[17.30]	17.60
6 Health	1.80	3.50	9.20	[2.80]	[8.50]	3.60
7 Transport	9.90	19.10	32.40	46.60	[42.40]	18.50
8 Communication	4.50	5.50	5.70	7.80	[8.70]	5.30
9 Recreation & culture	16.40	25.80	32.10	49.20	[51.90]	24.20
10 Education	[0.00]	[0.30]	[0.10]	[2.80]	[7.80]	[0.40]
11 Restaurants & hotels	7.20	9.70	15.90	22.30	[19.30]	10.10
12 Miscellaneous goods & services	10.90	17.30	28.10	67.80	[108.70]	19.60
1-12 All expenditure groups	122.50	163.60	216.20	330.50	[369.00]	163.60
13 Other expenditure items	18.60	25.60	30.40	38.50	[110.30]	25.60
Total expenditure	141.10	189.20	246.70	368.90	[479.30]	189.20
Average weekly expenditure per person (£)						
Total expenditure	141.10	189.20	246.70	368.90	[479.30]	189.20

Note: The commodity and service categories are not comparable with those in publications before 2001-02
1 Mainly dependent on state pension and not economically active - see definitions in Appendix B
2 Lower boundary of 2003-04 gross income quintile groups (£ per week)
3 Excluding mortgage interest payments, council tax and Northern Ireland rates

A28 Expenditure of one adult non-retired households by gross income quintile group
2001-02 — 2003-04
based on weighted data

	Lowest twenty per cent	Second quintile group	Third quintile group	Fourth quintile group	Highest twenty per cent	All house-holds
Lower boundary of group (£ per week)[1]		193	351	558	828	
Average grossed number of households (thousands)	1,140	950	850	450	220	3,600
Total number of households in sample (over 3 years)	1,012	845	720	366	176	3,119
Total number of persons in sample (over 3 years)	1,012	845	720	366	176	3,119
Total number of adults in sample (over 3 years)	1,012	845	720	366	176	3,119
Weighted average number of persons per household	1.0	1.0	1.0	1.0	1.0	1.0
Commodity or service	Average weekly household expenditure (£)					
1 Food & non-alcoholic drinks	17.90	21.90	22.60	23.80	26.60	21.30
2 Alcoholic drinks, tobacco & narcotics	8.20	7.90	8.70	9.60	11.30	8.60
3 Clothing & footwear	5.20	9.60	12.30	16.90	30.90	11.00
4 Housing (net)[2], fuel & power	25.70	34.10	36.90	38.30	47.70	33.50
5 Household goods & services	11.20	16.40	22.30	29.00	41.00	19.20
6 Health	1.30	2.60	2.90	3.70	4.30	2.50
7 Transport	15.90	29.40	45.60	80.10	76.90	38.20
8 Communication	5.70	7.60	9.80	10.70	13.20	8.20
9 Recreation & culture	20.20	26.20	37.80	57.50	72.90	33.80
10 Education	[1.30]	[0.70]	1.80	[3.60]	[7.40]	1.90
11 Restaurants & hotels	11.70	17.00	26.00	39.90	54.60	22.60
12 Miscellaneous goods & services	9.30	17.00	23.60	28.70	46.20	19.30
1-12 All expenditure groups	133.40	190.30	250.30	341.60	433.20	220.20
13 Other expenditure items	14.60	36.90	62.60	84.10	138.60	48.00
Total expenditure	148.00	227.20	312.90	425.70	571.80	268.20
Average weekly expenditure per person (£)						
Total expenditure	148.00	227.20	312.90	425.70	571.80	268.20

Note: The commodity and service categories are not comparable with those in publications before 2001-02
1 Lower boundary of 2003-04 gross income quintile groups (£ per week)
2 Excluding mortgage interest payments, council tax and Northern Ireland rates

A29 Expenditure of one adult households with children by gross income quintile group

2001-02 — 2003-04

based on weighted data and including children's expenditure

	Lowest twenty per cent	Second quintile group	Third quintile group	Fourth quintile group	Highest twenty per cent	All house- holds
Lower boundary of group (£ per week)[1]		193	351	558	828	
Average grossed number of households (thousands)	630	410	310	110	30	1,480
Total number of households in sample (over 3 years)	648	428	323	106	26	1,531
Total number of persons in sample (over 3 years)	1,701	1,287	886	288	71	4,233
Total number of adults in sample (over 3 years)	648	428	323	106	26	1,531
Weighted average number of persons per household	2.6	2.9	2.7	2.7	2.8	2.7

Commodity or service	Average weekly household expenditure (£)					
1 Food & non-alcoholic drinks	30.80	36.10	38.00	46.80	52.00	35.30
2 Alcoholic drinks, tobacco & narcotics	8.00	8.80	8.90	10.80	10.00	8.70
3 Clothing & footwear	14.70	23.00	27.10	26.40	76.10	21.80
4 Housing (net)[2], fuel & power	22.10	37.00	42.90	40.70	32.90	32.30
5 Household goods & services	13.90	17.10	29.00	30.50	90.80	20.60
6 Health	0.70	1.60	2.00	5.80	[9.00]	1.90
7 Transport	12.40	23.40	39.60	68.70	91.90	26.60
8 Communication	7.40	11.60	13.20	14.10	18.20	10.50
9 Recreation & culture	20.70	32.30	46.30	69.00	93.50	34.20
10 Education	1.30	3.10	3.90	16.20	[46.90]	4.40
11 Restaurants & hotels	13.70	19.80	29.10	35.50	46.40	20.90
12 Miscellaneous goods & services	11.40	21.00	35.10	50.80	80.70	23.20
1-12 All expenditure groups	157.30	235.00	315.10	415.50	648.30	240.30
13 Other expenditure items	9.10	24.50	45.40	73.10	170.30	28.60
Total expenditure	166.30	259.50	360.50	488.60	818.60	269.00
Average weekly expenditure per person (£)						
Total expenditure	63.80	88.30	134.10	182.40	296.40	98.80

Note: The commodity and service categories are not comparable with those in publications before 2001-02
1 Lower boundary of 2003-04 gross income quintile groups (£ per week)
2 Excluding mortgage interest payments, council tax and Northern Ireland rates

A30 Expenditure of two adult households with children by gross income quintile group

2001-02 — 2003-04

based on weighted data and including children's expenditure

	Lowest twenty per cent	Second quintile group	Third quintile group	Fourth quintile group	Highest twenty per cent	All house-holds
Lower boundary of group (£ per week)[1]		193	351	558	828	
Average grossed number of households (thousands)	190	510	1,160	1,570	1,530	4,960
Total number of households in sample (over 3 years)	178	508	1,133	1,514	1,427	4,760
Total number of persons in sample (over 3 years)	664	2,040	4,466	5,870	5,563	18,603
Total number of adults in sample (over 3 years)	356	1,016	2,266	3,028	2,854	9,520
Weighted average number of persons per household	3.7	4.0	3.9	3.8	3.9	3.9

Commodity or service	Average weekly household expenditure (£)					
1 Food & non-alcoholic drinks	43.20	48.80	51.60	59.20	71.60	59.50
2 Alcoholic drinks, tobacco & narcotics	13.50	13.00	13.70	13.40	14.00	13.70
3 Clothing & footwear	20.40	22.40	25.90	34.50	46.80	34.50
4 Housing (net)[2], fuel & power	29.80	37.10	40.90	37.80	47.50	41.20
5 Household goods & services	19.60	26.20	29.10	39.30	64.50	42.60
6 Health	2.10	1.50	2.80	4.50	7.30	4.50
7 Transport	37.00	40.20	55.50	74.80	120.10	79.20
8 Communication	8.60	11.80	11.90	13.10	15.70	13.30
9 Recreation & culture	31.30	45.10	56.50	79.20	113.40	79.20
10 Education	[6.80]	3.70	4.40	6.30	34.70	14.40
11 Restaurants & hotels	19.30	27.10	32.40	45.60	63.20	45.00
12 Miscellaneous goods & services	18.80	23.00	31.30	45.20	76.30	48.30
1-12 All expenditure groups	250.50	299.90	356.10	452.90	675.10	475.50
13 Other expenditure items	23.60	35.90	57.00	87.70	145.90	90.70
Total expenditure	274.10	335.80	413.00	540.70	821.10	566.30
Average weekly expenditure per person (£)						
Total expenditure	74.80	84.60	106.20	140.90	213.20	146.70

Note: The commodity and service categories are not comparable with those in publications before 2001-02
1 Lower boundary of 2003-04 gross income quintile groups (£ per week)
2 Excluding mortgage interest payments, council tax and Northern Ireland rates

A31 Expenditure of one man one woman non-retired households by gross income quintile group

2001-02 — 2003-04

based on weighted data

	Lowest twenty per cent	Second quintile group	Third quintile group	Fourth quintile group	Highest twenty per cent	All house-holds
Lower boundary of group (£ per week)[1]		193	351	558	828	
Average grossed number of households (thousands)	310	650	1,160	1,460	1,420	5,000
Total number of households in sample (over 3 years)	285	591	1,021	1,245	1,146	4,288
Total number of persons in sample (over 3 years)	570	1,182	2,042	2,490	2,292	8,576
Total number of adults in sample (over 3 years)	570	1,182	2,042	2,490	2,292	8,576
Weighted average number of persons per household	2.0	2.0	2.0	2.0	2.0	2.0

Commodity or service	Average weekly household expenditure (£)					
1 Food & non-alcoholic drinks	35.60	39.20	42.00	42.90	50.20	43.80
2 Alcoholic drinks, tobacco & narcotics	11.60	11.90	13.20	13.40	16.20	13.80
3 Clothing & footwear	11.60	12.10	18.30	23.60	38.20	24.30
4 Housing (net)[2], fuel & power	32.50	32.50	38.20	37.50	48.70	39.90
5 Household goods & services	21.50	28.00	28.20	38.70	57.00	38.90
6 Health	2.50	4.90	4.70	6.70	12.10	7.30
7 Transport	41.30	39.00	59.30	78.90	123.50	79.50
8 Communication	6.20	7.90	9.20	10.80	13.80	10.60
9 Recreation & culture	38.50	44.30	55.80	66.60	93.10	67.00
10 Education	[2.30]	[0.70]	1.80	1.50	5.50	2.70
11 Restaurants & hotels	19.60	23.60	30.30	40.90	64.50	41.60
12 Miscellaneous goods & services	21.40	19.90	29.50	37.20	54.00	37.00
1-12 All expenditure groups	244.60	264.00	330.40	398.80	576.80	406.30
13 Other expenditure items	23.50	36.10	53.20	74.10	138.40	79.40
Total expenditure	268.10	300.10	383.70	472.80	715.20	485.70
Average weekly expenditure per person (£)						
Total expenditure	134.00	150.10	191.80	236.40	357.60	242.90

Note: The commodity and service categories are not comparable with those in publications before 2001-02
1 Lower boundary of 2003-04 gross income quintile groups (£ per week)
2 Excluding mortgage interest payments, council tax and Northern Ireland rates

A32

Expenditure of one man one woman retired households mainly dependent on state income[1] by gross income quintile group

2001-02 — 2003-04

based on weighted data and including children's expenditure

	Lowest twenty per cent	Second quintile group	Third quintile group	Fourth quintile group	Highest twenty per cent	All house-holds
Lower boundary of group (£ per week)[2]		193	351	558	828	
Average grossed number of households (thousands)	300	350	10	0	0	660
Total number of households in sample (over 3 years)	283	315	8	0	0	606
Total number of persons in sample (over 3 years)	566	630	16	0	0	1,212
Total number of adults in sample (over 3 years)	566	630	16	0	0	1,212
Weighted average number of persons per household	2.0	2.0	2.0	0	0	2.0

Commodity or service	Average weekly household expenditure (£)					
1 Food & non-alcoholic drinks	36.80	38.80	[42.90]	..	..	37.90
2 Alcoholic drinks, tobacco & narcotics	5.20	7.20	[4.10]	..	..	6.30
3 Clothing & footwear	5.70	8.40	[18.30]	..	..	7.30
4 Housing (net)[3], fuel & power	24.10	28.30	[13.80]	..	..	26.40
5 Household goods & services	13.30	18.60	[69.00]	..	..	16.70
6 Health	2.50	4.50	[6.10]	..	..	3.70
7 Transport	15.80	21.70	[15.30]	..	..	18.90
8 Communication	4.80	4.80	[6.60]	..	..	4.80
9 Recreation & culture	25.90	28.60	[23.80]	..	..	27.50
10 Education	[0.00]	[0.00]	[0.00]	..	..	[0.00]
11 Restaurants & hotels	8.10	11.70	[10.70]	..	..	10.10
12 Miscellaneous goods & services	14.40	15.10	[16.00]	..	..	14.70
1-12 All expenditure groups	156.70	187.70	[226.70]	..	..	174.30
13 Other expenditure items	15.10	19.00	[7.00]	..	..	17.30
Total expenditure	171.80	206.70	[233.60]	..	..	191.60
Average weekly expenditure per person (£)						
Total expenditure	85.90	103.30	[116.80]	..	..	95.80

Note: The commodity and service categories are not comparable with those in publications before 2001-02
1 Mainly dependent on state pension and not economically active - see definitions in Appendix B
2 Lower boundary of 2003-04 gross income quintile groups (£ per week)
3 Excluding mortgage interest payments, council tax and Northern Ireland rates

A33 Expenditure of one man one woman retired households not mainly dependent on state pension[1] by gross income quintile group
2001-02 — 2003-04
based on weighted data

	Lowest twenty per cent	Second quintile group	Third quintile group	Fourth quintile group	Highest twenty per cent	All house-holds
Lower boundary of group (£ per week)[2]		193	351	558	828	
Average grossed number of households (thousands)	60	870	640	230	90	1,900
Total number of households in sample (over 3 years)	47	778	564	202	85	1,676
Total number of persons in sample (over 3 years)	94	1,556	1,128	404	170	3,352
Total number of adults in sample (over 3 years)	94	1,556	1,128	404	170	3,352
Weighted average number of persons per household	2.0	2.0	2.0	2.0	2.0	2.0

Commodity or service	Average weekly household expenditure (£)					
1 Food & non-alcoholic drinks	37.70	42.00	46.30	50.90	60.70	45.40
2 Alcoholic drinks, tobacco & narcotics	8.30	8.30	9.60	11.90	13.80	9.50
3 Clothing & footwear	7.00	11.20	16.20	20.60	25.70	14.40
4 Housing (net)[3], fuel & power	26.60	28.00	28.30	34.90	43.00	29.70
5 Household goods & services	17.50	20.20	28.80	46.50	58.60	28.00
6 Health	1.10	5.40	10.60	9.40	15.00	7.90
7 Transport	18.60	33.50	50.20	56.80	89.80	44.00
8 Communication	5.80	5.80	7.00	8.60	11.40	6.80
9 Recreation & culture	22.00	41.50	52.70	74.10	111.00	51.80
10 Education	[0.90]	[0.40]	[0.10]	[0.90]	[10.10]	[1.00]
11 Restaurants & hotels	10.80	15.90	25.70	38.10	46.60	23.20
12 Miscellaneous goods & services	13.60	18.60	30.10	41.30	59.90	27.20
1-12 All expenditure groups	169.90	230.80	305.70	394.10	545.80	289.00
13 Other expenditure items	15.50	25.30	34.80	51.10	129.90	36.10
Total expenditure	185.40	256.10	340.50	445.20	675.70	325.10
Average weekly expenditure per person (£)						
Total expenditure	92.70	128.10	170.20	222.60	337.80	162.60

Note: The commodity and service categories are not comparable with those in publications before 2001-02
1 Mainly dependent on state pension and not economically active - see definitions in Appendix B
2 Lower boundary of 2003-04 gross income quintile groups (£ per week)
3 Excluding mortgage interest payments, council tax and Northern Ireland rates

A34 Household expenditure by tenure

2003-04

based on weighted data and including children's expenditure

	Owners			Social rented from		
	Owned outright	Buying with a mortgage [1]	All	Council [2]	Registered Social Landlord [3]	All
Grossed number of households (thousands)	7,380	9,880	17,250	3,050	1,780	4,830
Total number of households in sample	2,093	2,858	4,951	893	491	1,384
Total number of persons in sample	4,055	8,241	12,296	2,003	1,056	3,059
Total number of adults in sample	3,713	5,606	9,319	1,365	715	2,080
Weighted average number of persons per household	1.9	2.8	2.4	2.2	2.1	2.2
Commodity or service	**Average weekly household expenditure (£)**					
1 Food & non-alcoholic drinks	42.70	51.90	47.90	32.20	32.60	32.40
2 Alcoholic drinks, tobacco & narcotics	9.20	13.40	11.60	11.30	11.10	11.20
3 Clothing & footwear	17.50	32.20	25.90	12.90	13.40	13.10
4 Housing (net)[6], fuel & power	27.40	32.50	30.30	37.60	42.10	39.30
5 Household goods & services	29.80	44.20	38.00	15.30	13.70	14.70
6 Health	7.60	5.10	6.20	1.50	2.60	1.90
7 Transport	53.40	86.30	72.20	19.50	22.80	20.80
8 Communication	8.50	14.30	11.80	7.60	8.20	7.80
9 Recreation & culture	56.90	74.70	67.10	31.20	29.60	30.60
10 Education	3.80	7.90	6.20	0.70	0.90	0.80
11 Restaurants & hotels	28.20	47.90	39.50	17.00	18.40	17.50
12 Miscellaneous goods & services	30.40	47.20	40.00	13.50	13.90	13.70
1-12 All expenditure groups	315.40	457.60	396.80	200.40	209.30	203.70
13 Other expenditure items	40.20	109.40	79.80	13.40	12.50	13.00
Total expenditure	355.60	567.00	476.60	213.70	221.70	216.70
Average weekly expenditure per person (£)						
Total expenditure	184.70	201.60	195.90	97.30	106.10	100.40

Note: The commodity and service categories are not comparable to those in publications before 2001-02

1 Including shared owners (who own part of the equity and pay mortgage, part rent).

2 "Council" includes local authorities, New Towns and Scottish Homes, but see note 3 below.

3 Formerly Housing Associations

A34 Household expenditure by tenure (cont.)

2003-04

based on weighted data and including children's expenditure

	Private rented [4]				All tenures
	Rent free	Rent paid, unfurn- ished [5]	Rent paid, furnished	All	
Grossed number of households (thousands)	350	1,590	650	2,590	24,670
Total number of households in sample	99	447	167	713	7,048
Total number of persons in sample	190	1,051	369	1,610	16,965
Total number of adults in sample	155	730	333	1,218	12,617
Weighted average number of persons per household	1.8	2.3	2.2	2.2	2.4
Commodity or service	**Average weekly household expenditure (£)**				
1 Food & non-alcoholic drinks	36.90	35.60	32.10	34.90	43.50
2 Alcoholic drinks, tobacco & narcotics	9.00	14.10	14.40	13.50	11.70
3 Clothing & footwear	18.70	19.80	18.80	19.40	22.70
4 Housing (net)[6], fuel & power	17.80	97.80	135.90	96.40	39.00
5 Household goods & services	11.50	21.90	7.80	17.00	31.30
6 Health	2.70	3.10	4.80	3.40	5.00
7 Transport	49.00	58.00	64.70	58.50	60.70
8 Communication	9.80	13.00	16.00	13.30	11.20
9 Recreation & culture	34.60	41.70	45.20	41.60	57.30
10 Education	[4.10]	4.40	16.80	7.40	5.20
11 Restaurants & hotels	26.50	32.80	52.60	36.90	34.90
12 Miscellaneous goods & services	26.40	28.20	28.80	28.10	33.60
1-12 All expenditure groups	246.90	370.30	437.90	370.40	356.20
13 Other expenditure items	32.00	31.30	39.30	33.40	61.90
Total expenditure	278.90	401.60	477.20	403.80	418.10
Average weekly expenditure per person (£)					
Total expenditure	151.90	174.40	212.50	181.50	177.40

Note: The commodity and service categories are not comparable to those in publications before 2001-02

4 All tenants whose accommodation goes with the job of someone in the household are allocated to "rented privately", even if the landlord is a local authority or housing association or Housing Action Trust, or if the accommodation is rent free. Squatters are also included in this category.

5 "Unfurnished" includes the answers: "partly furnished".

6 Excludes mortage interest paymenst, council tax and Northern Ireland rates

A35

Household expenditure
by UK Countries and Government Office Regions
based on weighted data and including children's expenditure

2001-02 — 2003-04

	North East	North West	Yorks & the Humber	East Midlands	West Midlands	East	London
Average grossed number of households (thousands)	1,040	2,820	2,140	1,730	2,130	2,250	2,860
Total number of households in sample (over 3 years)	945	2,342	1,755	1,471	1,774	1,883	1,922
Total number of persons in sample (over 3 years)	2,290	5,586	4,086	3,551	4,441	4,506	4,685
Total number of adults in sample (over 3 years)	1,686	4,166	3,083	2,668	3,228	3,409	3,424
Weighted average number of persons per household	2.4	2.3	2.3	2.4	2.4	2.4	2.5

Commodity or service	Average weekly household expenditure (£)						
1 Food & non-alcoholic drinks	38.50	40.80	38.10	42.70	41.40	45.70	44.60
2 Alcoholic drinks, tobacco & narcotics	10.90	12.50	11.60	11.40	11.10	10.10	10.50
3 Clothing & footwear	19.50	22.50	19.40	20.00	21.80	22.40	27.50
4 Housing (net)[1], fuel & power	28.60	33.20	32.30	31.60	32.30	37.80	57.00
5 Household goods & services	24.70	28.20	27.70	30.20	29.20	32.90	34.30
6 Health	3.10	3.40	4.10	3.80	4.20	6.70	6.20
7 Transport	48.40	55.80	54.10	60.60	54.30	68.50	61.30
8 Communication	9.30	9.60	9.20	10.00	10.30	11.00	14.80
9 Recreation & culture	50.70	57.10	52.60	55.80	53.60	59.10	57.00
10 Education	3.30	4.50	4.20	3.90	2.80	5.40	10.20
11 Restaurants & hotels	30.70	33.00	34.00	35.40	31.60	33.40	44.00
12 Miscellaneous goods & services	24.60	32.00	27.40	30.60	29.70	34.30	39.00
1-12 All expenditure groups	292.40	332.50	314.80	336.10	322.30	367.50	406.30
13 Other expenditure items	43.30	51.10	49.00	55.00	53.30	63.70	79.20
Total expenditure	335.70	383.60	363.70	391.10	375.60	431.20	485.50
Average weekly expenditure per person (£)							
Total expenditure	141.60	163.40	158.90	164.00	153.60	182.00	194.30

Note: The commodity and service categories are not comparable with those in publications before 2001-02
1 Excluding mortgage interest payments, council tax and Northern Ireland rates

A35 Household expenditure
by UK Countries and Government Office Regions (cont.)

2001-02 — 2003-04

based on weighted data and including children's expenditure

	South East	South West	England	Wales	Scotland	Northern Ireland	United Kingdom
Average grossed number of households (thousands)	3,380	2,160	20,510	1,230	2,120	630	24,490
Total number of households in sample (over 3 years)	2,853	1,934	16,879	1,082	1,755	1,732	21,448
Total number of persons in sample (over 3 years)	6,942	4,448	40,535	2,581	4,027	4,530	51,673
Total number of adults in sample (over 3 years)	5,223	3,427	30,314	1,893	3,079	3,227	38,513
Weighted average number of persons per household	2.3	2.2	2.4	2.3	2.3	2.7	2.4

Commodity or service	Average weekly household expenditure (£)						
1 Food & non-alcoholic drinks	45.30	42.70	42.60	40.60	42.80	46.70	42.60
2 Alcoholic drinks, tobacco & narcotics	10.90	10.90	11.10	10.90	14.10	13.80	11.40
3 Clothing & footwear	24.90	18.70	22.40	18.50	24.10	30.90	22.60
4 Housing (net)[1], fuel & power	41.90	36.40	38.20	33.40	32.40	31.00	37.30
5 Household goods & services	34.20	29.80	30.80	27.20	28.10	32.20	30.40
6 Health	6.80	5.10	5.10	3.10	3.60	3.10	4.80
7 Transport	73.30	57.80	60.80	47.30	50.90	54.10	59.10
8 Communication	11.60	9.90	10.90	8.80	9.90	10.90	10.70
9 Recreation & culture	64.30	52.70	56.80	53.10	50.10	48.10	55.80
10 Education	7.40	5.30	5.60	2.90	4.10	3.80	5.30
11 Restaurants & hotels	36.40	30.40	34.90	30.30	31.00	36.80	34.40
12 Miscellaneous goods & services	39.40	32.10	33.30	26.10	27.90	33.20	32.40
1-12 All expenditure groups	396.50	331.90	352.50	302.30	319.00	344.50	346.80
13 Other expenditure items	76.90	58.20	61.40	46.30	51.30	48.60	59.40
Total expenditure	473.40	390.10	413.80	348.60	370.30	393.00	406.20
Average weekly expenditure per person (£)							
Total expenditure	203.70	174.10	175.10	149.20	158.40	147.40	171.50

Note: The commodity and service categories are not comparable with those in publications before 2001-02
1 Excluding mortgage interest payments, council tax and Northern Ireland rates

A36 Household expenditure as a percentage of total expenditure by UK Countries and Government Office Regions

2001-02 — 2003-04

based on weighted data and including children's expenditure

	North East	North West	Yorks & the Humber	East Midlands	West Midlands	East	London
Average grossed number of households (thousands)	1,040	2,820	2,140	1,730	2,130	2,250	2,860
Total number of households in sample (over 3 years)	945	2,342	1,755	1,471	1,774	1,883	1,922
Total number of persons in sample (over 3 years)	2,290	5,586	4,086	3,551	4,441	4,506	4,685
Total number of adults in sample (over 3 years)	1,686	4,166	3,083	2,668	3,228	3,409	3,424
Weighted average number of persons per household	2.4	2.3	2.3	2.4	2.4	2.4	2.5

Commodity or service	Percentage of total expenditure						
1 Food & non-alcoholic drinks	11	11	10	11	11	11	9
2 Alcoholic drinks, tobacco & narcotics	3	3	3	3	3	2	2
3 Clothing & footwear	6	6	5	5	6	5	6
4 Housing (net)[1], fuel & power	9	9	9	8	9	9	12
5 Household goods & services	7	7	8	8	8	8	7
6 Health	1	1	1	1	1	2	1
7 Transport	14	15	15	15	14	16	13
8 Communication	3	2	3	3	3	3	3
9 Recreation & culture	15	15	14	14	14	14	12
10 Education	1	1	1	1	1	1	2
11 Restaurants & hotels	9	9	9	9	8	8	9
12 Miscellaneous goods & services	7	8	8	8	8	8	8
1-12 All expenditure groups	87	87	87	86	86	85	84
13 Other expenditure items	13	13	13	14	14	15	16
Total expenditure	100	100	100	100	100	100	100

Note: The commodity and service categories are not comparable with those in publications before 2001-02
1 Excluding mortgage interest payments, council tax and Northern Ireland rates

A36 Household expenditure as a percentage of total expenditure by UK Countries and Government Office Regions (cont.)

2001-02 — 2003-04

based on weighted data and including children's expenditure

	South East	South West	England	Wales	Scotland	Northern Ireland	United Kingdom
Average grossed number of households (thousands)	3,380	2,160	20,510	1,230	2,120	630	24,490
Total number of households in sample (over 3 years)	2,853	1,934	16,879	1,082	1,755	1,732	21,448
Total number of persons in sample (over 3 years)	6,942	4,448	40,535	2,581	4,027	4,530	51,673
Total number of adults in sample (over 3 years)	5,223	3,427	30,314	1,893	3,079	3,227	38,513
Weighted average number of persons per household	2.3	2.2	2.4	2.3	2.3	2.7	2.4
Commodity or service	**Percentage of total expenditure**						
1 Food & non-alcoholic drinks	10	11	10	12	12	12	10
2 Alcoholic drinks, tobacco & narcotics	2	3	3	3	4	4	3
3 Clothing & footwear	5	5	5	5	7	8	6
4 Housing (net)[1], fuel & power	9	9	9	10	9	8	9
5 Household goods & services	7	8	7	8	8	8	7
6 Health	1	1	1	1	1	1	1
7 Transport	15	15	15	14	14	14	15
8 Communication	2	3	3	3	3	3	3
9 Recreation & culture	14	14	14	15	14	12	14
10 Education	2	1	1	1	1	1	1
11 Restaurants & hotels	8	8	8	9	8	9	8
12 Miscellaneous goods & services	8	8	8	8	8	8	8
1-12 All expenditure groups	84	85	85	87	86	88	85
13 Other expenditure items	16	15	15	13	14	12	15
Total expenditure	100	100	100	100	100	100	100

Note: The commodity and service categories are not comparable with those in publications before 2001-02
1 Excluding mortgage interest payments, council tax and Northern Ireland rates

A37 Detailed household expenditure by UK Countries and Government Office Regions

2001-02 — 2003-04

based on weighted data and including children's expenditure

	North East	North West	Yorks & the Humber	East Midlands	West Midlands	East	London
Average grossed number of households (thousands)	1,040	2,820	2,140	1,730	2,130	2,250	2,860
Total number of households in sample (over 3 years)	945	2,342	1,755	1,471	1,774	1,883	1,922
Total number of persons in sample (over 3 years)	2,290	5,586	4,086	3,551	4,441	4,506	4,685
Total number of adults in sample (over 3 years)	1,686	4,166	3,083	2,668	3,228	3,409	3,424
Weighted average number of persons per household	2.4	2.3	2.3	2.4	2.4	2.4	2.5

Commodity or service	Average weekly household expenditure (£)						
1 Food & non-alcoholic drinks	**38.50**	**40.80**	**38.10**	**42.70**	**41.40**	**45.70**	**44.60**
1.1 Food	35.10	37.30	35.00	39.10	37.90	41.80	40.50
1.1.1 Bread, rice and cereals	3.60	3.80	3.50	3.90	3.80	3.90	3.90
1.1.2 Pasta products	0.30	0.30	0.30	0.30	0.20	0.30	0.40
1.1.3 Buns, cakes, biscuits etc.	2.60	2.60	2.50	2.80	2.60	3.00	2.50
1.1.4 Pastry (savoury)	0.60	0.60	0.60	0.60	0.50	0.70	0.60
1.1.5 Beef (fresh, chilled or frozen)	1.10	1.30	1.30	1.40	1.40	1.40	1.20
1.1.6 Pork (fresh, chilled or frozen)	0.50	0.60	0.60	0.60	0.60	0.60	0.50
1.1.7 Lamb (fresh, chilled or frozen)	0.40	0.60	0.50	0.50	0.70	0.60	0.90
1.1.8 Poultry (fresh, chilled or frozen)	1.30	1.50	1.30	1.50	1.50	1.70	1.80
1.1.9 Bacon and ham	0.90	1.00	0.90	0.90	0.90	0.80	0.70
1.1.10 Other meat and meat preparations	4.80	4.90	4.40	4.80	4.60	5.10	4.30
1.1.11 Fish and fish products	1.50	1.60	1.70	1.70	1.50	2.10	2.30
1.1.12 Milk	2.10	2.20	2.10	2.30	2.20	2.10	1.90
1.1.13 Cheese and curd	1.10	1.20	1.10	1.40	1.40	1.60	1.40
1.1.14 Eggs	0.40	0.40	0.40	0.40	0.40	0.40	0.50
1.1.15 Other milk products	1.30	1.30	1.20	1.50	1.30	1.60	1.50
1.1.16 Butter	0.20	0.20	0.20	0.20	0.20	0.20	0.30
1.1.17 Margarine, other vegetable fats and peanut butter	0.40	0.40	0.40	0.50	0.50	0.50	0.40
1.1.18 Cooking oils and fats	0.10	0.20	0.20	0.20	0.20	0.20	0.10
1.1.19 Fresh fruit	1.80	2.00	2.00	2.30	2.20	2.70	2.90
1.1.20 Other fresh, chilled or frozen fruits	0.20	0.20	0.20	0.20	0.20	0.20	0.30
1.1.21 Dried fruit and nuts	0.30	0.20	0.30	0.30	0.30	0.40	0.40
1.1.22 Preserved fruit and fruit based products	0.10	0.10	0.10	0.20	0.10	0.20	0.10
1.1.23 Fresh vegetables	2.20	2.60	2.60	3.00	3.00	3.50	3.90
1.1.24 Dried vegetables	0.60	0.60	0.60	0.70	0.60	0.70	0.70
1.1.25 Other preserved or processed vegetables	0.30	0.30	0.30	0.30	0.30	0.40	0.40
1.1.26 Potatoes	0.70	0.70	0.70	0.80	0.80	0.80	0.80
1.1.27 Other tubers and products of tuber vegetables	1.30	1.20	1.00	1.20	1.30	1.20	1.00
1.1.28 Sugar and sugar products	0.20	0.20	0.20	0.30	0.30	0.30	0.20
1.1.28 Jams, marmalades	0.20	0.20	0.20	0.20	0.20	0.20	0.20
1.1.30 Chocolate	1.30	1.30	1.20	1.50	1.30	1.30	1.10
1.1.31 Confectionery products	0.60	0.60	0.60	0.60	0.60	0.60	0.50
1.1.32 Edible ices and ice cream	0.50	0.40	0.40	0.50	0.50	0.60	0.60
1.1.33 Other food products	1.60	1.80	1.60	1.80	1.60	1.90	1.90
1.2 Non-alcoholic drinks	3.40	3.50	3.10	3.60	3.60	3.80	4.10
1.2.1 Coffee	0.50	0.50	0.50	0.50	0.50	0.50	0.40
1.2.2 Tea	0.40	0.50	0.40	0.50	0.50	0.50	0.40
1.2.3 Cocoa and powdered chocolate	0.10	0.10	0.10	0.10	0.10	0.10	0.10
1.2.4 Fruit and vegetable juices	0.70	0.80	0.70	0.90	0.80	1.10	1.30
1.2.5 Mineral or spring waters	0.10	0.20	0.10	0.20	0.10	0.20	0.30
1.2.6 Soft drinks	1.60	1.40	1.20	1.40	1.50	1.50	1.60

Note: The commodity and service categories are not comparable with those in publications before 2001-02
The numbering system is sequential, it does not use actual COICOP codes

A37   Detailed household expenditure   2001-02 — 2003-04
         by UK Countries and Government Office Regions (cont.)
         based on weighted data and including children's expenditure

	South East	South West	England	Wales	Scotland	Northern Ireland	United Kingdom
Average grossed number of households (thousands)	3,380	2,160	20,510	1,230	2,120	630	24,490
Total number of households in sample (over 3 years)	2,853	1,934	16,879	1,082	1,755	1,732	21,448
Total number of persons in sample (over 3 years)	6,942	4,448	40,535	2,581	4,027	4,530	51,673
Total number of adults in sample (over 3 years)	5,223	3,427	30,314	1,893	3,079	3,227	38,513
Weighted average number of persons per household	2.3	2.2	2.4	2.3	2.3	2.7	2.4

Commodity or service	Average weekly household expenditure (£)						
1 Food & non-alcoholic drinks	**45.30**	**42.70**	**42.60**	**40.60**	**42.80**	**46.70**	**42.60**
1.1 Food	41.50	39.30	39.00	37.30	38.70	42.50	39.00
1.1.1 Bread, rice and cereals	3.80	3.60	3.80	3.50	4.00	4.80	3.80
1.1.2 Pasta products	0.30	0.30	0.30	0.30	0.40	0.30	0.30
1.1.3 Buns, cakes, biscuits etc.	2.80	2.90	2.70	2.60	2.70	3.50	2.70
1.1.4 Pastry (savoury)	0.70	0.60	0.60	0.50	0.60	0.60	0.60
1.1.5 Beef (fresh, chilled or frozen)	1.30	1.40	1.30	1.20	1.70	2.40	1.40
1.1.6 Pork (fresh, chilled or frozen)	0.60	0.60	0.60	0.50	0.50	0.60	0.60
1.1.7 Lamb (fresh, chilled or frozen)	0.70	0.60	0.60	0.70	0.30	0.40	0.60
1.1.8 Poultry (fresh, chilled or frozen)	1.60	1.50	1.50	1.40	1.50	1.80	1.50
1.1.9 Bacon and ham	0.80	0.90	0.80	1.00	1.00	1.20	0.90
1.1.10 Other meat and meat preparations	4.90	4.40	4.70	5.00	5.40	5.10	4.80
1.1.11 Fish and fish products	2.00	1.70	1.80	1.60	1.60	1.40	1.80
1.1.12 Milk	2.10	2.20	2.10	2.10	2.10	2.90	2.10
1.1.13 Cheese and curd	1.60	1.50	1.40	1.20	1.30	1.10	1.40
1.1.14 Eggs	0.40	0.40	0.40	0.40	0.40	0.40	0.40
1.1.15 Other milk products	1.70	1.50	1.40	1.30	1.30	1.40	1.40
1.1.16 Butter	0.30	0.30	0.20	0.30	0.30	0.40	0.30
1.1.17 Margarine, other vegetable fats and peanut butter	0.50	0.50	0.40	0.50	0.40	0.50	0.40
1.1.18 Cooking oils and fats	0.10	0.10	0.10	0.10	0.10	0.10	0.10
1.1.19 Fresh fruit	2.80	2.70	2.50	2.10	2.10	2.10	2.40
1.1.20 Other fresh, chilled or frozen fruits	0.30	0.20	0.20	0.20	0.20	0.20	0.20
1.1.21 Dried fruit and nuts	0.40	0.50	0.40	0.30	0.20	0.20	0.30
1.1.22 Preserved fruit and fruit based products	0.20	0.20	0.10	0.10	0.10	0.20	0.10
1.1.23 Fresh vegetables	3.60	3.20	3.20	2.70	2.30	2.30	3.00
1.1.24 Dried vegetables	0.70	0.70	0.70	0.60	0.70	0.70	0.70
1.1.25 Other preserved or processed vegetables	0.40	0.30	0.30	0.30	0.30	0.40	0.30
1.1.26 Potatoes	0.80	0.70	0.80	0.80	0.70	1.20	0.80
1.1.27 Other tubers and products of tuber vegetables	1.10	1.10	1.10	1.30	1.40	1.40	1.20
1.1.28 Sugar and sugar products	0.30	0.30	0.30	0.30	0.30	0.20	0.30
1.1.28 Jams, marmalades	0.20	0.20	0.20	0.20	0.20	0.30	0.20
1.1.30 Chocolate	1.40	1.40	1.30	1.30	1.40	1.40	1.30
1.1.31 Confectionery products	0.50	0.50	0.60	0.60	0.60	0.70	0.60
1.1.32 Edible ices and ice cream	0.60	0.50	0.50	0.50	0.50	0.50	0.50
1.1.33 Other food products	2.00	1.80	1.80	1.70	1.90	1.90	1.80
1.2 Non-alcoholic drinks	3.80	3.40	3.60	3.30	4.10	4.20	3.70
1.2.1 Coffee	0.50	0.60	0.50	0.50	0.50	0.40	0.50
1.2.2 Tea	0.50	0.50	0.50	0.40	0.30	0.50	0.50
1.2.3 Cocoa and powdered chocolate	0.10	0.10	0.10	0.10	0.10	0.00	0.10
1.2.4 Fruit and vegetable juices	1.10	1.00	1.00	0.80	0.90	0.90	0.90
1.2.5 Mineral or spring waters	0.20	0.10	0.20	0.10	0.20	0.30	0.20
1.2.6 Soft drinks	1.40	1.10	1.40	1.50	2.20	2.20	1.50

Note: The commodity and service categories are not comparable with those in publications before 2001-02
The numbering system is sequential, it does not use actual COICOP codes

A37 Detailed household expenditure by UK Countries and Government Office Regions (cont.)
2001-02 — 2003-04

based on weighted data and including children's expenditure

	North East	North West	Yorks & the Humber	East Midlands	West Midlands	East	London
Commodity or service	\multicolumn{7}{c}{Average weekly household expenditure (£)}						
2 Alcoholic drink, tobacco & narcotics	**10.90**	**12.50**	**11.60**	**11.40**	**11.10**	**10.10**	**10.50**
2.1 Alcoholic drinks	5.40	6.70	5.50	6.20	5.60	5.80	5.80
2.1.1 Spirits and liqueurs (brought home)	1.00	1.40	0.90	1.20	1.20	1.00	1.10
2.1.2 Wines, fortified wines (brought home)	2.10	3.00	2.50	3.10	2.40	2.90	3.20
2.1.3 Beer, lager, ciders and Perry (brought home)	2.20	2.10	2.00	1.80	1.80	1.70	1.40
2.1.4 Alcopops (brought home)	0.10	0.20	0.10	0.10	0.10	0.20	0.10
2.2 Tobacco and narcotics	5.50	5.80	6.10	5.20	5.50	4.40	4.70
2.2.1 Cigarettes	5.00	5.20	5.30	4.70	4.90	4.00	4.10
2.2.2 Cigars, other tobacco products and narcotics	0.50	0.60	0.80	0.50	0.60	0.40	0.60
3 Clothing & footwear	**19.50**	**22.50**	**19.40**	**20.00**	**21.80**	**22.40**	**27.50**
3.1 Clothing	15.90	17.80	15.80	15.90	17.70	18.50	22.20
3.1.1 Men's outer garments	4.10	4.30	4.00	3.40	4.70	4.50	5.90
3.1.2 Men's under garments	0.30	0.40	0.30	0.40	0.40	0.50	0.50
3.1.3 Women's outer garments	6.50	7.60	6.70	7.30	7.40	8.20	9.50
3.1.4 Women's under garments	1.00	1.30	1.10	1.10	1.50	1.50	1.10
3.1.5 Boys' outer garments (5-15)	1.00	0.80	0.90	0.70	0.80	0.70	0.90
3.1.6 Girls' outer garments (5-15)	1.30	1.20	0.80	1.10	1.10	1.10	1.30
3.1.7 Infants' outer garments (under 5)	0.60	0.60	0.60	0.60	0.50	0.60	0.70
3.1.8 Children's under garments (under 16)	0.40	0.50	0.30	0.30	0.40	0.40	0.40
3.1.9 Accessories	0.60	0.60	0.50	0.60	0.60	0.60	0.90
3.1.10 Haberdashery, clothing materials and clothing hire	0.20	0.20	0.30	0.20	0.20	0.20	0.50
3.1.11 Dry cleaners, laundry and dyeing	0.10	0.30	0.20	0.20	0.20	0.30	0.60
3.2 Footwear	3.60	4.70	3.60	4.00	4.10	3.90	5.20
4 Housing (net)[1], fuel & power	**28.60**	**33.20**	**32.30**	**31.60**	**32.30**	**37.80**	**57.00**
4.1 Actual rentals for housing	19.90	20.90	19.30	15.20	19.60	20.80	46.50
4.1.1 Gross rent	19.90	20.70	19.30	15.10	19.50	20.70	46.50
4.1.2 less housing benefit, rebates & allowances rec'd	12.40	11.80	9.40	7.50	10.00	7.70	15.10
4.1.3 Net rent	7.40	8.90	9.90	7.70	9.50	13.00	31.40
4.1.4 Second dwelling rent	[0.00]	[0.20]	[0.00]	[0.00]	[0.10]	[0.00]	[0.00]
4.2 Maintenance and repair of dwelling	5.30	7.10	6.20	7.30	6.40	7.30	8.50
4.3 Water supply and miscellaneous services relating to the dwelling	4.50	5.40	5.10	4.80	4.90	5.70	6.10
4.4 Electricity, gas and other fuels	11.40	11.60	11.10	11.80	11.50	11.80	10.80
4.4.1 Electricity	5.50	5.50	5.40	5.60	5.60	5.80	5.30
4.4.2 Gas	5.40	5.80	5.30	5.50	5.50	4.80	5.50
4.4.3 Other fuels	0.50	0.30	0.50	0.70	0.40	1.20	0.10

Note: The commodity and service categories are not comparable with those in publications before 2001-02
The numbering system is sequential, it does not use actual COICOP codes
1 Excluding mortgage interest payments, council tax and Northern Ireland rates

A37 Detailed household expenditure by UK Countries and Government Office Regions (cont.)

2001-02 — 2003-04

based on weighted data and including children's expenditure

Commodity or service	South East	South West	England	Wales	Scotland	Northern Ireland	United Kingdom
	Average weekly household expenditure (£)						
2 Alcoholic drink, tobacco & narcotics	**10.90**	**10.90**	**11.10**	**10.90**	**14.10**	**13.80**	**11.40**
2.1 Alcoholic drinks	6.20	6.20	6.00	5.80	6.30	5.20	6.00
2.1.1 Spirits and liqueurs (brought home)	1.10	1.40	1.20	1.10	2.00	1.20	1.20
2.1.2 Wines, fortified wines (brought home)	3.40	3.20	2.90	2.50	2.50	2.30	2.90
2.1.3 Beer, lager, ciders and Perry (brought home)	1.50	1.50	1.70	2.00	1.70	1.50	1.70
2.1.4 Alcopops (brought home)	0.20	0.10	0.10	0.10	0.20	0.20	0.10
2.2 Tobacco and narcotics	4.70	4.80	5.10	5.10	7.80	8.60	5.50
2.2.1 Cigarettes	4.10	4.00	4.50	4.40	7.10	8.10	4.80
2.2.2 Cigars, other tobacco products and narcotics	0.60	0.70	0.60	0.70	0.70	0.50	0.60
3 Clothing & footwear	**24.90**	**18.70**	**22.40**	**18.50**	**24.10**	**30.90**	**22.60**
3.1 Clothing	20.60	15.40	18.20	14.80	19.60	24.40	18.30
3.1.1 Men's outer garments	4.80	3.70	4.50	3.10	5.10	6.20	4.50
3.1.2 Men's under garments	0.50	0.40	0.40	0.30	0.40	0.50	0.40
3.1.3 Women's outer garments	9.60	6.90	8.00	6.90	7.90	10.40	8.00
3.1.4 Women's under garments	1.40	1.20	1.30	0.90	1.20	1.30	1.20
3.1.5 Boys' outer garments (5-15)	0.80	0.50	0.80	0.80	1.10	1.50	0.80
3.1.6 Girls' outer garments (5-15)	1.10	1.00	1.10	0.90	1.50	1.80	1.20
3.1.7 Infants' outer garments (under 5)	0.60	0.40	0.60	0.70	0.80	1.00	0.60
3.1.8 Children's under garments (under 16)	0.30	0.30	0.40	0.40	0.50	0.50	0.40
3.1.9 Accessories	0.70	0.60	0.70	0.50	0.70	0.80	0.70
3.1.10 Haberdashery, clothing materials and clothing hire	0.30	0.20	0.30	0.20	0.20	0.20	0.20
3.1.11 Dry cleaners, laundry and dyeing	0.30	0.20	0.30	0.20	0.20	0.20	0.30
3.2 Footwear	4.30	3.30	4.20	3.70	4.50	6.50	4.30
4 Housing (net)[1], fuel & power	**41.90**	**36.40**	**38.20**	**33.40**	**32.40**	**31.00**	**37.30**
4.1 Actual rentals for housing	22.10	18.40	23.50	17.00	20.20	15.70	22.70
4.1.1 Gross rent	22.10	18.40	23.50	16.80	20.20	15.70	22.70
4.1.2 *less* housing benefit, rebates & allowances rec'd	7.80	7.90	10.00	9.10	10.80	9.00	10.00
4.1.3 Net rent	14.30	10.50	13.50	7.60	9.40	6.70	12.70
4.1.4 Second dwelling rent	[0.00]	[0.00]	[0.10]	[0.26]	[0.00]	[0.00]	0.10
4.2 Maintenance and repair of dwelling	9.70	7.90	7.60	7.70	5.40	7.10	7.40
4.3 Water supply and miscellaneous services relating to the dwelling	6.00	6.00	5.50	5.70	5.20	0.30	5.40
4.4 Electricity, gas and other fuels	11.90	12.00	11.60	12.10	12.40	16.90	11.80
4.4.1 Electricity	6.00	6.30	5.70	5.90	6.80	7.90	5.80
4.4.2 Gas	5.30	4.50	5.30	5.40	4.80	0.70	5.10
4.4.3 Other fuels	0.60	1.10	0.60	0.80	0.90	8.40	0.80

Note: The commodity and service categories are not comparable with those in publications before 2001-02
The numbering system is sequential, it does not use actual COICOP codes
1 Excluding mortgage interest payments, council tax and Northern Ireland rates

A37 Detailed household expenditure by UK Countries and Government Office Regions (cont.)

2001-02 — 2003-04

based on weighted data and including children's expenditure

		North East	North West	Yorks & the Humber	East Midlands	West Midlands	East	London
Commodity or service				Average weekly household expenditure (£)				
5	**Household goods & services**	**24.70**	**28.20**	**27.70**	**30.20**	**29.20**	**32.90**	**34.30**
5.1	Furniture and furnishings, carpets and other floor coverings	12.80	15.10	14.60	14.80	15.30	16.30	19.10
	5.1.1 Furniture and furnishings	9.10	11.60	11.10	10.90	11.40	12.60	14.70
	5.1.2 Floor coverings	3.70	3.50	3.50	3.90	3.90	3.80	4.40
5.2	Household textiles	2.00	1.80	1.70	2.10	3.00	2.50	2.00
5.3	Household appliances	3.00	3.20	3.20	4.30	2.80	3.80	3.70
5.4	Glassware, tableware and household utensils	1.30	1.40	1.40	1.50	1.20	2.00	1.70
5.5	Tools and equipment for house and garden	2.00	2.30	2.40	3.20	2.50	3.00	2.60
5.6	Goods and services for routine household maintenance	3.60	4.50	4.50	4.40	4.40	5.30	5.20
	5.6.1 Cleaning materials	1.90	1.90	1.90	2.10	2.10	2.30	2.00
	5.6.2 Household goods and hardware	1.00	1.00	1.00	1.10	1.00	1.20	1.10
	5.6.3 Domestic services, carpet cleaning & repair of furniture	0.80	1.60	1.60	1.20	1.30	1.80	2.10
6	**Health**	**3.10**	**3.40**	**4.10**	**3.80**	**4.20**	**6.70**	**6.20**
6.1	Medical products, appliances and equipment	2.20	2.40	3.20	2.60	2.90	3.80	3.20
	6.1.1 Medicines, prescriptions, healthcare products & equipt.	1.10	1.50	1.70	1.50	2.00	1.80	1.80
	6.1.2 Spectacles, lenses, accessories and repairs	1.10	0.90	1.50	1.20	0.90	2.00	1.40
6.2	Hospital services	0.90	1.00	0.90	1.20	1.30	3.00	3.10
7	**Transport**	**48.40**	**55.80**	**54.10**	**60.60**	**54.30**	**68.50**	**61.30**
7.1	Purchase of vehicles	21.10	27.20	26.60	29.80	24.70	30.70	23.00
	7.1.1 Purchase of new cars and vans	8.60	10.50	11.40	11.00	9.40	13.40	10.00
	7.1.2 Purchase of second hand cars or vans	12.10	16.10	14.90	17.90	14.90	16.50	11.90
	7.1.3 Purchase of motorcycles and other vehicles	0.40	0.60	0.30	0.90	0.40	0.80	1.20
7.2	Operation of personal transport	19.90	21.10	20.50	24.80	23.60	27.50	21.60
	7.2.1 Spares and accessories	2.70	1.40	1.40	2.00	1.80	2.50	1.70
	7.2.2 Petrol, diesel and other motor oils	12.70	13.80	13.10	15.90	15.60	16.80	11.90
	7.2.3 Repairs and servicing	3.30	4.10	4.40	5.10	4.40	5.80	5.70
	7.2.4 Other motoring costs	1.20	1.70	1.70	1.80	1.70	2.40	2.20
7.3	Transport services	7.40	7.50	7.00	5.90	6.10	10.40	16.70
	7.3.1 Rail and tube fares	1.00	1.00	0.90	0.90	1.00	3.60	3.90
	7.3.2 Bus and coach fares	2.00	1.60	1.70	1.30	1.30	0.90	2.10
	7.3.3 Combined fares	0.20	0.10	0.10	[0.00]	[0.10]	0.50	5.60
	7.3.4 Other travel and transport	4.10	4.80	4.20	3.60	3.80	5.30	5.10

Note: The commodity and service categories are not comparable with those in publications before 2001-02
The numbering system is sequential, it does not use actual COICOP codes

A37 Detailed household expenditure by UK Countries and Government Office Regions (cont.)

2001-02 — 2003-04

based on weighted data and including children's expenditure

	South East	South West	England	Wales	Scotland	Northern Ireland	United Kingdom
Commodity or service							

Commodity or service	Average weekly household expenditure (£)						
5 Household goods & services	**34.20**	**29.80**	**30.80**	**27.20**	**28.10**	**32.20**	**30.40**
5.1 Furniture and furnishings, carpets and other floor coverings	17.30	14.70	15.90	13.90	13.80	18.60	15.70
5.1.1 Furniture and furnishings	12.90	11.20	12.00	10.50	11.00	14.00	11.90
5.1.2 Floor coverings	4.50	3.50	3.90	3.40	2.80	4.60	3.80
5.2 Household textiles	2.10	2.00	2.10	1.80	2.00	1.80	2.10
5.3 Household appliances	4.10	3.30	3.50	4.00	4.80	2.60	3.60
5.4 Glassware, tableware and household utensils	2.10	2.00	1.70	1.20	1.30	1.60	1.60
5.5 Tools and equipment for house and garden	3.30	2.70	2.70	2.40	2.20	3.30	2.70
5.6 Goods and services for routine household maintenance	5.20	5.00	4.80	3.90	4.00	4.30	4.70
5.6.1 Cleaning materials	2.20	2.00	2.10	2.00	1.90	2.10	2.00
5.6.2 Household goods and hardware	1.20	1.20	1.10	1.00	1.00	1.10	1.10
5.6.3 Domestic services, carpet cleaning & repair of furniture	1.70	1.90	1.60	0.90	1.00	1.10	1.50
6 Health	**6.80**	**5.10**	**5.10**	**3.10**	**3.60**	**3.10**	**4.80**
6.1 Medical products, appliances and equipment	3.80	3.20	3.10	2.20	2.60	2.10	3.00
6.1.1 Medicines, prescriptions, healthcare products & equipt.	2.10	1.60	1.70	1.30	1.30	1.20	1.70
6.1.2 Spectacles, lenses, accessories and repairs	1.80	1.50	1.40	0.90	1.30	0.90	1.30
6.2 Hospital services	3.00	1.90	2.00	0.90	0.90	1.00	1.80
7 Transport	**73.30**	**57.80**	**60.80**	**47.30**	**50.90**	**54.10**	**59.10**
7.1 Purchase of vehicles	34.80	26.30	27.70	20.40	22.30	23.30	26.80
7.1.1 Purchase of new cars and vans	15.90	10.40	11.50	6.00	9.70	12.30	11.10
7.1.2 Purchase of second hand cars or vans	17.70	14.80	15.40	13.80	12.20	10.10	14.90
7.1.3 Purchase of motorcycles and other vehicles	1.20	1.00	0.80	0.50	0.40	0.90	0.80
7.2 Operation of personal transport	29.30	25.60	24.10	22.00	20.80	23.70	23.70
7.2.1 Spares and accessories	2.90	2.20	2.10	1.60	1.90	1.50	2.00
7.2.2 Petrol, diesel and other motor oils	17.40	15.60	14.90	14.60	13.50	17.20	14.80
7.2.3 Repairs and servicing	6.90	5.70	5.30	4.20	4.00	3.70	5.10
7.2.4 Other motoring costs	2.20	2.10	2.00	1.70	1.40	1.30	1.90
7.3 Transport services	9.20	6.00	8.90	4.90	7.90	7.10	8.50
7.3.1 Rail and tube fares	3.00	1.20	2.00	0.60	1.20	0.30	1.80
7.3.2 Bus and coach fares	0.90	1.20	1.40	1.10	2.00	1.10	1.40
7.3.3 Combined fares	0.60	[0.00]	1.00	[0.00]	0.10	[0.00]	0.80
7.3.4 Other travel and transport	4.70	3.60	4.50	3.20	4.60	5.70	4.40

Note: The commodity and service categories are not comparable with those in publications before 2001-02
The numbering system is sequential, it does not use actual COICOP codes

A37 Detailed household expenditure by UK Countries and Government Office Regions (cont.)

2001-02 — 2003-04

based on weighted data and including children's expenditure

	North East	North West	Yorks & the Humber	East Midlands	West Midlands	East	London
Commodity or service	\multicolumn{7}{c}{Average weekly household expenditure (£)}						
8 Communication	**9.30**	**9.60**	**9.20**	**10.00**	**10.30**	**11.00**	**14.80**
8.1 Postal services	0.40	0.40	0.50	0.40	0.40	0.50	0.60
8.2 Telephone and telefax equipment	0.80	0.60	0.50	0.80	0.70	0.50	0.90
8.3 Telephone and telefax services	8.00	8.50	8.30	8.80	9.20	10.00	13.30
9 Recreation & culture	**50.70**	**57.10**	**52.60**	**55.80**	**53.60**	**59.10**	**57.00**
9.1 Audio-visual, photographic and information processing equipment	7.50	8.40	8.00	7.40	8.20	7.50	9.00
9.1.1 Audio equipment and accessories, CD players	2.10	2.30	2.40	2.10	2.00	2.50	2.70
9.1.2 TV, video and computers	5.10	5.40	4.80	4.40	5.60	4.00	5.50
9.1.3 Photographic, cine and optical equipment	0.20	0.70	0.70	0.90	0.60	0.90	0.80
9.2 Other major durables for recreation and culture	0.70	[2.10]	[2.20]	[3.80]	1.80	3.20	0.80
9.3 Other recreational items and equipment, gardens and pets	8.20	9.30	8.40	10.50	9.30	11.00	9.20
9.3.1 Games, toys and hobbies	2.20	2.20	2.10	2.40	2.10	2.30	2.60
9.3.2 Computer software and games	1.10	1.00	1.10	0.80	1.20	1.20	0.90
9.3.3 Equipment for sport, camping and open-air recreation	1.20	0.80	0.60	1.30	0.80	0.90	0.70
9.3.4 Horticultural goods, garden equipment and plants	1.90	2.40	2.20	2.90	2.60	3.20	2.90
9.3.5 Pets and pet food	1.80	2.90	2.40	3.10	2.60	3.50	2.00
9.4 Recreational and cultural services	17.40	17.30	15.70	16.30	15.10	17.00	19.40
9.4.1 Sports admissions, subscriptions, leisure class fees and equipment hire	4.00	4.80	3.80	4.70	4.10	5.50	7.50
9.4.2 Cinema, theatre and museums etc.	1.30	1.60	1.20	1.50	1.50	1.50	2.30
9.4.3 TV, video, satellite rental, cable subscriptions, TV licences and the Internet	5.10	5.30	4.50	5.10	4.60	5.00	5.00
9.4.4 Miscellaneous entertainments	1.00	1.00	0.80	1.20	0.90	1.20	1.00
9.4.5 Development of film, deposit for film development, passport photos, holiday and school photos	0.30	0.50	0.30	0.30	0.40	0.50	0.80
9.4.6 Gambling payments	5.60	4.10	5.00	3.60	3.60	3.40	2.80
9.5 Newspapers, books and stationery	5.60	6.20	5.50	6.50	5.70	6.70	7.40
9.5.1 Books	1.00	1.30	1.10	1.50	1.10	1.50	2.30
9.5.2 Diaries, address books, cards etc.	1.80	2.00	1.60	2.00	1.90	2.00	2.10
9.5.3 Newspapers	1.90	1.90	1.80	1.90	1.70	1.90	1.90
9.5.4 Magazines and periodicals	0.90	1.10	1.00	1.10	0.90	1.20	1.10
9.6 Package holidays	11.40	13.80	12.70	11.20	13.60	13.80	11.30
9.6.1 Package holidays - UK	0.70	0.80	1.20	1.20	0.80	1.00	0.90
9.6.2 Package holidays - abroad	10.70	12.90	11.50	10.00	12.70	12.80	10.50
10 Education	**3.30**	**4.50**	**4.20**	**3.90**	**2.80**	**5.40**	**10.20**
10.1 Education fees	3.20	4.10	4.00	3.60	2.60	5.10	9.70
10.2 Payments for school trips, other ad-hoc expenditure	0.10	0.30	0.30	0.20	0.20	0.30	0.50

Note: The commodity and service categories are not comparable with those in publications before 2001-02
The numbering system is sequential, it does not use actual COICOP codes

A37 Detailed household expenditure by UK Countries and Government Office Regions (cont.)

2001-02 — 2003-04

based on weighted data and including children's expenditure

Commodity or service	South East	South West	England	Wales	Scotland	Northern Ireland	United Kingdom
			Average weekly household expenditure (£)				
8 Communication	**11.60**	**9.90**	**10.90**	**8.80**	**9.90**	**10.90**	**10.70**
8.1 Postal services	0.60	0.60	0.50	0.40	0.40	0.40	0.50
8.2 Telephone and telefax equipment	0.60	0.50	0.70	0.20	0.60	0.60	0.60
8.3 Telephone and telefax services	10.30	8.80	9.70	8.20	8.90	9.90	9.60
9 Recreation & culture	**64.30**	**52.70**	**56.80**	**53.10**	**50.10**	**48.10**	**55.80**
9.1 Audio-visual, photographic and information processing equipment	9.90	7.30	8.30	9.10	7.00	5.70	8.20
9.1.1 Audio equipment and accessories, CD players	3.30	2.10	2.50	1.70	2.20	1.70	2.40
9.1.2 TV, video and computers	5.70	4.50	5.10	6.70	4.20	3.60	5.10
9.1.3 Photographic, cine and optical equipment	1.00	0.70	0.80	0.70	0.60	0.40	0.70
9.2 Other major durables for recreation and culture	2.10	0.90	2.00	2.80	0.80	1.70	1.90
9.3 Other recreational items and equipment, gardens and pets	12.20	11.20	10.10	9.90	8.30	8.90	9.90
9.3.1 Games, toys and hobbies	2.40	2.40	2.30	2.30	2.20	2.90	2.30
9.3.2 Computer software and games	1.10	0.90	1.00	1.30	1.20	1.00	1.10
9.3.3 Equipment for sport, camping and open-air recreation	1.30	1.20	0.90	1.00	0.90	0.80	0.90
9.3.4 Horticultural goods, garden equipment and plants	3.80	3.20	2.90	2.30	2.00	2.30	2.80
9.3.5 Pets and pet food	3.60	3.60	2.90	3.00	2.10	1.80	2.80
9.4 Recreational and cultural services	18.00	15.70	17.00	14.50	16.50	15.40	16.80
9.4.1 Sports admissions, subscriptions, leisure class fees and equipment hire	6.00	5.00	5.20	3.40	4.40	4.50	5.00
9.4.2 Cinema, theatre and museums etc.	2.00	1.60	1.70	1.10	1.80	1.50	1.70
9.4.3 TV, video, satellite rental, cable subscriptions, TV licences and the Internet	5.10	4.40	4.90	5.30	5.00	4.20	4.90
9.4.4 Miscellaneous entertainments	1.20	1.00	1.00	0.80	0.90	1.30	1.00
9.4.5 Development of film, deposit for film development, passport photos, holiday and school photos	0.70	0.60	0.50	0.40	0.30	0.40	0.50
9.4.6 Gambling payments	3.00	3.00	3.60	3.60	4.10	3.40	3.70
9.5 Newspapers, books and stationery	7.00	6.80	6.50	5.80	7.00	6.20	6.50
9.5.1 Books	1.80	1.60	1.50	1.20	1.70	1.20	1.50
9.5.2 Diaries, address books, cards etc.	2.30	2.10	2.00	1.80	1.80	1.50	2.00
9.5.3 Newspapers	1.80	1.90	1.90	1.80	2.60	2.40	1.90
9.5.4 Magazines and periodicals	1.10	1.20	1.10	1.00	1.00	1.00	1.10
9.6 Package holidays	15.00	10.90	12.90	10.90	10.50	10.30	12.50
9.6.1 Package holidays - UK	0.70	0.70	0.90	0.70	0.30	0.60	0.80
9.6.2 Package holidays - abroad	14.30	10.20	12.00	10.20	10.20	9.80	11.70
10 Education	**7.40**	**5.30**	**5.60**	**2.90**	**4.10**	**3.80**	**5.30**
10.1 Education fees	7.10	5.10	5.30	2.60	3.90	3.40	5.00
10.2 Payments for school trips, other ad-hoc expenditure	0.30	0.20	0.30	0.30	0.20	0.40	0.30

Note: The commodity and service categories are not comparable with those in publications before 2001-02
The numbering system is sequential, it does not use actual COICOP codes

A37 Detailed household expenditure by UK Countries and Government Office Regions (cont.)

2001-02 — 2003-04

based on weighted data and including children's expenditure

	North East	North West	Yorks & the Humber	East Midlands	West Midlands	East	London
Commodity or service	Average weekly household expenditure (£)						
11 Restaurants & hotels	**30.70**	**33.00**	**34.00**	**35.40**	**31.60**	**33.40**	**44.00**
11.1 Catering services	28.20	29.20	29.80	30.30	27.30	27.90	38.10
11.1.1 Restaurant and café meals	8.60	10.00	9.60	11.50	9.30	11.50	15.10
11.1.2 Alcoholic drinks (away from home)	10.00	9.40	9.20	9.00	8.40	7.20	9.70
11.1.3 Take away meals eaten at home	3.80	3.40	3.60	3.50	3.70	3.40	4.40
11.1.4 Other take-away and snack food	4.00	4.30	4.00	3.70	3.60	3.80	6.40
11.1.5 Contract catering (food) and canteens	1.80	2.10	3.30	2.60	2.20	2.00	2.40
11.2 Accommodation services	2.50	3.70	4.30	5.10	4.40	5.50	5.90
11.2.1 Holiday in the UK	1.70	2.10	2.30	2.80	2.80	2.80	2.10
11.2.2 Holiday abroad	0.80	1.60	1.70	2.20	1.60	2.70	3.80
11.2.3 Room hire	[0.00]	[0.00]	[0.30]	[0.00]	[0.00]	[0.00]	[0.00]
12 Miscellaneous goods & services	**24.60**	**32.00**	**27.40**	**30.60**	**29.70**	**34.30**	**39.00**
12.1 Personal care	7.40	8.70	7.80	8.80	7.80	9.20	9.60
12.1.1 Hairdressing, beauty treatment	1.80	2.70	2.40	2.50	2.20	2.80	2.80
12.1.2 Toilet paper	0.60	0.60	0.60	0.70	0.70	0.80	0.70
12.1.3 Toiletries and soap	1.60	1.80	1.60	1.90	1.70	2.00	2.30
12.1.4 Baby toiletries and accessories (disposable)	0.50	0.50	0.50	0.60	0.50	0.60	0.70
12.1.5 Hair products, cosmetics and electrical personal appliances	2.80	3.00	2.70	3.10	2.70	3.20	3.20
12.2 Personal effects	2.30	3.10	3.00	2.50	2.90	2.60	3.60
12.3 Social protection	1.60	2.50	1.80	1.60	2.30	3.50	4.30
12.4 Insurance	10.50	13.50	11.50	14.00	13.40	14.70	16.20
12.4.1 Household insurances - structural, contents and appliances	3.90	4.40	3.90	4.70	4.20	4.80	5.50
12.4.2 Medical insurance premiums	0.50	0.90	0.80	1.10	1.20	1.80	2.30
12.4.3 Vehicle insurance including boat insurance	6.10	8.00	6.70	8.10	7.80	7.80	8.30
12.4.4 Non-package holiday, other travel insurance	[0.00]	0.20	[0.10]	0.20	[0.20]	0.30	0.10
12.5 Other services n.e.c	2.80	4.30	3.10	3.70	3.30	4.40	5.20
12.5.1 Moving house	1.20	1.70	1.40	2.20	1.40	3.00	3.10
12.5.2 Bank, building society, post office, credit card charges	0.20	0.30	0.30	0.30	0.30	0.40	0.50
12.5.3 Other services and professional fees	1.40	2.20	1.50	1.20	1.50	1.00	1.60
1-12 All expenditure groups	**292.40**	**332.50**	**314.80**	**336.10**	**322.30**	**367.50**	**406.30**

Note: The commodity and service categories are not comparable with those in publications before 2001-02
The numbering system is sequential, it does not use actual COICOP codes

A37 Detailed household expenditure by UK Countries and Government Office Regions (cont.)

2001-02 — 2003-04

based on weighted data and including children's expenditure

	South East	South West	England	Wales	Scotland	Northern Ireland	United Kingdom
Commodity or service			Average weekly household expenditure (£)				
11 Restaurants & hotels	**36.40**	**30.40**	**34.90**	**30.30**	**31.00**	**36.80**	**34.40**
11.1 Catering services	30.30	25.40	30.00	26.60	27.40	34.50	29.70
11.1.1 Restaurant and café meals	12.60	10.70	11.30	9.10	9.30	12.10	11.10
11.1.2 Alcoholic drinks (away from home)	8.50	7.50	8.70	8.50	7.60	8.80	8.60
11.1.3 Take away meals eaten at home	3.40	2.50	3.50	3.40	3.70	5.60	3.60
11.1.4 Other take-away and snack food	3.90	3.10	4.20	3.70	4.60	5.30	4.20
11.1.5 Contract catering (food) and canteens	1.90	1.60	2.20	1.90	2.20	2.60	2.20
11.2 Accommodation services	6.00	5.00	4.90	3.70	3.60	2.20	4.70
11.2.1 Holiday in the UK	2.60	2.40	2.40	2.00	1.80	0.80	2.30
11.2.2 Holiday abroad	3.20	2.60	2.40	1.70	1.70	1.50	2.30
11.2.3 Room hire	[020]	[.10]	0.10	[0.00]	[0.00]	[0.00]	0.10
12 Miscellaneous goods & services	**39.40**	**32.10**	**33.30**	**26.10**	**27.90**	**33.20**	**32.40**
12.1 Personal care	9.90	8.70	8.80	7.30	8.50	10.00	8.80
12.1.1 Hairdressing, beauty treatment	3.30	2.80	2.70	1.80	2.40	3.00	2.60
12.1.2 Toilet paper	0.70	0.70	0.70	0.70	0.70	0.80	0.70
12.1.3 Toiletries and soap	2.10	1.90	1.90	1.70	1.90	2.10	1.90
12.1.4 Baby toiletries and accessories (disposable)	0.50	0.50	0.50	0.40	0.50	0.80	0.50
12.1.5 Hair products, cosmetics and electrical personal appliances	3.30	2.90	3.00	2.60	3.00	3.30	3.00
12.3 Personal effects	4.00	2.80	3.10	2.50	3.10	2.40	3.10
12.3 Social protection	2.40	2.00	2.60	2.00	2.00	2.50	2.50
12.4 Insurance	16.90	13.90	14.30	11.10	10.90	14.80	13.80
12.4.1 Household insurances - structural, contents and appliances	5.20	4.40	4.70	3.90	4.00	3.70	4.50
12.4.2 Medical insurance premiums	2.50	1.50	1.50	0.80	0.60	0.80	1.40
12.4.3 Vehicle insurance including boat insurance	9.00	7.80	7.90	6.30	6.10	10.20	7.70
12.4.4 Non-package holiday, other travel insurance	0.20	0.20	0.20	[0.10]	0.20	[0.20]	0.20
12.5 Other services n.e.c	6.30	4.70	4.40	3.20	3.40	3.50	4.30
12.5.1 Moving house	3.80	3.00	2.50	1.70	1.40	0.80	2.30
12.5.2 Bank, building society, post office, credit card charges	0.40	0.40	0.40	0.30	0.40	0.50	0.40
12.5.3 Other services and professional fees	2.00	1.30	1.60	1.20	1.60	2.20	1.60
1-12 All expenditure groups	**396.50**	**331.90**	**352.50**	**302.30**	**319.00**	**344.50**	**346.80**

Note: The commodity and service categories are not comparable with those in publications before 2001-02
The numbering system is sequential, it does not use actual COICOP codes

A37 Detailed household expenditure by UK Countries and Government Office Regions (cont.)

2001-02 — 2003-04

based on weighted data and including children's expenditure

	North East	North West	Yorks & the Humber	East Midlands	West Midlands	East	London
Commodity or service	**Average weekly household expenditure (£)**						
13 Other expenditure items	**43.30**	**51.10**	**49.00**	**55.00**	**53.30**	**63.70**	**79.20**
13.1 Housing: mortgage interest payments, council tax etc.	31.20	34.90	30.60	38.00	36.50	44.40	49.30
13.2 Licences, fines and transfers	1.90	2.80	2.30	3.20	2.70	3.20	[6.40]
13.3 Holiday spending	3.50	5.40	6.40	6.60	5.80	7.30	11.30
13.4 Money transfers and credit	6.80	8.10	9.60	7.20	8.30	8.80	12.30
13.4.1 Money, cash gifts given to children	0.10	0.10	0.20	0.20	0.10	0.10	0.10
13.4.2 Cash gifts and donations	5.60	6.60	8.20	5.60	6.90	7.00	9.90
13.4.3 Club instalment payments (child) and interest on credit cards	1.10	1.40	1.30	1.40	1.20	1.70	2.20
Total expenditure	**335.70**	**383.60**	**363.70**	**391.10**	**375.60**	**431.20**	**485.50**
14 Other items recorded							
14.1 Life assurance, contributions to pension funds	15.30	18.60	24.30	20.50	19.30	23.70	24.80
14.2 Other insurance inc. Friendly Societies	0.50	0.90	1.20	1.30	1.00	1.20	1.10
14.3 Income tax, payments less refunds	49.60	60.80	58.60	68.70	63.70	88.70	116.20
14.4 National insurance contributions	16.60	18.50	17.00	19.60	19.40	22.20	26.70
14.5 Purchase or alteration of dwellings, mortgages	28.20	30.70	23.30	40.70	27.30	[81.70]	[204.70]
14.6 Savings and investments	7.70	7.10	5.80	7.90	5.80	9.40	7.10
14.7 Pay off loan to clear other debt	2.60	2.50	3.00	2.80	2.20	2.70	2.50
14.8 Windfall receipts from gambling etc.	[8.20]	2.00	3.70	[4.40]	1.30	1.40	1.00

Note: The commodity and service categories are not comparable with those in publications before 2001-02
The numbering system is sequential, it does not use actual COICOP codes

A37 Detailed household expenditure by UK Countries and Government Office Regions (cont.)

2001-02 — 2003-04

based on weighted data and including children's expenditure

	South East	South West	England	Wales	Scotland	Northern Ireland	United Kingdom
Commodity or service	Average weekly household expenditure (£)						
13 Other expenditure items	**76.90**	**58.20**	**61.40**	**46.30**	**51.30**	**48.60**	**59.40**
13.1 Housing: mortgage interest payments, council tax etc.	51.50	40.60	41.10	29.70	35.40	26.60	39.60
13.2 Licences, fines and transfers	3.30	3.10	3.40	2.30	2.30	2.60	3.20
13.3 Holiday spending	8.80	5.80	7.20	6.30	4.90	7.60	7.00
13.4 Money transfers and credit	13.20	8.60	9.70	8.00	8.70	11.80	9.60
13.4.1 Money, cash gifts given to children	0.10	0.10	0.10	[060]	0.20	0.30	0.20
13.4.2 Cash gifts and donations	11.00	6.90	7.90	6.30	7.20	10.60	7.90
13.4.3 Club instalment payments (child) and interest on credit cards	2.20	1.60	1.60	1.00	1.40	0.90	1.60
Total expenditure	**473.40**	**390.10**	**413.80**	**348.60**	**370.30**	**393.00**	**406.20**
14 Other items recorded							
14.1 Life assurance, contributions to pension funds	26.30	19.50	22.00	17.40	20.30	17.70	21.50
14.2 Other insurance inc. Friendly Societies	1.70	1.40	1.20	1.00	0.80	0.60	1.10
14.3 Income tax, payments less refunds	100.10	66.30	78.80	53.40	63.60	50.40	75.50
14.4 National insurance contributions	23.10	17.70	20.60	16.80	18.90	16.80	20.20
14.5 Purchase or alteration of dwellings, mortgages	64.40	65.30	69.30	27.50	20.60	21.40	61.70
14.6 Savings and investments	7.70	8.10	7.40	5.70	4.70	4.40	7.00
14.7 Pay off loan to clear other debt	3.10	2.60	2.70	1.90	2.40	0.60	2.60
14.8 Windfall receipts from gambling etc.	1.50	1.30	2.30	1.30	1.90	1.40	2.20

Note: The commodity and service categories are not comparable with those in publications before 2001-02
The numbering system is sequential, it does not use actual COICOP codes

A38 Household expenditure by urban/rural areas (GB) 2001-02 — 2003-04

based on weighted data and including children's expenditure

	London built-up area	Other metro-politan built-up areas	Other urban					Rural
			popu-lation over 250K	popu-lation 100K to 250K	popu-lation 25K to 100K	popu-lation 10K to 25K	popu-lation 3K to 10K	
Average number of grossed households (thousands)	3,320	3,500	3,210	2,510	3,380	2,000	1,960	3,990
Total number of households in sample (over 3 years)	2,313	2,816	2,743	2,133	2,876	1,705	1,679	3,451
Total number of persons in sample (over 3 years)	5,624	6,831	6,506	5,084	6,824	4,090	3,873	8,311
Total number of adults in sample (over 3 years)	4,141	4,983	4,912	3,776	5,098	3,061	3,031	6,284
Weighted average number of persons per household	2.5	2.4	2.3	2.3	2.3	2.4	2.3	2.4

Commodity or service	Average weekly household expenditure (£)							
1 Food & non-alcoholic drinks	45.00	38.30	41.40	40.00	41.60	42.90	43.20	47.00
2 Alcoholic drinks, tobacco & narcotics	10.50	11.90	11.90	11.40	11.10	11.60	10.80	11.60
3 Clothing & footwear	27.20	21.50	20.80	21.60	21.50	22.40	20.80	22.30
4 Housing (net)[1], fuel & power	55.50	32.60	35.30	36.10	33.60	34.10	32.00	36.90
5 Household goods & services	34.40	25.20	28.50	27.60	28.30	27.70	31.20	37.00
6 Health	6.60	3.30	3.80	4.60	5.20	5.30	4.80	5.40
7 Transport	63.50	44.90	54.10	59.00	55.40	57.00	62.60	74.70
8 Communication	14.40	9.40	10.30	10.10	10.10	9.70	10.10	10.70
9 Recreation & culture	59.80	49.20	56.00	54.70	55.20	53.60	53.30	62.90
10 Education	9.70	3.60	4.50	3.90	3.40	4.00	4.20	7.80
11 Restaurants & hotels	43.60	31.90	34.70	32.60	30.40	34.10	30.80	34.70
12 Miscellaneous goods & services	39.80	27.10	30.40	30.80	28.90	30.80	30.70	38.10
1-12 All expenditure groups	410.00	299.00	331.80	332.40	324.70	333.10	334.40	389.00
13 Other expenditure items	81.30	45.30	53.60	54.10	51.60	58.90	58.20	71.60
Total expenditure	491.30	344.30	385.40	386.50	376.30	392.00	392.50	460.60
Average weekly expenditure per person (£)								
Total expenditure	198.60	146.30	165.90	165.40	160.50	165.90	171.50	194.90

Note: The commodity and service categories are not comparable with those in publications before 2001-02
1 Excluding mortgage interest payments and council tax

A39 Government Office Regions of the United Kingdom

A40　Income and source of income by household composition　　　2003-04
based on weighted data

	Grossed number of house-holds	Number of house-holds in the sample	Disposable	Gross	Wages and salaries	Self employ-ment	Invest-ments	Annuities and pensions[1]	Social security benefits[2]	Other sources
	(000s)	Number	£	£	Percentage of gross weekly household income					
All households	**24,670**	**7,048**	**464**	**570**	*67*	*9*	*3*	*7*	*13*	*1*
Composition of household										
One adult	6,970	1,952	236	284	*52*	*5*	*5*	*13*	*24*	*1*
Retired households mainly dependent on state pensions[3]	1,090	308	128	129	*0*	*0*	*1*	*5*	*94*	*0*
Other retired households	2,190	601	203	226	*0*	*0*	*12*	*38*	*49*	*1*
Non-retired households	3,690	1,043	288	364	*76*	*8*	*3*	*4*	*8*	*1*
One adult, one child	770	248	252	285	*59*	*7*	*1*	*2*	*27*	*4*
One adult, two or more children	680	249	268	294	*45*	*3*	*0*	*0*	*45*	*6*
One man and one woman	7,520	2,108	499	614	*62*	*8*	*4*	*13*	*13*	*1*
Retired households mainly dependent on state pensions[3]	580	163	209	210	*0*	*0*	*2*	*7*	*90*	*0*
Other retired households	1,960	556	366	402	*6*	*1*	*8*	*42*	*42*	*1*
Non-retired households	4,990	1,389	584	743	*76*	*10*	*3*	*7*	*4*	*1*
Two men or two women	630	173	472	572	*66*	*10*	*3*	*6*	*13*	*1*
One man one woman, one child	1,700	499	607	774	*80*	*11*	*2*	*1*	*5*	*1*
One man one woman, two children	2,270	711	631	799	*78*	*11*	*2*	*1*	*7*	*1*
One man one woman, three children	670	230	703	890	*75*	*13*	*1*	*0*	*9*	*1*
Two adults, four or more children	180	72	609	742	*61*	*18*	*1*	*0*	*19*	*1*
Three adults	1,580	344	678	830	*73*	*9*	*3*	*6*	*8*	*1*
Three adults, one or more children	760	222	727	881	*76*	*10*	*1*	*2*	*9*	*2*
Four or more adults	530	113	804	973	*81*	*4*	*0*	*4*	*6*	*4*
Four or more adults, one or more children	260	79	853	1,048	*72*	*17*	*0*	*2*	*7*	*2*

1 Other than social security benefits
2 Excluding housing benefit and council tax benefit (rates rebate in Northern Ireland) - see definitions in Appendix B
3 Mainly dependent on state pension and not economically active - see definitions in Appendix B

A41　Income and source of income by age of household reference person　　　2003-04
based on weighted data

	Grossed number of house-holds	Number of house-holds in the sample	Disposable	Gross	Wages and salaries	Self employ-ment	Invest-ments	Annuities and pensions[1]	Social security benefits[2]	Other sources
Age of household reference person	(000s)	Number	£	£	Percentage of gross weekly household income					
Under 30	2,540	682	431	535	*82*	*7*	*1*	*0*	*7*	*3*
30 and under 50	9,640	2,877	570	722	*80*	*10*	*2*	*1*	*7*	*1*
50 and under 65	6,120	1,725	509	628	*67*	*11*	*4*	*9*	*8*	*1*
65 and under 75	3,280	965	314	349	*13*	*2*	*7*	*34*	*43*	*1*
75 and over	3,090	799	230	247	*7*	*0*	*9*	*28*	*55*	*0*

1 Other than social security benefits
2 Excluding housing benefit and council tax benefit (rates rebate in Northern Ireland) - see definitions in Appendix B

A42   Income and source of income by gross income quintile group   2003-04
based on weighted data

| Gross income quintile group | Grossed number of house-holds | Number of house-holds in the sample | Weekly household income | | Source of income | | | | | |
			Dispo-sable	Gross	Wages and salaries	Self employ-ment	Invest-ments	Annuities and pensions[1]	Social security benefits[2]	Other sources
	(000s)	Number	£	£	Percentage of gross weekly household income					
Lowest twenty per cent	4,940	1,423	121	124	7	2	3	8	77	2
Second quintile group	4,930	1,458	243	266	30	4	4	17	44	2
Third quintile group	4,930	1,434	384	450	59	6	3	12	17	2
Fourth quintile group	4,930	1,399	554	681	76	7	2	7	7	1
Highest twenty per cent	4,930	1,334	1018	1,330	79	12	3	3	2	1

1 Other than social security benefits
2 Excluding housing benefit and council tax benefit (rates rebate in Northern Ireland) - see definitions in Appendix B

A43   Income and source of income by household tenure   2003-04
based on weighted data

| Tenure of dwelling[3] | Grossed number of house-holds | Number of house-holds in the sample | Weekly household income | | Source of income | | | | | |
			Dispo-sable	Gross	Wages and salaries	Self employ-ment	Invest-ments	Annuities and pensions[1]	Social security benefits[2]	Other sources
	(000s)	Number	£	£	Percentage of gross weekly household income					
Owners										
Owned outright	7,380	2,093	411	487	42	8	8	21	21	1
Buying with a mortgage[3]	9,880	2,858	623	795	81	10	1	2	5	1
All	17,250	4,951	533	664	69	9	3	8	10	1
Social rented from										
Council	3,050	893	230	253	47	2	0	4	46	1
Registered social landlord[4]	1,780	491	232	255	46	4	0	4	44	2
All	4,830	1,384	231	254	46	3	0	4	45	1
Private rented										
Rent free	350	99	367	429	55	11	10	5	14	4
Rent paid, unfurnished	1,590	447	440	536	74	10	2	2	10	2
Rent paid, furnished	650	167	487	604	82	5	2	1	3	8
All	2,590	713	442	539	74	8	3	2	9	4

1 Other than social security benefits
2 Excluding housing benefit and council tax benefit (rates rebate in Northern Ireland) - see definitions in Appendix B
3 See footnotes in Table A34
4 Formerly housing association

A44 Income and source of income by UK Countries and Government Office Regions
based on weighted data

2001-02 — 2003-04

| | Average number of grossed house-holds | Total number of house-holds (over 3 years) | Weekly household income | | Source of income | | | | | |
			Dispo-sable	Gross	Wages and salaries	Self employ-ment	Invest-ments	Annuities and pensions[1]	Social security benefits[2]	Other sources
Government Office Regions	(000s)	Number	£	£	Percentage of gross weekly household income					
United Kingdom	24,490	21,448	453	554	68	8	3	7	12	1
North East	1,040	945	385	458	68	4	2	6	18	1
North West	2,820	2,342	406	489	67	7	2	8	15	1
Yorkshire and the Humber	2,140	1,755	393	474	66	6	3	8	15	1
East Midlands	1,730	1,471	439	532	69	8	3	7	12	1
West Midlands	2,130	1,774	417	505	68	8	3	6	14	1
East	2,250	1,883	478	594	69	8	3	7	11	1
London	2,860	1,922	591	740	71	12	4	4	8	1
South East	3,380	2,853	526	658	68	10	4	8	9	1
South West	2,160	1,934	428	517	62	9	5	9	14	1
England	20,510	16,879	463	568	68	9	4	7	12	1
Wales	1,230	1,082	388	461	64	6	2	10	17	1
Scotland	2,120	1,755	412	500	69	5	2	7	14	2
Northern Ireland	630	1,732	390	461	65	8	2	5	19	1

1 Other than social security benefits
2 Excluding housing benefit and council tax benefit (rates rebate in Northern Ireland) - see definitions in Appendix B

A45 Income and source of income by GB urban/rural area
based on weighted data

2001-02 — 2003-04

| | Average number of grossed house-holds | Total number of house-holds (over 3 years) | Weekly household income | | Source of income | | | | | |
			Dispo-sable	Gross	Wages and salaries	Self employ-ment	Invest-ments	Annuities and pensions[1]	Social security benefits[2]	Other sources
GB urban rural areas	(000s)	Number	£	£	Percentage of gross weekly household income					
Urban										
London built-up area	3,320	2,313	588	738	71	11	4	5	8	1
Other metropolitan built up areas	3,500	2,816	377	451	68	5	2	6	17	1
Other urban:										
population over 250k	3,210	2,743	420	508	67	7	3	8	14	2
population 100k to 250k	2,510	2,133	415	505	70	6	2	7	13	1
population 25k to 100k	3,380	2,876	419	508	68	7	3	8	14	1
population 10k to 25k	2,000	1,705	446	537	65	9	4	8	14	1
population 3k to 10k	1,960	1,679	435	528	65	7	4	10	13	1
Rural	3,990	3,451	510	634	66	10	5	8	9	1

1 Other than social security benefits
2 Excluding housing benefit and council tax benefit - see definitions in Appendix B

A46 Income and source of income by socio-economic class

2003-04

based on weighted data

| | Grossed number of house-holds | Number of house-holds in the sample | Weekly household income | | Source of income | | | | | |
			Dispo-sable	Gross	Wages and salaries	Self employ-ment	Invest-ments	Annuities and pensions[1]	Social security benefits[2]	Other sources
Gross income quintile group	(000s)	Number	£	£	Percentage of gross weekly household income					
Large employers/higher managerial	1,210	337	864	1172	89	2	3	4	2	1
Higher professional	1,590	451	828	1083	73	16	4	4	2	1
Lower managerial and professional	4,920	1,398	634	810	84	5	2	4	4	1
Intermediate	1,680	496	447	553	81	2	2	5	8	1
Small employers	1,580	461	553	637	22	63	3	3	8	0
Lower supervisory	1,980	563	468	579	85	2	1	3	8	1
Semi-routine	2,500	730	348	410	75	1	1	4	17	2
Routine	2,330	690	342	402	72	2	1	4	21	1
Long-term unemployed[3]	490	157	214	227	22	3	0	4	63	8
Students	310	83	256	275	48	0	2	1	9	39
Occupation not stated[4]	6,090	1,682	257	281	8	1	8	32	51	1

1 Other than social security benefits
2 Excluding housing benefit and council tax benefit (rates rebate in Northern Ireland) - see definitions in Appendix B
3 Includes those who have never worked
4 Includes those who are economically inactive - see definitions in Appendix B

A47 Income and source of income 1970 to 2003-04

| | Grossed number of house-holds | Number of house-holds in the sample | Weekly household income[1] | | | | Source of income | | | | | |
| | | | Current prices | | 2003-04 prices | | Wages and salaries | Self employ-ment | Invest-ments | Annuities and pensions[2] | Social security benefits[3] | Other sources |
			Dispo-sable	Gross	Dispo-sable	Gross						
	(000s)	Number	£	£	£	£	Percentage of gross weekly household income					
1970		6,393	28	34	274	330	77	7	4	3	9	1
1980		6,944	115	140	308	377	75	6	3	3	13	1
1990		7,046	258	317	373	459	67	10	6	5	11	1
1995-96		6,797	307	381	373	463	64	9	5	7	14	2
1996-97		6,415	325	397	385	471	65	9	4	7	14	1
1997-98		6,409	343	421	394	483	67	8	4	7	13	1
1998-99[4]	24,660	6,630	371	457	413	509	68	8	4	7	12	1
1999-2000	25,340	7,097	391	480	429	526	66	10	5	7	12	1
2000-01	25,030	6,637	409	503	436	535	67	9	4	7	12	1
2001-02[5]	24,450	7,473	442	541	464	567	69	9	4	7	11	1
2002-03	24,350	6,927	453	552	466	568	68	8	3	7	12	1
2003-04	24,670	7,048	464	570	464	570	67	9	3	7	13	1

1 Does not include imputed income from owner-occupied and rent-free households.
2 Other than social security benefits.
3 Excluding housing benefit and council tax benefit (rates rebate in Northern Ireland) and their predecessors in earlier years - see appendix B.
4 Based on grossed data from 1998-99
5 From 2001-02 onwards, weighting is based on the population estimates from the 2001 census

A48 Characteristics of households

2003-04

based on weighted data

	% * of all house- holds	Grossed number of house- holds (000s)	House- holds in sample (number)		% * of all house- holds	Grossed number of house- holds (000s)	House- holds in sample (number)
Total number of households	100	24,670	7,048	**Composition of household (cont)**			
				Four adults	2	480	101
Size of household							
One person	28	6,980	1,953	Four adults, one child	1	140	38
Two persons	36	8,930	2,531	Four adults, two or more children	0	70	26
Three persons	15	3,800	1,028				
Four persons	14	3,440	1,019	Five adults	0	30	8
Five persons	5	1,120	367				
Six persons	1	290	106	Five adults, one or more children	0	40	11
Seven persons	0	80	35				
Eight persons	0	20	8	All other households without children	0	10	4
Nine or more persons	0	0	1	All other households with children	0	10	4
Composition of household				**Number of economically active**			
One adult	28	6,970	1,952	**persons in household**			
Retired households mainly				No person	33	8,070	2,321
dependent on state pensions[1]	4	1,090	308	One person	29	7,040	2,060
Other retired households	9	2,190	601	More than one person	39	9,560	2,667
Non-retired households	15	3,690	1,043	Two persons	30	7,340	2,114
One man	12	3,040	838	Three persons	7	1,680	419
Aged under 65	9	2,130	567	Four persons	2	500	123
Aged 65 and over	4	910	271	Five persons	0	40	10
One woman	16	3,940	1,114	Six or more persons	0	0	1
Aged under 60	5	1,330	409				
Aged 60 and over	11	2,610	705				
One adult, one child	3	770	248	**Households with married women**	50	12,240	3,526
One man, one child	0	100	28	Households with married women			
One woman, one child	3	670	220	economically active	29	7,060	2,012
One adult, two or more children	3	680	249	With no dependent children	15	3,640	958
One man, two or more children	0	60	21	With dependent children	14	3,420	1,054
One woman, two or more children	3	620	228	One child	5	1,280	362
				Two children	7	1,650	527
One man, one woman	30	7,520	2,108	Three children	2	400	133
Retired households mainly				Four or more children	0	90	32
dependent on state pensions[1]	2	580	163				
Other retired households	8	1,960	556	Households with married women			
Non-retired households	20	4,990	1,389	not economically active	21	5,180	1,514
Two men or two women	3	630	173	With no dependent children	16	3,970	1,119
				With dependent children	5	1,210	395
Two adults with children	20	4,960	1,560	One child	2	390	115
One man one woman, one child	7	1,700	499	Two children	2	530	167
Two men or two women, one child	0	90	31	Three children	1	200	77
One man one woman, two children	9	2,270	711	Four or more children	0	90	36
Two men or two women, two children	0	30	10				
One man one woman, three children	3	670	230	**Economic status of household reference person**			
Two men or two women, three children	0	20	7	Economically active	62	15,180	4,344
Two adults, four children	1	150	59	Employee at work	52	12,820	3,660
Two adults, five children	0	20	9	Full-time	45	10,980	3,098
Two adults, six or more children	0	10	4	Part-time	7	1,840	562
Three adults	6	1,580	344	Government-supported training	0	10	4
Three adults with children	3	760	222	Unemployed	2	450	132
Three adults, one child	2	470	129	Self-employed	8	1,890	548
Three adults, two children	1	200	62				
Three adults, three children	0	60	20	Economically inactive	38	9,490	2,704
Three adults, four or more children	0	30	11				

A48 Characteristics of households (cont.)   2003-04
based on weighted data

	% * of all house- holds	Grossed number of house- holds (000s)	House- holds in sample (number)		% * of all house- holds	Grossed number of house- holds (000s)	House- holds in sample (number)
Age of household reference person				**GB urban/rural areas 2001-02 -- 2003-04**			
15 and under 20 years	0	80	25	Urban			
20 and under 25 years	3	800	230	London built-up area	14	3,320	2,313
25 and under 30 years	7	1,660	427	Other metropolitan built up areas	15	3,500	2,816
				Other urban:			
30 and under 35 years	9	2,160	630	population over 250k	13	3,210	2,743
35 and under 40 years	10	2,580	783	population 100k to 250k	11	2,510	2,133
40 and under 45 years	11	2,660	797	population 25k to 100k	14	3,380	2,876
				population 10k to 25k	8	2,000	1,705
45 and under 50 years	9	2,230	667	population 3k to 10k	8	1,960	1,679
50 and under 55 years	9	2,210	624	Rural	17	3,990	3,451
55 and under 60 years	9	2,190	614				
				Tenure of dwelling[4]			
60 and under 65 years	7	1,720	487	Owners			
65 and under 70 years	7	1,690	508	Owned outright	30	7,380	2,093
70 and under 75 years	6	1,590	457	Buying with a mortgage	40	9,880	2,858
				All	70	17,250	4,951
75 and under 80 years	6	1,400	387	Social rented from			
80 and under 85 years	5	1,120	274	Council	12	3,050	893
85 and under 90 years	2	420	103	Registered social landlord	7	1,780	491
90 years or more	1	150	35	All	20	4,830	1,384
				Private rented			
				Rent free	1	350	99
Government Office Regions and Countries				Rent paid, unfurnished	6	1,590	447
2001-02 -- 2003-04				Rent paid, furnished	3	650	167
United Kingdom	100	24,490	21,448	All	10	2,590	713
North East	4	1,040	945	**Households with durable goods**			
North West	12	2,820	2,342	Car/van	75	18,540	5,332
Yorkshire and the Humber	9	2,140	1,755	One	44	10,830	3,135
				Two	25	6,270	1,812
East Midlands	7	1,730	1,471	Three or more	6	1,450	385
West Midlands	9	2,130	1,774				
East	9	2,250	1,883	Central heating, full or partial	94	23,160	6,640
				Fridge-freezer or deep freezer	96	23,600	6,742
London	12	2,860	1,922	Washing machine	94	23,200	6,659
South East	14	3,380	2,853	Tumble dryer	57	13,940	4,018
South West	9	2,160	1,934	Dishwasher	31	7,650	2,243
				Microwave oven	89	22,060	6,333
England	84	20,510	16,879				
Wales	5	1,230	1,082	Telephone	92	22,820	6,517
Scotland	9	2,120	1,755	Mobile phone	76	18,720	5,262
Northern Ireland	3	630	1,732	Video recorder	90	22,190	6,362
				Satellite receiver[5]	49	12,180	3,540
Socio-economic class of household reference person				Compact disc player	86	21,100	6,001
Large employers/higher managerial	5	1,210	337	Home computer	58	14,300	4,061
Higher professional	6	1,590	451	Internet connection	49	11,970	3,382
Lower managerial and professional	20	4,920	1,398				
Intermediate	7	1,680	496				
Small employers	6	1,580	461				
Lower supervisory	8	1,980	563				
Semi-routine	10	2,500	730				
Routine	9	2,330	690				
Long-term unemployed[2]	2	490	157				
Students	1	310	83				
Occupation not stated[3]	25	6,090	1,682				

* Based on grossed number of households
1 Mainly dependent on state pension and not economically active - see definitions in Appendix B.
2 Includes those who have never worked
3 Includes those who are economically inactive
4 See footnotes in Table A34
5 Includes digital and cable receivers

A49 Characteristics of persons

2003-04

based on weighted data

	Males				Females				All persons			
	Percentage* of		Grossed number of persons (000s)	Persons in the sample (number)	Percentage* of		Grossed number of persons (000s)	Persons in the sample (number)	%* of	Grossed number of persons (000s)	Persons in the sample (number)
	all males	all persons			all females	all persons			all persons		
All persons	100	49	28,270	8,139	100	51	29,880	8,826	100	58,150	16,965
Adults	76	37	21,560	5,945	78	40	23,330	6,672	77	44,890	12,617
Persons aged under 60	57	28	16,200	4,425	56	29	16,690	4,862	57	32,890	9,287
Persons aged 60 or under 65	5	2	1,430	396	5	3	1,530	434	5	2,960	830
Persons aged 65 or under 70	5	2	1,300	387	5	2	1,350	394	5	2,650	781
Persons aged 70 or over	9	5	2,630	737	13	6	3,760	982	11	6,390	1,719
Children	24	12	6,710	2,194	22	11	6,550	2,154	23	13,260	4,348
Children under 2 years of age	2	1	680	209	2	1	550	173	2	1,220	382
Children aged 2 or under 5	4	2	1,140	360	3	2	1,010	320	4	2,150	680
Children aged 5 or under 16	14	7	4,060	1,364	14	7	4,190	1,416	14	8,240	2,780
Children aged 16 or under 18	3	1	830	261	3	1	810	245	3	1,650	506
Economic activity											
Persons active (aged 16 or over)	55	27	15,510	4,256	45	23	13,450	3,837	50	28,960	8,093
Persons not active	45	22	12,760	3,883	55	28	16,430	4,989	50	29,190	8,872
Men 65 or over and women 60 or over	13	6	3,610	1,030	20	10	6,010	1,639	17	9,620	2,669
Others (Including children under 16)	32	16	9,150	2,853	35	18	10,420	3,350	34	19,580	6,203

* Based on grossed number of households

A50 Percentage of households with durable goods 1970 to 2003-04

based on weighted data

	Car/ van	Central heating[1]	Washing machine	Tumble dryer	Dish-washer	Micro-wave	Tele-phone	Mobile phone	Video recorder	Satellite receiver[2]	Cd player	Home computer	Internet connec-tion
1970	52	30	65	--	--	--	35	--	--	--	--	--	--
1975	57	47	72	--	--	--	52	--	--	--	--	--	--
1980	60	59	79	--	--	--	72	--	--	--	--	--	--
1985	63	69	83	--	--	--	81	--	30	--	--	13	--
1990	67	79	86	--	--	--	87	--	61	--	--	17	--
1994-95	69	84	89	50	18	67	91	--	76	--	46	--	--
1995-96	70	85	91	50	20	70	92	--	79	--	51	--	--
1996-97	69	87	91	51	20	75	93	16	82	19	59	27	--
1997-98	70	89	91	51	22	77	94	20	84	26	63	29	--
1998-99	72	89	92	51	24	80	95	26	86	27	68	32	9
1998-99*	72	89	92	51	23	79	95	27	85	28	68	33	10
1999-2000*	71	90	91	52	23	80	95	44	86	32	72	38	19
2000-01*	72	91	92	53	25	84	93	47	87	40	77	44	32
2001-02[3] *	74	92	93	54	27	86	94	64	90	43	80	49	39
2002-03*	74	93	94	56	29	87	94	70	90	45	83	55	45
2003-04*	75	94	94	57	31	89	92	76	90	49	86	58	49

-- Data not available.
* Based on weighted data and including children's expenditure
1 Full or partial.
2 Includes digital and cable receivers
3 From 2001-02 onwards, weighting is based on the population figures from the 2001 census

A51 Percentage[1] of households with durable goods by income group and household composition

2003-04

based on weighted data and including children's expenditure

	Central heating[2]	Washing machine	Tumble dryer	Micro-wave	Dish-washer	CD player
All households	94	94	57	89	31	86
Gross income decile group						
Lowest ten per cent	90	80	32	79	7	60
Second decile group	91	86	43	84	8	65
Third decile group	92	91	48	86	14	76
Fourth decile group	93	94	48	89	22	85
Fifth decile group	93	97	57	92	26	90
Sixth decile group	95	97	60	92	30	93
Seventh decile group	95	99	62	92	40	95
Eighth decile group	97	99	70	94	42	97
Ninth decile group	97	99	70	94	48	97
Highest ten per cent	98	99	75	93	73	98
Household composition						
One adult, retired households [3]	88	78	26	75	4	45
One adult, non-retired households	90	88	42	86	17	85
One adult, one child	96	97	63	89	15	93
One adult, two or more children	95	98	68	93	20	90
One man and one woman, retired households[3]	94	94	45	83	10	67
One man and one woman, non-retired households	94	98	63	91	39	93
One man and one woman, one child	96	99	67	95	39	96
One man and one woman, two or more children	97	100	75	95	52	96
All other households without children	93	96	50	88	25	92
All other households with children	95	98	61	95	46	91

	Home computer	Internet connection	Tele-phone	Mobile phone	Satellite receiver[4]	Video recorder
All households	58	49	92	76	49	90
Gross income decile group						
Lowest ten per cent	23	15	78	47	20	72
Second decile group	23	15	87	48	28	78
Third decile group	30	21	90	61	37	88
Fourth decile group	47	37	93	75	45	92
Fifth decile group	55	42	93	78	51	94
Sixth decile group	69	55	94	85	58	94
Seventh decile group	73	63	96	90	60	95
Eighth decile group	82	70	97	90	67	95
Ninth decile group	84	77	98	92	62	97
Highest ten per cent	93	90	99	93	66	96
Household composition						
One adult, retired households[3]	6	4	96	23	15	66
One adult, non-retired households	49	40	83	76	38	84
One adult, one child	56	34	76	85	47	93
One adult, two or more children	61	40	79	87	54	94
One man and one woman, retired households [3]	13	13	99	41	31	88
One man and one woman, non-retired households	71	61	96	86	57	94
One man and one woman, one child	77	65	94	90	65	96
One man and one woman, two or more children	87	76	96	90	70	98
All other households without children	69	58	93	82	51	90
All other households with children	76	63	90	88	68	96

1 See table A52 for number of recording households.
2 Full or partial.
3 Mainly dependent on state pension and not economically active - see appendix B.
4 Includes digital and cable receivers

A52

Percentage of households with cars
by income group, tenure and household composition
based on weighted data

2003-04

	One car/van	Two cars/vans	Three or more cars/vans	All with cars/vans	Grossed number of house-holds (000s)	House-holds in the sample (number)
All households	44	25	6	75	24,670	7,048
Gross income decile group						
Lowest ten per cent	26	3	0	29	2,470	703
Second decile group	36	4	0	40	2,470	720
Third decile group	52	6	1	59	2,470	729
Fourth decile group	60	12	1	73	2,460	729
Fifth decile group	61	19	3	83	2,470	715
Sixth decile group	57	26	5	88	2,460	719
Seventh decile group	51	34	6	91	2,470	712
Eighth decile group	44	43	8	94	2,470	687
Ninth decile group	33	50	14	97	2,470	681
Highest ten per cent	21	55	22	97	2,460	653
Tenure of dwelling[1]						
Owners						
Owned outright	52	22	5	79	7,377	2,093
Buying with a mortgage	44	40	9	93	9,877	2,858
All	47	32	8	87	17,254	4,951
Social rented from						
Council	31	6	1	38	3,047	893
Registered social landlord [2]	31	5	2	38	1,780	491
All	31	6	1	38	4,830	1,384
Private rented						
Rent free	52	18	3	74	350	99
Rent paid, unfurnished	49	19	3	70	1,590	447
Rent paid, furnished	38	13	5	56	650	167
All	47	17	3	67	2,590	713
Household composition						
One adult, retired mainly dependent on state pensions[3]	21	1	0	21	1,090	308
One adult, other retired	39	3	0	41	2,190	601
One adult, non-retired	61	6	1	68	3,690	1,043
One adult, one child	50	5	1	55	770	248
One adult, two or more children	45	3	0	47	680	249
One man and one woman, retired dependent on state pensions[3]	62	4	1	67	580	163
One man and one woman, other retired	63	18	2	83	1,960	556
One man and one woman, non-retired	43	40	6	89	4,990	1,389
One man and one woman, one child	41	44	6	91	1,700	499
One man and one woman, two children	39	49	6	94	2,270	711
One man and one woman, three children	38	46	9	92	670	230
Two adults, four or more children	39	38	3	80	180	72
Three adults	28	35	21	85	1,580	344
Three adults, one or more children	28	40	20	89	760	222
All other households without children	35	30	15	80	1,160	286
All other households with children	26	26	24	76	400	127

1 See footnotes in Table A34
2 Formerly housing association
3 Mainly dependent on state pension and not economically active - see appendix B

A53 Percentage of households with durable goods by UK Countries and Government Office Region
2001-02 — 2003-04
based on weighted data

	North East	North West	Yorks and the Humber	East Midlands	West Midlands	East	London
Average number of grossed households (thousands)	1,040	2,820	2,140	1,730	2,130	2,250	2,860
Total number of households in sample (over 3 years)	945	2,342	1,755	1,471	1,774	1,883	1,922
Percentage of households							
by Government Office Region and country							
Car/van	62	72	70	78	75	81	67
One	39	43	44	44	43	44	44
Two	18	24	21	27	25	30	18
Three or more	4	5	5	7	7	7	5
Central heating full or partial	97	91	89	95	91	94	94
Fridge-freezer or deep freezer	95	92	94	96	94	95	91
Washing machine	97	95	95	97	96	96	95
Tumble dryer	56	57	54	59	59	56	45
Dishwasher	19	24	23	29	26	35	29
Microwave	92	90	90	90	89	86	81
Telephone	94	92	92	96	93	95	93
Mobile phone	68	68	73	73	73	71	69
Video recorder	92	90	90	92	91	92	86
Satellite receiver	49	48	44	47	44	45	45
CD player	82	83	80	84	81	85	82
Home computer	48	53	50	54	54	58	61
Internet connection	38	42	39	45	41	48	52

	South East	South West	England	Wales	Scotland	Northern Ireland	United Kingdom
Average number of grossed households (thousands)	3,380	2,160	20,510	1,230	2,120	630	24,490
Total number of households in sample (over 3 years)	2,853	1,934	16,879	1,082	1,755	1,732	21,448
Percentage of households							
by Government Office Region and country							
Car/van	83	82	75	76	67	73	74
One	44	46	44	46	43	47	44
Two	30	28	25	24	20	23	24
Three or more	8	8	6	5	4	3	6
Central heating full or partial	95	91	93	93	93	97	93
Fridge-freezer or deep freezer	94	93	94	94	96	95	94
Washing machine	97	95	96	97	94	92	96
Tumble dryer	58	55	55	58	57	52	56
Dishwasher	39	31	29	24	26	33	29
Microwave	87	85	87	91	89	87	87
Telephone	95	94	94	90	92	91	93
Mobile phone	77	68	71	65	69	51	70
Video recorder	92	88	90	90	91	87	90
Satellite receiver[1]	45	40	45	56	47	46	46
CD player	87	81	83	81	86	73	83
Home computer	60	53	55	47	49	44	54
Internet connection	51	43	45	36	41	35	44

1 Includes digital and cable receivers

A54 Percentage of households by size, composition and age in each gross income decile group

2003-04

based on weighted data

	Lowest ten per cent	Second decile group	Third decile group	Fourth decile group	Fifth decile group	Sixth decile group
Lower boundary of group (£ per week)		124	193	263	351	445
Grossed number of households (thousands)	2,470	2,470	2,470	2,460	2,470	2,460
Number of households in the sample	703	720	729	729	715	719
Size of household						
One person	77	60	37	36	23	17
Two persons	17	25	45	48	42	43
Three persons	4	10	8	8	16	17
Four persons	1	5	5	5	13	15
Five persons	0	1	4	2	3	5
Six or more persons	0	0	0	1	2	3
All sizes	100	100	100	100	100	100
Household composition						
One adult, retired mainly dependent on state pensions[1]	26	15	2	0	0	0
One adult, other retired	18	28	18	13	5	2
One adult, non-retired	33	16	16	22	18	15
One adult, one child	10	3	3	6	3	3
One adult, two or more children	2	9	6	3	4	2
One man and one woman, retired mainly dependent on state pensions[1]	0	8	13	2	0	0
One man and one woman, other retired	0	3	14	22	18	10
One man and one woman, non-retired	6	8	11	16	18	26
One man and one woman, one child	1	2	3	3	7	11
One man and one woman, two children	1	2	3	3	9	11
One man and one woman, three children	0	0	2	1	2	4
Two adults, four or more children	0	0	0	1	0	2
Three adults	1	1	2	2	6	4
Three adults, one or more children	0	0	1	2	3	3
All other households without children	1	2	4	3	5	5
All other households with children	1	1	1	1	1	1
All compositions	100	100	100	100	100	100
Age of household reference person						
15 and under 20 years	1	0	0	0	0	0
20 and under 25 years	5	5	2	3	6	3
25 and under 30 years	6	4	6	6	7	9
30 and under 35 years	5	3	6	8	9	10
35 and under 40 years	6	7	6	7	7	12
40 and under 45 years	6	5	5	8	10	13
45 and under 50 years	5	4	4	5	8	10
50 and under 55 years	6	4	5	6	7	10
55 and under 60 years	9	4	6	8	11	9
60 and under 65 years	8	9	8	10	7	6
65 and under 70 years	7	10	12	13	11	6
70 and under 75 years	8	12	14	10	7	4
75 and under 80 years	11	14	13	8	5	4
80 and under 85 years	11	12	9	5	4	2
85 and under 90 years	5	5	3	3	1	1
90 years or more	1	2	1	0	1	0
All ages	100	100	100	100	100	100

1 Mainly dependent on state pension and not economically active - see appendix B

A54 Percentage of households by size, composition and age in each gross income decile group (cont.)

2003-04

based on weighted data

	Seventh decile group	Eighth decile group	Ninth decile group	Highest ten per cent	All house- holds
Lower boundary of group (£ per week)	558	673	828	1092	
Grossed number of households (thousands)	2,470	2,470	2,470	2,460	24,670
Number of households in the sample	712	687	681	653	7,048
Size of household					
One person	13	9	7	4	28
Two persons	38	37	35	32	36
Three persons	22	21	25	24	15
Four persons	20	23	22	29	14
Five persons	5	8	8	10	5
Six or more persons	2	3	2	3	2
All sizes	100	100	100	100	100
Household composition					
One adult, retired mainly dependent on state pensions[1]	0	0	0	0	4
One adult, other retired	2	1	0	0	9
One adult, non-retired	11	9	7	3	15
One adult, one child	1	1	1	0	3
One adult, two or more children	1	0	1	0	3
One man and one woman, retired mainly dependent on state pensions[1]	0	0	0	0	2
One man and one woman, other retired	5	4	2	1	8
One man and one woman, non-retired	31	28	29	28	20
One man and one woman, one child	10	10	11	10	7
One man and one woman, two children	16	18	13	16	9
One man and one woman, three children	3	4	5	5	3
Two adults, four or more children	1	1	1	1	1
Three adults	10	10	14	13	6
Three adults, one or more children	4	5	7	8	3
All other households without children	3	6	7	10	5
All other households with children	1	3	3	4	2
All compositions	100	100	100	100	100
Age of household reference person					
15 and under 20 years	0	0	0	0	0
20 and under 25 years	3	3	2	1	3
25 and under 30 years	9	7	7	6	7
30 and under 35 years	11	14	11	11	9
35 and under 40 years	15	16	14	16	10
40 and under 45 years	14	15	17	15	11
45 and under 50 years	10	12	15	17	9
50 and under 55 years	11	11	14	15	9
55 and under 60 years	10	10	11	11	9
60 and under 65 years	6	7	4	5	7
65 and under 70 years	4	2	2	1	7
70 and under 75 years	3	3	2	1	6
75 and sender 80 years	1	1	1	0	6
80 and under 85 years	1	1	1	0	5
85 and under 90 years	0	0	0	0	2
90 years or more	0	0	0	0	1
All ages	100	100	100	100	100

1 Mainly dependent on state pension and not economically active - see appendix B

A55 Percentage of households by economic activity status, tenure and socio-economic class in each gross income decile group   2003-04

based on weighted data

	Lowest ten per cent	Second decile group	Third decile group	Fourth decile group	Fifth decile group	Sixth decile group
Lower boundary of group (£ per week)		124	193	263	351	445
Grossed number of households (thousands)	2,470	2,470	2,470	2,460	2,470	2,460
Number of households in the sample	703	720	729	729	715	719
Number of economically active persons in household						
No person	80	79	66	44	27	14
One person	19	19	29	44	51	38
Two persons	2	2	5	10	20	41
Three persons	0	0	0	1	2	5
Four or more persons	0	0	0	0	0	1
All economically active persons	100	100	100	100	100	100
Tenure of dwelling[1]						
Owners						
Owned outright	25	38	42	43	38	29
Buying with a mortgage	6	8	15	24	34	51
All	31	46	57	67	71	79
Social rented from						
Council	34	27	22	12	10	8
Registered social landlord [2]	19	16	11	10	6	3
All	54	43	33	22	16	11
Private rented						
Rent free	2	2	2	1	2	1
Rent paid, unfurnished	9	6	5	6	7	7
Rent paid, furnished	3	2	2	3	3	1
All	15	11	10	11	12	9
All tenures	100	100	100	100	100	100
Socio-economic class						
Higher managerial and professional						
Large employers/higher managerial	1	0	0	0	1	3
Higher professional	2	0	1	2	3	6
Lower managerial and professional	4	4	6	12	16	23
Intermediate	4	3	6	9	9	10
Small employers	5	4	5	6	9	7
Lower supervisory	3	5	4	7	8	11
Semi-routine	13	11	12	12	15	13
Routine	15	11	10	11	10	12
Long-term unemployed[3]	7	4	4	2	1	1
Students	3	1	2	1	2	1
Occupation not stated[4]	44	54	50	37	26	15
All occupational groups	100	100	100	100	100	100

1 See footnotes in Table A34
2 Formerly housing association
3 Includes those who have never worked
4 Includes those who are economically inactive

A55 Percentage of households by economic activity status and tenure in each gross income decile group (cont.) 2003-04
based on weighted data

	Seventh decile group	Eighth decile group	Ninth decile group	Highest ten per cent	All house-holds
Lower boundary of group (£ per week)	558	673	828	1092	
Grossed number of households (thousands)	2,470	2,470	2,470	2,460	24,670
Number of households in the sample	712	687	681	653	7,048
Number of economically active persons in household					
No person	8	4	3	2	33
One person	31	24	16	15	29
Two persons	51	55	57	54	30
Three persons	9	15	17	18	7
Four or more persons	1	2	6	11	2
All economically active persons	100	100	100	100	100
Tenure of dwelling[1]					
Owners					
Owned outright	24	20	20	21	30
Buying with a mortgage	60	66	68	69	40
All	83	85	88	90	70
Social rented from					
Council	4	4	1	0	12
Registered social landlord [2]	3	2	1	0	7
All	6	6	3	1	20
Private rented					
Rent free	1	0	1	0	1
Rent paid, unfurnished	7	4	5	6	6
Rent paid, furnished	2	3	3	3	3
All	10	8	9	9	10
All tenures	100	100	100	100	100
Socio-economic class					
Higher managerial and professional					
Large employers/higher managerial	6	7	11	20	5
Higher professional	7	9	12	23	6
Lower managerial and professional	27	32	38	37	20
Intermediate	9	8	7	4	7
Small employers	8	7	6	7	6
Lower supervisory	15	13	10	4	8
Semi-routine	10	7	6	3	10
Routine	9	9	6	1	9
Long-term unemployed[3]	0	1	0	0	2
Students	1	1	0	0	1
Occupation not stated[4]	8	6	5	2	25
All occupational groups	100	100	100	100	100

1 See footnotes in Table A34
2 Formerly housing association
3 Includes those who have never worked
4 Includes those who are economically inactive

Methodology

Section B1

Description and response rate of the survey

The survey

The Expenditure and Food Survey (EFS) is a voluntary sample survey of private households. The basic unit of the survey is the household. In the 2001-02 survey the EFS adopted the harmonised definition used in other government household surveys: a group of people living at the same address with common housekeeping, that is sharing household expenses such as food and bills, or sharing a living room (see Section B4). The previous definition differed from the harmonised definition by requiring both common housekeeping **and** a shared living room. This resulted in the EFS having slightly more one person households and fewer large households than the other surveys.

Each individual aged 16 or over in the household visited is asked to keep diary records of daily expenditure for two weeks. Information about regular expenditure, such as rent and mortgage payments, is obtained from a household interview along with retrospective information on certain large, infrequent expenditures such as those on vehicles. Since 1998-99 the results have also included information from simplified diaries kept by children aged between 7 and 15. The effects of including children's expenditure were shown in Appendix F of Family Spending for 1998-99 and again for 1999-2000. The analysis is not repeated this year as inclusion of the data is now a standard feature of the survey.

Detailed questions are asked about the income of each adult member of the household. In addition, personal information such as age, sex and marital status is recorded for each household member. Paper versions of the computerised household and income questionnaires can be obtained from ONS at the address given in the Introduction.

The survey has been conducted each year since 1957. The survey is continuous, interviews being spread evenly over the year to ensure that seasonal effects are covered. From time to time changes are made to the information sought. Some changes reflect new forms of expenditure or new sources of income, especially benefits. Others are the result of new requirements by the survey's users. An important example is the re-definition of housing costs for owner occupiers in 1992 (see Section B5).

The sample design

The EFS sample for Great Britain is a multi-stage stratified random sample with clustering. It is drawn from the Small Users file of the Postcode Address File - the Post Office's list of addresses. All Scottish offshore islands and the Isles of Scilly are excluded from the sample because of excessive interview travel costs. Postal sectors (ward size) are the primary sample unit. Six hundred and seventy two postal sectors are randomly selected during the year after being arranged in strata defined by Government Office Regions (sub-divided into metropolitan and non-metropolitan areas) and two 1991 Census variables - socio-economic group and ownership of cars. These were new stratifiers introduced for the 1996-97 survey. The Northern Ireland sample is drawn as a random sample of addresses from the Valuation and Lands Agency list.

Response to the survey

Great Britain

Some 12,096 households are selected each year for the EFS in Great Britain, but it is never possible to get full response. A small number cannot be contacted at all, and in other households one or more members decline to co-operate. Six thousand two hundred and ninety-nine households in Great Britain co-operated fully in the survey in 2003-04, that is they answered the household questionnaire and all adults in the household answered the income questionnaire and kept the expenditure diary. A further 133 households provided sufficient information to be included as valid responses. The overall response rate for the 2003-04 EFS was 58 per cent in Great Britain. This compares with 58 per cent in 2002-03.

Details of response are shown in the following table.

Response in 2003-04 - Great Britain

		No of households or addresses	Percentage of effective sample
i.	Sampled addresses	12,096	-
ii.	Ineligible addresses: businesses, institutions, empty, demolished/derelict	1,103	-
iii.	Extra households (multi-household addresses)	127	-
iv.	Total eligible (i.e. i less ii, plus iii)	11,120	100.0
v.	Co-operating households (which includes 133 partials)	6,432	57.8
vi.	Refusals	3,884	34.9
vii.	Households at which no contact could be obtained	804	7.2

Northern Ireland

In the Northern Ireland survey, the eligible sample was 1,064 households. The number of co-operating households who provided usable data was 616, giving a response rate of 58 per cent. Northern Ireland is over-sampled in order to provide a large enough sample for some separate analysis. The re-weighting procedure compensates for the over-sampling.

The fieldwork

The fieldwork is conducted by the Office for National Statistics (ONS) in Great Britain and by the Northern Ireland Statistics and Research Agency of the Department of Finance and Personnel in Northern Ireland using almost identical questionnaires. Households at the selected addresses are visited and asked to co-operate in the survey. In order to maximise response, interviewers make at least four separate calls, and sometimes many more, at different times of day on households which are difficult to contact. Interviews are conducted by Computer Assisted Personal Interviewing (CAPI) using portable computers. During the interview, information is collected about the household, about certain regular payments such as rent, gas, electricity and telephone accounts, about expenditure on certain large items (for example vehicle purchases over the previous 12 months), and about income. Each individual aged 16 or over in the household keeps a detailed record of expenditure every day for two weeks. Children aged between 7 and 15 are also asked to keep a simplified diary of daily expenditure. In 2003-04 a total of 2,149 children aged between 7 and 15 in responding households in the UK were asked to complete expenditure diaries; 192 or about 8 per cent did not do so. This number includes both refusals and children who had no expenditure during the two weeks. Information provided by all members of the household is kept strictly confidential. If all persons aged 16 and over in the household co-operate, each is subsequently paid £10 for the trouble involved. Children who keep a diary are given a £5 payment.

In the last two months of the 1998-99 survey, as an experiment, a small book of postage stamps was enclosed with the introductory letter sent to every address. It seemed to help with response and the measure has become a permanent feature of the survey. It is difficult to quantify the exact effect on response but the cognitive work that was carried out as part of the Expenditure and Food Survey development indicated that it was having a positive effect.

A new strategy for reissues was adopted in 1999-2000 and has continued since. Addresses where there had been no contact or a refusal, but were judged suitable for reissue, were accumulated to form complete batches consisting only of reissues. The interviewers dealing with them were specially selected and given extra briefing. The information from households converted from non-responding to responding was included with the data for the quarter of the year when the interview was carried out. The increase in response rate, however, was attributed to the original month of issue. In 2003-04 some 1,526 addresses were reissued, of which 134 were converted into responding households, this added 1.2 percentage points to the response rate.

Eligible response

Under EFS rules, a refusal by just one person to respond to the income section of the questionnaire invalidates the response of the whole household. Similarly, a refusal by the household's main shopper to complete the two-week expenditure diary also results in an invalid response.

Proxy Interviews – while questions about general household affairs are put to all household members or to a main household informant, questions about work and income are put to the individual members of the household. Where a member of the household is not present during the household interview, another member of the household (e.g. spouse) may be able to provide information about the absent person. The individual's interview is then identified as a proxy interview.

In 2001-02, the EFS began including households that contained a proxy interview. In that year, 12 per cent of all responding households contained at least one proxy interview. In 2003-04 the percentage of responding households with a proxy interview was also 12 per cent. Analysis of the 2002-03 data revealed that the inclusion of proxy interviews increased response from above average income households. For the 2002-03 survey, the average gross normal weekly household income was some three per cent higher than it would have been if proxy interviews had not been accepted. The analysis showed a similar difference for average total expenditure.

Short Income – all adult members of a household must supply information about their income. This information is quite detailed, and a small number of respondents are reluctant to provide it. For these people, we accept responses to a reduced set of questions, called short income.

From 2001-02, the EFS began including households that contained a short income section. In that year, 0.5 per cent of households contained at least one short income response. In 2003-04, 0.3 per cent did so.

Reliability

Great care is taken in collecting information from households and comprehensive checks are applied during processing, so that errors in recording and processing are minimised. The main factors that affect the reliability of the survey results are sampling variability, non-response bias and some incorrect reporting of certain items of expenditure and income. Measures of sampling variability are given alongside some results in this report and are discussed in detail in Section B3.

The households which decline to respond to the survey tend to differ in some respects from those which co-operate. It is therefore possible that their patterns of expenditure and income also differ. A comparison was made of the households responding in the 1991 FES with those not responding, based on information from the 1991 Census of Population (A comparison of the Census characteristics of respondents and non-respondents to the 1991 FES by K Foster, ONS Survey Methodology Bulletin No. 38, Jan 1996). Results from the study indicate that response was lower than average in Greater London, higher in non-metropolitan areas and that non-response tended to increase with increasing age of the head of the household, up to age 65. Households that contained three or more adults, or where the head was born outside the United Kingdom or was classified to an ethnic minority group, were also more likely than others to be non-responding. Non-response was also above average where the head of the household had no post-school qualifications, was self-employed, or was in a manual social class group. The data are now re-weighted to compensate for the main non-response biases identified from the 1991 Census comparison, as described in Section B6. ONS is currently undertaking a similar comparative exercise, with the 2001 Census data, which will result in an update of the non-response weights.

Checks are included in the CAPI program which are applied to the responses given during the interview. Other procedures are also in place to ensure that users are provided with high quality data. For example, quality control is carried out to ensure that any outliers are genuine, and checks are made on any unusual changes in average spending compared with the previous year.

When aspects of the survey change, rigorous tests are used to ensure the proposed changes are sensible and work both in the field and on the processing system. For example, in 1996-97 an improved set of questions was introduced on income from self-employment. This was developed by focus groups and then tested by piloting before being introduced into the main survey.

The information obtained by the survey does not permit the construction of household accounts in the form of an income-expenditure balance sheet. The definitions of weekly household expenditure and income used are such that it is not to be expected that expenditure and income will balance, either for an individual household or even when averaged over a group of households. Hence, the difference between expenditure and income is not a measure of savings or dis-savings.

Imputation of missing information

Although EFS response is generally based on complete households responding, there are areas in the survey for which missing information is imputed. This falls into two broad categories:

(i)   Specific items of information missing from a response. These missing values are imputed on a case by case basis using other information collected in the interview. The procedure is used, for example, for council tax payments and for interest received on savings.

(ii) Imputation of a complete diary case. Where a response is missing a diary from a household member, this information is imputed using information from respondents with similar characteristics.

Section B2

Uses of the survey

EFS Expenditure Data

Retail Prices Index - The main reason, historically, for instituting a regular survey on expenditure by households has been to provide information on spending patterns for the Retail Prices Index (RPI). The RPI plays a vital role in the uprating of state pensions and welfare benefits and in general economic policy and analysis. The RPI measures the change in the cost of a selection of goods and services representative of the expenditure of the vast majority of households. The pattern of expenditure gradually changes from one year to the next, and the composition of the basket needs to be kept up-to-date. Accordingly, regular information is required on spending patterns and much of this is supplied by the EFS. The expenditure weights for the general RPI need to relate to people within given income limits, for which the EFS is the only source of information.

Consumers' expenditure and GDP - EFS data on spending are an important source used in compiling national estimates of consumers' expenditure which are published regularly in United Kingdom National Accounts (ONS Blue Book). Consumers' expenditure estimates feed into the National Accounts and estimates of GDP. They will also provide the weights for the Harmonised Index of Consumer prices (HICP) which is calculated by each member of the European Union, and for Purchasing Power Parities (PPPs) for international price comparisons. EFS data are also used in the estimation of taxes on expenditure, in particular VAT.

Regional accounts - EFS expenditure information is one of the sources used by ONS to derive regional estimates of consumers' expenditure. It is also used in compiling some of the other estimates for the regional accounts.

Pay Review Bodies governing the salaries of HM Armed Forces and the medical and dental professions receive estimates of the minimum valuation of the benefit of a company car. This is based on EFS data on the cost of buying and running private cars.

The Statistical Office of the European Communities (Eurostat) collates information from family budget surveys conducted by the member states. The EFS is the UK's contribution to this. The UK is one of only a few countries with such a regular, continuous and detailed survey.

Other Government uses - The Department of Trade and Industry and the Department for Transport, both use EFS expenditure data in their own fields, e.g. - relating to energy, housing, cars and transport. Several other government publications include EFS expenditure data, such as *Social Trends, Regional Trends* and the *Social Focus* series.

Non-Government uses - There are also numerous users outside Central Government, including academic researchers and business and market researchers.

EFS Income Data

Redistribution of income - EFS information on income and expenditure is used to study how Government taxes and benefits affect household income. The Government's interdepartmental tax benefit model is based on the EFS and enables the economic effects of policy measures to be analysed across households. This model is used by HM Treasury, Inland Revenue and HM Customs and Excise to estimate the impact on different households of possible changes in taxes and benefits.

Non-Government users - As with the expenditure data, EFS income data are also studied extensively outside Government. In particular, academic researchers in the economic and social science areas of many universities use the EFS. For example the Institute for Fiscal Studies uses EFS data in research it carries out both for Government and on its own account to inform public debate.

Other EFS Data

The Department for Environment, Food and Rural Affairs (DEFRA) publishes separate reports using EFS data on food expenditure to estimate consumption and nutrient intake.

The Office for National Statistics uses the information on access to the Internet in a quarterly analysis of Internet access. The Department for Transport uses EFS data to monitor and forecast levels of car ownership and use, and in studies on the effects of motoring taxes.

<u>Note</u>: **Great care is taken to ensure complete confidentiality of information and to protect the identity of EFS households. Only anonymised data are supplied to users.**

Section B3

Standard errors and estimates of precision

Because the EFS is a survey of a sample of households and not of the whole population, the results are liable to differ to some degree from those that would have been obtained if every single household had been covered. Some of the differences will be systematic, in that lower proportions of certain types of household respond than of others. That aspect is discussed in Section B1 and B6. This section discusses the effect of sampling variability, the differences in expenditure and income between the households in the sample and in the whole population that arise from random chance. The degree of possible error will depend on the sample size and how widely particular categories of expenditure (or income) vary between households. This "sampling error" is smallest for the average expenditure of large groups of households on items purchased frequently and when the level of spending does not vary greatly between households. Conversely it is largest for small groups of households, and for items purchased infrequently or for which expenditure varies considerably between households. A numerical measure of the likely magnitude of such differences (between the sample estimate and the value of the entire population) is provided by the quantity known as the standard error.

The calculation of standard errors takes into account the fact that the EFS sample is drawn in two stages, first a sample of areas (primary sampling units) then a sample of addresses within each of these areas. The main features of the sample design are described in Section B1of this Appendix. The calculation also takes account of the effect of weighting. The two-stage sample increases sampling variability slightly, but the weighting reduces it for some items.

Standard errors for detailed expenditure items are presented in relative terms in **Table A1** (standard error as a percentage of the average to which it refers). As the calculation of full standard errors is complex, this is the only table where they are shown. **Tables B1** and **B2** in this section show the design factor (DEFT), a measure of the efficiency of the survey's sample design. The DEFT is calculated by dividing the 'full' standard error by the standard error that would have applied if the survey had used a simple random sample ('simple method').

Table B1
Percentage standard errors of expenditure of households and number of recording households   2003-04

Commodity or service	Weighted average weekly household expenditure (£)	Percentage standard error Simple method	Design factor (DEFT)	Percentage standard error Full method	Households recording expenditure Recording households in sample	Percentage of all households
All expenditure groups	**356.20**	*1.0*	**1.0**	*1.0*	7,048	*100*
Food and non-alcoholic drinks	43.50	*0.8*	1.0	*0.8*	7,007	*99*
Alcoholic drink and tobacco	11.70	*1.9*	1.1	*2.0*	4,597	*65*
Clothing and footwear	22.70	*2.1*	1.0	*2.1*	4,895	*69*
Housing, fuel and power	39.00	*1.6*	1.0	*1.7*	7,018	*100*
Household goods and services	31.30	*2.8*	0.9	*2.6*	6,558	*93*
Health	5.00	*6.6*	1.0	*6.5*	3,604	*51*
Transport	60.70	*2.5*	1.1	*2.6*	6,200	*88*
Communication	11.20	*1.4*	1.2	*1.8*	6,763	*96*
Recreation and culture	57.30	*1.9*	1.0	*1.9*	6,988	*99*
Education	5.20	*9.0*	1.0	*9.0*	647	*9*
Restaurants and hotels	34.90	*1.4*	1.2	*1.6*	6,337	*90*
Miscellaneous	33.60	*1.9*	1.0	*1.9*	6,914	*98*

Table B2
Percentage standard errors of income of households and number of recording households   2003-04

Source of income	Weighted average weekly household income (£)	Percentage standard error Simple method	Design factor (DEFT)	Percentage standard error Full method	Households recording income Recording households in sample	Percentage of all households
Gross household income	**570**	*1.2*	**1.1**	*1.3*	7,048	*100*
Wages and salaries	384	*1.6*	1.1	*1.7*	4,277	*61*
Self-employment	50	*6.6*	1.1	*7.1*	797	*11*
Investments	17	*5.6*	1.0	*5.5*	3,949	*56*
Annuities and pensions (other than social security benefits)	41	*3.2*	0.9	*2.8*	1,960	*28*
Social security benefits	72	*1.3*	0.8	*1.0*	5,037	*71*
Other sources	6	*6.4*	1.1	*7.0*	1,218	*17*

Using the standard errors – confidence intervals

A good way of using standard errors is to calculate 95% confidence intervals from them. Simplifying a little, these can be taken to mean that there is only a 5% chance that the true population value lies outside that confidence interval. The 95% confidence interval is calculated as 1.96 times the standard error on either side of the mean. For example the average expenditure on alcoholic drink and tobacco is £11.70 and the corresponding percentage standard error (full method) is 2.0%. The amount either side of the mean for 95% confidence is then:

1.96 x (2.0 ÷100) x £11.70 = £0.50 (rounded to nearest 10p)
Lower limit is 11.70 – 0.50 = £11.30 (rounded to nearest 10p)
Upper limit is 11.70 + 0.50 = £12.20 (rounded to nearest 10p)

Similar calculations can be carried out for other estimates of expenditure and income. The 95% confidence intervals for main expenditure categories are given in **Table B3**.

Table B3
95 per cent confidence intervals for average household expenditure   2003-04

Commodity or service	Weighted average weekly household expenditure (£)	95% confidence interval	
		Lower limit	Upper limit
All expenditure groups	**356.20**	**349.10**	**363.40**
Food and non-alcoholic drinks	43.50	42.90	44.20
Alcoholic drink and tobacco	11.70	11.30	12.20
Clothing and footwear	22.70	21.80	23.70
Housing, fuel and power	39.00	37.70	40.30
Household goods and services	31.30	29.70	32.90
Health	5.00	4.40	5.70
Transport	60.70	57.60	63.80
Communication	11.20	10.80	11.60
Recreation and culture	57.30	55.20	59.40
Education	5.20	4.30	6.20
Restaurants and hotels	34.90	33.80	36.00
Miscellaneous	33.60	32.40	34.90

Calculation of standard errors

Simple method

This formula treats the EFS sample as though it had arisen from a much simpler design with no multi-stage sampling, stratification, nor differential sampling and no nonresponse weights. The weights are used but only to estimate the true population standard deviation in what is, in fact, a weighted design. The method of calculation is as follows: Let n be the total number of responding households in the survey, x_r the expenditure on a particular item of the r-th household, w_r be the weight attached to household r, and $\bar{x}$ the average expenditure per household on that item (averaged over the n households). Then the standard error $\bar{x}$, $sesrs$ is given by:

$$sesrs = \sqrt{\frac{\sum_{r=1}^{n} w_r (x_r - \overline{x})^2}{(n-1)\sum_{r=1}^{n} w_r}}$$

Full method

In fact, the sample in Great Britain is a multi-stage, stratified, random sample described further in Section B1. First a sample of areas, the Primary Sampling Units (PSUs), is drawn from an ordered list. Then within each PSU a random sample of households is drawn. In Northern Ireland, however, the sample is drawn in a single stage and there is no clustering. The results are also weighted for non-response and calibrated to match the population separately by sex, by 5-year age ranges and by region, as described in section B6.

The method for calculating complex standard errors for the weighted estimates used on this survey is quite complex. First, we apply methods that take account of the clustering, stratification and differential sampling (and initial non-response weights) used in the design. Then we modify these to allow for the calibration weighting used on the survey. The exact formulae also depend on whether we are estimating standard errors for an estimated total or a mean or proportion. Here we outline the method for a total.

Consecutive PSUs in the ordered list are first grouped up into pairs, or triples at the end of a regional stratum. The standard error of a weighted total is estimated by:

$$sedes = \sqrt{\sum_h \frac{k_h}{k_h - 1} \sum_i (x_{hi} - \overline{x}_h)^2}$$

where the h denotes the stratum (PSU pairs or triples), k_h is the number of PSUs in the stratum h (either 2 or 3), the x_{hi} is the weighted total in PSU i and the $\overline{x}_h$ is the mean of these totals in stratum h. Further details of this method of estimating sampling errors are described in *A sampling Errors Manual* (B Butcher and D Elliot, ONS 1987).

The effect of the calibration weighting is calculated using a jackknife linearisation estimator. It uses the formula given above but with each household's expenditure, x_i, replaced by a residual from a linear regression of expenditure on the number of people in each household in each of the regions and age by sex categories used in the weighting.

The formulae have been expressed in terms of expenditures on a particular item, but of course they can also be applied to expenditures on groups of items, commodity groups and incomes from particular sources.

Section B4

Definitions

Major changes in definitions since 1991 are described in Section B5. Changes made between 1980 and 1990 are summarised in Appendix E of Family Spending 1994-95. For earlier changes see Annex 5 of Family Expenditure Survey 1980.

Household

A household comprises one person or a group of people who have the accommodation as their only or main residence and (for a group):

share the living accommodation, that is a living room or sitting room

or share meals together or have common housekeeping

Resident domestic servants are included. The members of a household are not necessarily related by blood or marriage. As the survey covers only private households, people living in hostels, hotels, boarding houses or institutions are excluded. Households are not excluded if some or all members are not British subjects, but no attempt is made to obtain information from households containing members of the diplomatic service of another country or members of the United States armed forces. Nor are attempts made to obtain information from Roman Catholic priests living in accommodation provided by the parish church.

Retired households

Retired households are those where the household reference person is retired. The household reference person is defined as retired if 65 years of age or more and male or 60 years of age or more and female, and economically inactive. Hence if, for example, a male household reference person is over 65 years of age, but working part-time or waiting to take up a part-time job, this household would not be classified as a retired household. For analysis purposes two categories are used in this report:

a.   "A retired household mainly dependent upon state pensions" is one in which at least three quarters of the total income of the household is derived from national insurance retirement and similar pensions, including housing and other benefits paid in supplement to or instead of such pensions. The term "national insurance retirement and similar pensions" includes national insurance disablement and war disability pensions, and income support in conjunction with these disability payments.

b.   "Other retired households" are retired households which do not fulfil the income conditions of "retired household mainly dependent upon state pensions" because more than a quarter of the household's income derives from occupational retirement pensions and/or income from investments, annuities etc.

Household reference person (HRP)

From 2001-02, the concept of household reference person (HRP) was adopted on all government-sponsored surveys, in place of head of household. The household reference person is the householder, i.e. the person who:

a.   owns the household accommodation, or
b.   is legally responsible for the rent of the accommodation, or
c.   has the household accommodation as an emolument or perquisite, or
d.   has the household accommodation by virtue of some relationship to the owner who is not a member of the household.

If there are joint householders the household reference person will be the one with the higher income. If the income is the same, then the eldest householder is taken.

A key difference between household reference person and head of household is that the household reference person must always be a householder, whereas the head of household was always the husband, who might not even be a householder himself.

Members of household

In most cases the members of co-operating households are easily identified as the people who satisfy the conditions in the definition of a household, above, and are present during the record-keeping period. However difficulties of definition arise where people are temporarily away from the household or else spend their time between two residences. The following rules apply in deciding whether or not such persons are members of the household:

a.   married persons living and working away from home for any period are included as members provided they consider the sampled address to be their main residence; in general, other people (e.g. relatives, friends, boarders) who are either temporarily absent or who spend their time between the sampled address and another address, are included as members if they consider the sampled address to be their main residence. However, there are exceptions which override the subjective main residence rule:

i.   Children under 16 away at school are included as members;

ii.   Older persons receiving education away from home, including children aged 16 and 17, are excluded unless they are at home for all or most of the record-keeping period.

iii.   Visitors staying temporarily with the household and others who have been in the household for only a short time are treated as members -provided they will be staying with the household for at least one month from the start of record-keeping.

Household composition

A consequence of these definitions is that household compositions quoted in this report include some households where certain members are temporarily absent. For example, "one adult and children" households will contain a few households where one parent is temporarily away from home.

Adult

In the report, persons who have reached the age of 18 or who are married are classed as adults.

Children

In the report, persons who are under 18 years of age, in full-time education and have never been married are classed as children.

However, in the definition of clothing, clothing for persons aged 16 years and over is classified as clothing for men and women; clothing for those aged five but under 16 as clothing for boys and girls; and clothing for those under five as babies clothing.

Spenders

Members of households who are aged 16 or more, excluding those who for special reasons are not capable of keeping diary record-books, are described as spenders.

Economically active

These are persons aged 16 or over who fall into the following categories:

a.   *Employees at work* - those who at the time of interview were working full-time or part-time as employees or were away from work on holiday. Part-time work is defined as normally working 30 hours a week or less (excluding meal breaks) including regularly worked overtime.

b.   *Employees temporarily away from work* - those who at the time of interview had a job but were absent because of illness or accident, temporary lay-off, strike etc.

c.   *Government supported training schemes* - those participating in government programmes and schemes who in the course of their participation receive training, such as Employment Training, including those who are also employees in employment.

d.   *Self-employed* - those who at the time of interview said they were self-employed.

e.   *Unemployed* - those who at time of interview were out of employment, and have sought work within the last four weeks and were available to start work within two weeks, or were waiting to start a job already obtained.

f.   *Unpaid family workers* - those working unpaid for their own or a relative's business. In this report, unpaid family workers are included under economically inactive in analyses by economic status (Tables A19 and A48) because insufficient information is available to assign them to an economic status group.

Economically inactive

a.   *Retired* - persons who have reached national insurance retirement age (60 and over for women, 65 and over for men) and are not economically active.

b.   *Unoccupied* - persons under national insurance retirement age who are not working, nor actively seeking work. This category includes certain self-employed persons such as mail order agents and baby-sitters who are not classified as economically active.

In this report, unpaid family workers are classified as economically inactive in analyses by economic status, although they are economically active by definition. This is because insufficient information is available to assign them to an economic status group.

National Statistics Socio-economic classification (NS-SEC)

From 2001, the National Statistics Socio-economic classification (NS-SEC) was adopted for all official surveys, in place of Social Class based on Occupation and Socio-economic group. NS-SEC is itself based on the Standard Occupational Classification 2000 (SOC2000) and details of employment status. Although NS-SEC is an occupationally based classification, there are procedures for classifying those not in work.

The main categories used for analysis in Family Spending are:

1 Higher managerial and professional occupations, sub-divided into:

    1.1 Large employers and higher managerial occupations

    1.2 Higher professional occupations

2 Lower managerial and professional occupations

3 Intermediate occupations

4 Small employers and own account workers

5 Lower supervisory and technical occupations

6 Semi-routine occupations

7 Routine occupations

8 Never worked and long-term unemployed

9 Students

10 Occupation not stated

11 Not classifiable for other reasons

The long-term unemployed are defined as those unemployed and seeking work for 12 months or more. Members of the armed forces, who were assigned to a separate category in Social Class, are included within the NS-SEC classification. Individuals that have retired within the last 12 months are classified according to their employment. Other retired individuals are assigned to the 'Not classifiable for other reasons' category.

Regions

These are the Government Office Regions as formed in 1994. See section B4 for more details.

Urban and rural areas

This classification is based on the population of the continuous built-up areas, irrespective of administrative boundaries derived by the Department for Transport, Local Government and the Regions (DTLR) based on the 1991 Census. Note that the metropolitan built-up areas are not the same as the metropolitan administrative districts. They exclude any rural areas within the metropolitan districts and include any built up areas adjoining them.

Expenditure

Any definition of expenditure is to some extent arbitrary, and the inclusion of certain types of payment is a matter of convenience or convention depending on the purpose for which the information is to be used. In the tables in this report, total expenditure represents current expenditure on goods and services. Total expenditure, defined in this way, excludes those recorded payments which are really savings or investments (e.g. purchases of national savings certificates, life assurance premiums, contributions to pension funds). Similarly, income tax payments, national insurance contributions, mortgage capital repayments and other payments for major additions to dwellings are excluded. Expenditure data are collected in the diary record-book and in the household schedule. Informants are asked to record in the diary any payments made during the 14 days of record-keeping, whether or not the goods or services paid for have been received. Certain types of expenditure which are usually regular though infrequent, such as insurance, licences and season tickets, and the periods to which they relate, are recorded in the household schedule as well as regular payments such as utility bills.

The cash purchase of motor vehicles is also entered in the household schedule. In addition, expenditure on some items purchased infrequently (thereby being subject to high sampling errors) has been recorded in the household schedule using a retrospective recall period of either three or 12 months. These items include carpets, furniture, holidays and some housing costs. In order to avoid duplication, all payments shown in the diary record-book which relate to items listed in the household or income schedules are omitted in the analysis of the data irrespective of whether there is a corresponding entry on the latter schedules. Amounts paid in respect of periods longer than a week are converted to weekly values.

Expenditure tables in this report show the 12 main commodity groups of spending and these are broken down into items which are numbered hierarchically (see section B5 which details a major change to the coding frame used from 2001-02). Table A1 shows a further breakdown in the items themselves into components which can be separately identified. The items are numbered as in the main expenditure tables and against each item or component are shown the average weekly household expenditure and percentage standard error.

Qualifications which apply to this concept of expenditure are described in the following paragraphs:

a. *Goods supplied from a household's own shop or farm*
   Spenders are asked to record and give the value of goods obtained from their own shop or farm, even if the goods are withdrawn from stock for personal use without payment. The value is included as expenditure.

b. *Hire purchase and credit sales agreements, and transactions financed by loans repaid by instalments*
   Expenditure on transactions under hire purchase or credit sales agreements, or financed by loans repaid by instalments, consists of all instalments which are still being paid at the date of interview, together with down payments on commodities acquired within the preceding three months. These two components (divided by the periods covered) provide the weekly averages which are included in the expenditure on the separate items given in the tables in this report.

c. *Club payments and budget account payments, instalments through mail order firms and similar forms of credit transaction*
   When goods are purchased by forms of credit other than hire purchase and credit sales agreement, the expenditure on them may be estimated either from the amount of the instalment which is paid or from the value of the goods which are acquired. Since the particular commodities to which the instalment relates may not be known, details of goods ordered through clubs, etc. during the month prior to the date of interview are recorded in the household schedule. The weekly equivalent of the value of the goods is included in the expenditure on the separate items given in the tables in this report. This procedure has the advantage of enabling club transactions to be related to specific articles. Although payments into clubs, etc. are shown in the diary record-book, these entries are excluded from expenditure estimates.

d. *Credit card transactions*
   From 1988 purchases made by credit card or charge card have been recorded in the survey on an *acquisition* basis rather than the formerly used payment basis. Thus, if a spender

acquired an item (by use of credit/charge card) during the two week survey period, the value of the item would be included as part of expenditure in that period whether or not any payment was made in this period to the credit card account. Payments made to the card account are ignored. However any payment of credit/charge card *interest* is included in expenditure if made in the two week period.

e. *Income Tax*

Amounts of income tax deducted under the PAYE scheme or paid directly by those who are employers or self-employed are recorded (together with information about tax refunds). For employers and the self-employed the amounts comprise the actual payments made in the previous twelve months and may not correspond to the tax due on the income arising in that period, e.g. if no tax has been paid but is due or if tax payments cover more than one financial year. However, the amounts of tax deducted at source from some of the items which appear in the Income Schedule are not directly available. Estimates of the tax paid on bank and building society interest and amounts deducted from dividends on stocks and shares are therefore made by applying the appropriate rates of tax. In the case of income tax paid at source on pensions and annuities, similar adjustments are made. These estimates mainly affect the relatively few households with high incomes from interest and dividends, and households including someone receiving a pension from previous employment.

f. *Rented dwellings*

Expenditure on rented dwellings is taken as the sum of expenditure on rent, rates, council tax, water rates etc. For local authority tenants the expenditure is gross rent less any rebate (including rebate received in the form of housing benefit), and for other tenants gross rent less any rent allowance received under statutory schemes including the Housing Benefit Scheme. Rebate on Council Tax or rates (Northern Ireland) is deducted from expenditure on Council Tax or rates. Receipts from sub-letting part of the dwelling are not deducted from housing costs but appear (net of the expenses of the sub-letting) as investment income. Average payments by households renting accommodation for repairs, maintenance and decorations are shown separately in the estimates of expenditure by such households in table A34 which gives housing expenditure by tenure type. Accommodation rented from a housing association is shown separately.

g. *Rent-free dwellings*

Rent-free dwellings are those owned by someone outside the household and where either no rent is charged or the rent is paid by someone outside the household. Households whose rent is paid directly to the landlord by the DSS do not live rent-free. Payments for Council Tax, water rates etc., are regarded as the cost of housing. Rebate on rates (Northern Ireland)/Council Tax/water rates(Scotland) (including rebate received in the form of housing benefit), is deducted from expenditure on rates/Council Tax/water rates. Receipts from sub-letting part of the dwelling are not deducted from housing costs but appear (net of the expenses of the sub-letting) as investment income.

h. *Owner-occupied dwellings*

In the EFS payments for water rates, ground rent, fuel, maintenance and repair of the dwelling, and other miscellaneous services related to the dwelling etc., are regarded as the cost of housing. Receipts from letting part of the dwelling are not deducted from housing costs but appear (net of the expenses of the letting) as investment income. Mortgage capital repayments and amounts paid for the outright purchase of the dwelling or for major structural alterations are not included as housing expenditure, but are entered under "Other items recorded", as are Council Tax, rates (Northern Ireland), and mortgage interest payments. Structural insurance is included in Miscellaneous goods and services.

i.   *Second-hand goods and part-exchange transactions*

The survey expenditure data are based on information about actual payments and therefore include payments for second-hand goods and part-exchange transactions. New payments only are included for part-exchange transactions, i.e. the costs of the goods obtained less the amounts allowed for the goods which are traded in. Receipts for goods sold or traded in are not included in income.

j.   *Business expenses*

The survey covers only private households and is concerned with payments made by members of households as private individuals. Spenders are asked to state whether expenditure which has been recorded on the schedules includes amounts which will be refunded as expenses from a business or organisation or which will be entered as business expenses for income tax purposes, e.g. rent, telephone charges, travelling expenses, meals out. Any such amounts are deducted from the recorded expenditure.

Income

The standard concept of income in the survey is, as far as possible, that of gross weekly cash income current at the time of interview, i.e. before the deduction of income tax actually paid, national insurance contributions and other deductions at source. However, for a few tables a concept of disposable income is used, defined as gross weekly cash income less the statutory deductions and payments of income tax (taking refunds into account) and national insurance contributions. Analysis in Chapter 3 of this volume and some other analyses of EFS data use "equivalisation" of incomes - i.e. adjustment of household income to allow for the different size and composition of each household. For more information see Chapter 3 of this volume. The cash levels of certain items of income (and expenditure) recorded in the survey by households receiving supplementary benefit were affected by the Housing Benefit Scheme introduced in stages from November 1982. From 1984 housing expenditure is given on a strictly net basis and all rent/council tax rebates and allowances and housing benefit are excluded from gross income.

Although information about most types of income is obtained on a current basis, some data, principally income from investment and from self-employment, are estimated over a twelve-month period.

The following are excluded from the assessment of income:

a.   money received by one member of the household from another (e.g. housekeeping money, dress allowance, children's pocket money) other than wages paid to resident domestic servants;

b.   withdrawals of savings, receipts from maturing insurance policies, proceeds from sale of financial and other assets (e.g. houses, cars, furniture, etc.), winnings from betting, lump-sum gratuities and windfalls such as legacies;

c.   the value of educational grants and scholarships not paid in cash;

d.   the value of income in kind, including the value of goods received free and the abatement in cost of goods received at reduced prices, and of bills paid by someone who is not a member of the household;

e.   loans and money received in repayment of loans.

Details are obtained of the income of each member of the household. The income of the household is taken to be the sum of the incomes of all its members. The information does not relate to a common or a fixed time period. Items recorded for periods greater than a week are converted to a weekly value.

Particular points relating to some components of income are as follows:

a.   *Wages and salaries of employees*
The normal gross wages or salaries of employees are taken to be their earnings. These are calculated by adding to the normal "take home" pay amounts deducted at source, such as income tax payments, national insurance contributions and other deductions, e.g. payments into firm social clubs, superannuation schemes, works transport, benevolent funds etc. Employees are asked to give the earnings actually received including bonuses and commission the last time payment was made and, if different, the amount usually received. It is the amount usually received which is regarded as the normal take-home pay. Additions are made so as to include in normal earnings the value of occasional payments, such as bonuses or commissions received quarterly or annually. One of the principal objects in obtaining data on income is to enable expenditure to be classified in ranges of normal income. Average household expenditure is likely to be based on the long-term expectations of the various members of the household as to their incomes rather than be altered by short-term changes affecting individuals. Hence if employees have been away from work without pay for 13 weeks or less they are regarded as continuing to receive their normal earnings instead of social security benefits, such as unemployment or sickness benefit, that they may be receiving. Otherwise, normal earnings are disregarded and current short-term social security benefits taken instead. Wages and salaries include any earnings from subsidiary employment as an employee and the earnings of HM Forces.

b.   *Income from self-employment*
Income from self-employment covers any personal income from employment other than as an employee; for example, as a sole trader, professional or other person working on his own account or in partnership, including subsidiary work on his own account by a person whose main job is as an employee. It is measured from estimates of income or trading profits, after deduction of business expenses but before deduction of tax, over the most recent twelve-month period for which figures can be given. Should either a loss have been made or no profit, income would be taken as the amounts drawn from the business for own use or as any other income received from the job or business. Persons working as mail order agents or baby-sitters, with no other employment, have been classified as unoccupied rather than as self-employed, and the earnings involved have been classified as earnings from "other sources" rather than self-employment income.

c.   *Income from investment*

Income from investments or from property, other than that in which the household is residing, is the amount received during the twelve months immediately prior to the date of the initial interview. It includes receipts from sub-letting part of the dwelling (net of the expenses of the sub-letting). If income tax has been deducted at source the gross amount is estimated by applying a conversion factor during processing.

d.   *Social security benefits*

Income from social security benefits does not include the short-term payments such as unemployment or sickness benefit received by an employee who has been away from work for 13 weeks or less, and who is therefore regarded as continuing to receive his normal earnings as described on page 190.

Quantiles

The quantiles of a distribution, e.g. of household expenditure or income, divide it into a number of equal parts; each of which contains the same number of households.

For example, the median of a distribution divides it into two equal parts, so that half the households in a distribution of household income will have income more than the median, and the other half will have income less than the median. Similarly, quartiles, quintiles and deciles divide the distribution into four, five and ten equal parts respectively.

Most of the analysis in Family Spending is done in terms of quintile groups and decile groups.

In the calculation of quantiles for this report, zero values are counted as part of the distribution.

Income headings
Headings used for identifying 2003-04 income information

	Source of income	
References in tables	Components separately identified	Explanatory notes
a. Wages and salaries	Normal "take-home" pay from main employment "Take-home" pay from subsidiary employment Employees' income tax deduction Employees' National Insurance contribution Superannuation contributions deducted from pay Other deductions	(i) In the calculation of household income in this report, where an employee has been away from work without pay for 13 weeks or less his normal wage or salary has been used in estimating his total income instead of social security benefits, such as unemployment or sickness benefits that he may have received. Otherwise such benefits are used in estimating total income (see notes at reference e) (ii) Normal income from wages and salaries is estimated by adding to the normal "take-home" pay deductions made at source last time paid, together with the weekly value of occasional additions to wages and salaries (see page 187). (iii) The components of wages and salaries for which figures are separately available amount in total to the normal earnings of employees, regardless of the operation of the 13 week rule in note (i) above. Thus the sum of the components listed here does not in general equal the wages and salaries figure in tables of this report.
b. Self-employment	Income from business or profession, including subsidiary self-employment	The earnings or profits of a trade or profession, after deduction of business expenses but before deduction of tax
c. Investments	Interest on building society shares and deposits Interest on bank deposits and savings accounts including National Savings Bank Interest on ISAs Interest on TESSAs Interest on Gilt-edged stock and War Loans Interest and dividends from stocks, shares, bonds, trusts, PEPs, debentures and other securities Rent or income from property, after deducting expenses but inclusive of income tax (including receipts from letting or sub-letting part of own residence, net of the expenses of the letting or sub-letting). Other unearned Income	

d. Annuities and pensions, other than social security	Annuities and income from trust or covenant Pensions from previous employers Personal pensions	
e. Social security benefits	Child benefit Guardian's allowance Invalid care allowance Retirement pension (National Insurance) or old person's pension Pension credit Widow's pension or widowed mother's allowance (NI) War disablement pension or war widow's pension Severe disablement allowance Care component of disability living allowance Mobility component of disability living allowance Attendance allowance Job seekers allowance, contributions based Job seekers allowance, income based Income support Working tax credit Child tax credit Incapacity benefit Statutory sick pay (from employer) Industrial injury disablement benefit Maternity allowance Statutory maternity pay Any other benefit including lump sums and grants Social security benefits excluded from income calculation by 13 week rule	i. The calculation of household income in this report takes account of the 13 week rule described at reference a, note (i) ii. The components of social security benefits for which figures are separately available amount in total to the benefits received in the week before interview. That is to say, they include amounts that are discounted from the total by the operation of the 13 week rule in note i. Thus the sum of the components listed here differs from the total of social security benefits used in the income tables of this report. iii Housing Benefit is treated as a reduction in housing costs and not as income
f. Other sources	Married person's allowance from husband/wife temporarily away from home Alimony or separation allowances; allowances for foster children, allowances from members of the Armed Forces or Merchant Navy, or any other money from friends or relatives, other than husband outside the household Benefits from trade unions, friendly societies etc., other than pensions Value of meal vouchers Earnings from intermittent or casual work over twelve months, not included in a or b above Student loans and money scholarships received by persons aged 16 and over and aged under 16. Other income of children under 16	e.g. from spare-time jobs or income from trusts or investments

STANDARD STATISTICAL REGION	COUNTY*	GOVERNMENT OFFICE REGION
NORTH	Cleveland* Durham Northumberland Tyne and Wear	NORTH EAST
	Cumbria	
NORTH WEST	Cheshire Greater Manchester Lancashire Merseyside	NORTH WEST
YORKSHIRE AND HUMBERSIDE	Humberside* North Yorkshire* South Yorkshire West Yorkshire	YORKSHIRE AND THE HUMBER
EAST MIDLANDS	Derbyshire Leicestershire Lincolnshire Northamptonshire Nottinghamshire	EAST MIDLANDS
WEST MIDLANDS	Hereford and Worcester Shropshire Staffordshire Warwickshire West Midlands	WEST MIDLANDS
EAST ANGLIA	Cambridgeshire Norfolk Suffolk	EAST OF ENGLAND
	Bedfordshire Essex Hertfordshire	
	Greater London	LONDON
SOUTH EAST	Berkshire Buckinghamshire East Sussex Hampshire Isle of Wight Kent Oxfordshire Surrey West Sussex	SOUTH EAST
SOUTH WEST	Avon* Cornwall Devon Dorset Gloucestershire Somerset Wiltshire	SOUTH WEST

* Counties prior to local government reorganisation

Section B5

Changes in definitions, 1991 to 2003-04

1991

No significant changes.

1992

Housing – Imputed rent for owner occupiers and households in rent-free accommodation was discontinued. For owner occupiers this had been the rent they would have had pay themselves to live in the property they own, and for households in rent-free accommodation it was the rent they would normally have had to pay. Up to 1990 these amounts were counted both as income and as a housing cost. Mortgage interest payments were counted as a housing cost for the first time in 1991.

1993

Council Tax - Council Tax was introduced to replace the Community Charge in Great Britain from April 1993.

1994-95

New expenditure items - The definition of expenditure was extended to include two items previously shown under "other payments recorded". These were:

        gambling payments;

        mortgage protection premiums.

Expenditure classifications - A new classification system for expenditures was introduced in April 1994. The system is hierarchical and allows more detail to be preserved than the previous system. New categories of expenditure were introduced and are shown in detail in table 7.1. The 14 main groups of expenditure were retained, but there were some changes in the content of these groups.

Gambling Payments - data on gambling expenditure and winnings are collected in the expenditure diary. Previously these were excluded from the definition of household expenditure used in the FES. The data are shown as memoranda items under the heading "Other payments recorded" on both gross and net bases. The net basis corresponds approximately to the treatment of gambling in the National Accounts. The introduction of the National Lottery stimulated a reconsideration of this treatment. From April 1994, (gross) gambling payments have been included as expenditure in "Leisure Services". Gambling winnings continued to be noted as a memorandum item under "Other items recorded". They are treated as windfall income. They do not form a part of normal household income, nor are they subtracted from gross gambling payments. This treatment is in line with the PRODCOM classification of the Statistical Office of the European Communities (SOEC) for expenditure in household budget surveys.

1995-96

Geographical overage - The FES geographical coverage was extended to mainland Scotland north of the Caledonian Canal.

Under 16s diaries - Two week expenditure diaries for 7-15 year olds were introduced following three feasibility pilot studies which found that children of that age group were able to cope with the task of keeping a two week expenditure record. Children are asked to record everything they buy with their own money but to exclude items bought with other people's money. Purchases are coded according to the same coding categories as adult diaries except for meals and snacks away from home which are coded as school meals, hot meals and snacks, and cold meals and snacks. Children who keep a diary are given a £5 incentive payment. A refusal to keep an under 16's diary does not invalidate the household from inclusion in the survey.

Pocket money given to children is still recorded separately in adult diaries; and money paid by adults for school meals and school travel is recorded in the Household Questionnaire. Double counting is eliminated at the processing stage.

Tables in Family Spending reports did not include the information from the children's diaries until the 1998-99 report. Appendix F in the 1998-99 and 1999-2000 reports show what difference the inclusion made.

1996-97

Self-employment - The way in which information about income from self-employment is collected was substantially revised in 1996-97 following various tests and pilot studies. The quality of such data was increased but this may have lead to a discontinuity. Full details are shown the Income Questionnaire, available from the address in the introduction.

Cable/satellite television - Information on cable and satellite subscriptions is now collected from the household questionnaire rather than from the diary, leading to more respondents reporting this expenditure.

Mobile phones - Expenditure on mobile phones was previously collected through the diary. From 1996/97 this has been included in the questionnaire.

Job seekers allowance (JSA) - Introduced in October 1996 as a replacement for Unemployment Benefit and any Income Support associated with the payment of Unemployment Benefit. Receipt of JSA is collected with NI Unemployment Benefit and with Income Support. In both cases the number of weeks a respondent has been in receipt of these benefits is taken as the number of weeks receiving JSA in the last 12 months and before that period the number of weeks receiving Unemployment Benefit/Income Support.

Retrospective recall - The period over which information is requested has been extended from 3 to 12 months for vehicle purchase and sale. Information on the purchase of car and motorcycle spare parts is no longer collected by retrospective recall. Instead expenditure on these items is collected through the diary.

State benefits - The lists of benefits specifically asked about was reviewed in 1996/97. See the Income Questionnaire for more information.

Sample stratifiers - New stratifiers were introduced in 1996/97 based on standard regions, socio-economic group and car ownership.

Government Office Regions - Regional analyses are now presented using the Government Office Regions (GORs) formed in 1994. Previously all regional analyses used Standard Statistical Regions (SSRs). For more information see Appendix F in the 1996-97 report.

1997-98

Bank/Building society service charges - Collection of information on service charges levied by banks has been extended to include building societies.

Payments from unemployment/redundancy insurances - Information is now collected on payments received from private unemployment and redundancy insurance policies. This information is then incorporated into the calculation of income from other sources.

Retired households - The definition of retired households has been amended to exclude households where the head of the household is economically active.

Rent-free tenure - The definition of rent-free tenure has been amended to include those households for which someone outside the household, except an employer or an organisation, is paying a rent or mortgage on behalf of the household.

National Lottery - From February 1997, expenditure on National lottery tickets was collected as three separate items: tickets for the Wednesday draw only, tickets for the Saturday draw only and tickets for both draws.

1998-99

Children's income – Three new expenditure codes were introduced: pocket money to children; money given to children for specific purposes and cash gifts to children. These replaced a single code covering all three categories.

Main job and last paid job – Harmonised questions were adopted.

1999-2000

Disabled Persons Tax Credit replaced Disability Working Allowance and *Working Families Tax Credit* replaced Family Credit from October 1999.

2000-01

Household definition – the definition was changed to the harmonised definition which has been in use in the Census and nearly all other government household surveys since 1981. The effect is to group together into a single household some people who would have been allocated to separate households on the previous definition. The effect is fairly small but not negligible.
Up to 1999-2000 the FES definition was based on the pre-1981 Census definition and required members to share eating and budgeting arrangements as well as shared living accommodation.

The definition of a household was:
One person or a group of people who have the accommodation as their only or main residence and (for a group)

    share the living accommodation, that is a living or sitting room

    and   share meals together (or have common housekeeping).

The harmonised definition is less restrictive:
One person or a group of people who have the accommodation as their only or main residence and (for a group)

    share the living accommodation, that is a living or sitting room

    or   share meals together or have common housekeeping.

The effect of the change is probably to increase average household size by 0.6 per cent.

Question reductions - A thorough review of the questionnaire showed that a number of questions were no longer needed by government users. These were cut from the 2000-01 survey to reduce the burden on respondents. The reduction was fairly small but it did make the interview flow better. All the questions needed for a complete record of expenditure and income were retained.

Redesigned diary - The diary was redesigned to be easier for respondent to keep and to look cleaner. The main change of substance was to delete the column for recording whether each item was purchased by credit, charge or shop card.

Ending of MIRAS - Tax relief on interest on loans for house purchase was abolished from April 2000. Questions related to MIRAS were therefore dropped. They included some that were needed to estimate the amount if the respondent did not know it. A number were retained for other purposes, however, such as the amount of the loan still outstanding which is still asked for households paying a reduced rate of interest because one of them works for the lender.

2001-02

Household reference person – this replaced the previous concept of head of household. The household reference person is the householder, i.e. the person who:

a.   owns the household accommodation, or
b.   is legally responsible for the rent of the accommodation, or
c.   has the household accommodation as an emolument or perquisite, or
d.   has the household accommodation by virtue of some relationship to the owner who is not a
        member of the household.

If there are joint householders the household reference person is the one with the higher income. If the income is the same, then the eldest householder is taken.

A key difference between household reference person and head of household is that the household reference person must always be a householder, whereas the head of household was always the husband, who might not even be a householder himself.

National Statistics Socio-economic classification (NS-SEC) – the National Statistics Socio-economic classification (NS-SEC) was adopted for all official surveys, in place of Social Class based on Occupation and Socio-economic group. NS-SEC is itself based on the Standard Occupational Classification 2000 (SOC2000) and details of employment status.

The long-term unemployed, which fall into a separate category, are defined as those unemployed and seeking work for 12 months or more. Members of the armed forces, who were assigned to a separate category in Social Class, are included within the NS-SEC classification. Residual groups that remain unclassified include students and those with inadequately described occupations.

COICOP – From 2001-02, the **C**lassification **O**f **I**ndividual **CO**nsumption by **P**urpose (COICOP/HBS, referred to as COICOP in this volume) was introduced as a new coding frame for expenditure items. COICOP has been adapted to the needs of Household Budget Surveys (HBS) across the EU and, as a consequence, is compatible with similar classifications used in national accounts and consumer price indices. This allows the production of indicators which are comparable Europe-wide, such as the Harmonised Indices of Consumer Prices (computed for all goods as well as sub-categories such as food and transport). The main categorisation of spending used in this volume (namely twelve categories relating to food and non-alcoholic beverages; alcoholic beverages, tobacco and narcotics; clothing and footwear; housing, fuel and power; fhousehold goods and services; health, transport; communication; recreation and culture; education; restaurants and hotels; and miscellaneous goods and services) is only comparable between the two frames at a broad level. Table 6.1 in this volume has been produced by mapping COICOP to the FES 14 main categories. However the two frames are not comparable for any smaller categories, leading to a break in trends between 2000-01 and 2001-02 for any level of detail below the main 12-fold categorisation. A complete listing of COICOP and COICOP plus (an extra level of detail added by individual countries for their own needs) is available on request from the address in the introduction.

Proxy interviews – While questions about general household affairs are put to all household members or to a main household informant, questions about work and income are put to the individual members of the household. Where a member of the household is not present during the household interview, another member of the household (e.g. spouse) may be able to provide information about the absent person. The individual's interview is then identified as a *proxy* interview. From 2001/02, the EFS began accepting responses that contained a proxy interview.

Short income – From 2001-02, the EFS accepted responses from households that answered the short income section. This was designed for respondents who were reluctant to provide more detailed income information.

2002-03

Main shopper – At the launch of the EFS in April 2001, the respondent responsible for buying the household's main shopping was identified as the Main Diary Keeper. From 2002-03, this term has been replaced by the "Main Shopper".

The importance of the Main Shopper is to ensure that we have obtained information on the bulk of the shopping in the household. Without this person's co-operation we have insufficient information to use the other diaries kept by members of the household in a meaningful way. The main shopper must therefore complete a diary for the interview to qualify as a full or partial interview. Without their participation, the outcome will be a refusal no matter who else is willing to complete a diary.

2003-04

Working Tax Credit replaced Disabled Persons Tax Credit and Working Families Tax Credit from April 2003.

Pension Credit replaces Minimum Income Guarantee from October 2003.

Child Tax Credit replaces Children's Tax Credit and Childcare Tax Credit from April 2003.

Section B6

Differential grossing

Since 1998-99 results have been based on data that have been grossed differentially (re-weighted) to reduce the effect of non-response bias. This section shows the effect on the 2003-04 results published in this report. The population weights are based on the latest population estimates from the 2001 census.

The grossing method used for the 2003-04 data is the same in principle as in previous years. As well as providing users with estimates of total spending by a single, agreed procedure, the grossing also re-weights the data. It is known from comparisons with the census (see section B1 on reliability) that response rates are higher in some groups than others, leading to sampled households not being fully representative of the population as a whole. The aim of re-weighting is to compensate for this non-response bias by giving higher weights to households in the groups that are under-represented. An example of such an under-represented group is households with three or more adults and no children.

Method used to produce the weights

The weights are produced in two stages, the first of which uses results from the census-linked study of survey non-respondents (*Weighting the FES to compensate for non-response, Part 1: An investigation into census-based weighting schemes*, Foster 1994). A statistical analysis[1] was used to identify ten groups with very different response rates. A weight was then assigned to each of those groups, based on the inverse of the response rate for the group. A group with a low response rate is therefore given a high initial weight. ONS is currently analysing data from the 2001 Census; this will result in an update to the non-response weights applied to the EFS data.

The second stage adjusts the weights so that there is an exact match with population estimates, for males and females in different age groups and separately for regions. An important feature of the EFS grossing is that this is done by adjusting the factors for whole households, not by adjusting the factors for individuals. The population figures being matched exclude people who are not covered by the EFS, that is those in bed-and-breakfast accommodation, hostels, residential care homes and other institutions. A so called calibration method [2] is used in this stage to produce the weights.

The grossing procedure is carried out separately for each quarter of the survey. The main reason is that sample sizes vary from quarter to quarter more than in the past. This is the result of re-issuing addresses where there had been a non-contact or a refusal to a new interviewer after an interval of a few months, so that there are more interviews in the later quarters of the year than in the first quarter. Spending patterns are seasonal and quarterly grossing counteracts any bias from the uneven spread of interviews through the year. Quarterly grossing results in small sample numbers in some of the age group/sex categories previously used in the grossing and they have been widened slightly to avoid this.

---

1 Chi-squared Auomatic Interaction Detector

2 Implemented by the CALMAR software package

The overall effect of differential grossing

Table B4 shows the effect of differential grossing (weighting) on the 2003-04 EFS data.

Weighting increased the estimate of total average expenditure by 80p a week, that is by 0.2 per cent. It had the largest impact on average weekly expenditure on housing, fuel and power, increasing the estimate of expenditure by 3.5 per cent; on health, increasing the expenditure estimate by 2.0 per cent; and transport costs by 1.7 per cent. It reduced the estimate of spending on education by 3.7 per cent. Weighting also increased the estimates of average income, by £7.20 a week (1.6 per cent) for disposable household income and by £11.20 a week (2.0 per cent) for gross household income, which is the income used in most tables in the report.

Table B4
The effect of weighting on expenditure

Commodity or service	Average weekly household expenditure		Absolute difference	Percentage difference
	Unweighted	Weighted as published		
All expenditure groups	**355.40**	**356.20**	**0.80**	*0.2*
Food and non-alcoholic drinks	44.20	43.50	-0.70	*-1.6*
Alcoholic drink and tobacco	11.70	11.70	0.00	*-0.1*
Clothing and footwear	23.30	22.70	-0.50	*-2.3*
Housing, fuel and power	37.70	39.00	1.30	*3.5*
Household goods and services	31.70	31.30	-0.50	*-1.5*
Health	5.00	5.00	0.10	*2.0*
Transport	59.70	60.70	1.00	*1.7*
Communication	11.10	11.20	0.10	*1.3*
Recreation and culture	57.20	57.30	0.10	*0.2*
Education	5.40	5.20	-0.20	*-3.7*
Restaurants and hotels	34.50	34.90	0.40	*1.1*
Miscellaneous	33.90	33.60	-0.30	*-0.8*
Weekly household income:				
Disposable	456.90	464.04	7.20	*1.6*
Gross	559.10	570.28	11.20	*2.0*

Re-weighting also has an effect on the variance of estimates. In an analysis on the 1999-2000 data weighting increased variance slightly for some items and reduced for others. Overall the effect was to reduce variance slightly.

Further information

Further information is available on the method used to produce the weights from the address given in the introduction.

Section B7

Index to tables in reports on the Family Expenditure Survey 1995-96 to 2000-01 and the Expenditure and Food Survey 2001-02 to 2003-04

					Table numbers in reports for				
2003-04 tables		2002-03	2001-02[1]	2000-01	1999-2000	1998-99	1997-98	1996-97	1995-96
Detailed expenditure and place of purchase									
A1	Detailed expenditure with full-method satndard errors	7.1	7.1	7.1	7.1	7.1	7.1	7.1	7.1
A2	expenditure on alcoholic drink by type of premises	7.2	7.2	7.2	7.2	7.2	7.2	7.2	7.2
A3	expenditure on food by place of purchase	7.3	7.3	7.3	7.3	7.3	7.3	7.3	7.3
..	expenditure on alcoholic drink by place of purchase	-	-	-	7.4	7.4	7.4	7.4	-
A4	expenditure on selected items by place of purchase	7.4	7.4	7.4	-	-	-	-	-
..	expenditure on petrol, diesel and other motor oils by place of purchase	-	-	-	7.5	7.5	7.5	7.5	-
..	selected household goods and personal goods and services by place of purchase	-	-	-	7.6	7.6	7.6	7.6	-
..	selected regular purchases by place of purchase	-	-	-	7.7	7.7	7.7	7.7	-
A5	expenditure on clothing and footwear by place of purchase	7.5	7.5	7.5	7.8	7.8	7.8	7.8	-
Expenditure by income									
A6	main items by gross income decile	1.1	1.1	1.1	1.1	1.1	1.1	1.1	1.1
A7	percentage on main items by gross income decile	1.2	1.2	1.2	1.2	1.2	1.2	1.2	1.2
A8	detailed expenditure by gross income decile	1.3	1.3	1.3	1.3	1.3	1.3	1.3	1.3
..	(housing expenditure in each tenure group)	-	-	-	-	-	-	1.4	1.4
A9	main items by disposable income decile	1.4	1.4	1.4	1.4	-	-	-	-
A10	percentage on main items by disposable income decile	1.5	1.5	1.5	1.5	-	-	-	-
Expenditure by age and income									
A11	main items by age of HRP	2.1	2.1	2.9	-	-	-	-	-
..	main items by age of head of household	-	-	2.1	2.1	2.1	2.1	2.1	2.1
A12	main items as a percentage by age of HRP	2.2	2.2	2.2	2.2	2.2	2.2	2.2	2.2
A13	detailed expenditure by age of HRP	2.3	2.3	2.3	2.3	2.3	2.3	2.3	2.3
A14	aged under 30 by income	2.4	2.4	2.4	2.4	2.4	2.4	2.4	2.4
A15	aged 30 and under 50 by income	2.5	2.5	2.5	2.5	2.5	2.5	2.5	2.5
A16	aged 50 and under 65 by income	2.6	2.6	2.6	2.6	2.6	2.6	2.6	2.6
A17	aged 65 and under 75 by income	2.7	2.7	2.7	2.7	2.7	2.7	2.7	2.7
A18	aged 75 or over by income	2.8	2.8	2.8	2.8	2.8	2.8	2.8	2.8
Expenditure by socio-economic characteristics									
A19	by economic activity status of HRP	3.1	3.1	3.9	-	-	-	-	-
..	by economic activity status of HoH	-	-	3.1	3.1	3.1	3.1	3.1	3.1
..	by occupation	-	-	3.2	3.2	3.2	3.2	3.2	3.2
A20	HRP is a full-time employee by income	3.2	3.2	3.3	3.3	3.3	3.3	3.3	3.3
A21	HRP is self-employed by income	3.3	3.3	3.4	3.4	3.4	3.4	3.4	3.4
..	by social class	-	-	3.5	3.5	3.5	3.5	3.5	3.5
A22	by number of persons working	3.4	3.4	3.6	3.6	3.6	3.6	3.6	3.6
A23	by age HRP completed continuous full-time education	3.5	3.5	3.7	3.7	3.7	3.7	3.7	3.7
..	by occupation of HRP	-	-	3.8	-	-	-	-	-
A24	by socio-economic class of HRP	3.6	3.6	-	-	-	-	-	-
Expenditure by composition, income and tenure									
A25	expenditure by household composition	4.1	4.1	4.1	4.1	4.1	4.1	4.1	4.1
A26	one adult retired households mainly dependent on state pensions	4.2	4.2	4.2	4.2	4.2	4.2	4.2	4.2
A27	one adult retired households not mainly dependent on state pensions	4.3	4.3	4.3	4.3	4.3	4.3	4.3	4.3
A28	one adult non-retired	4.4	4.4	4.4	4.4	4.4	4.4	4.4	4.4
A29	one adult with children	4.5	4.5	4.5	4.5	4.5	4.5	4.5	4.5
A30	two adults with children	4.6	4.6	4.6	4.6	4.6	4.6	4.6	4.6

.. Tables do not appear in the 2003-04 report
1 Household reference person (HRP) replaced head of household (HoH) in 2001-02

2003-04 tables		Table numbers in reports for							
		2002-03	2001-02[1]	2000-01	1999-2000	1998-99	1997-98	1996-97	1995-96
Expenditure by composition, income and tenure (cont.)									
A31	one man one woman non-retired	4.7	4.7	4.7	4.7	4.7	4.7	4.7	4.7
A32	one man one woman retired mainly dependent on state pensions	4.8	4.8	4.8	4.8	4.8	4.8	4.8	4.8
A33	one man one woman retired not mainly dependent on state pensions	4.9	4.9	4.9	4.9	4.9	4.9	4.9	4.9
A34	household expenditure by tenure	4.10	4.10	4.10	4.10	4.10	4.10	4.10	4.10
..	household expenditure by type of dwelling	-	-	-	-	4.11	4.11	4.11	4.11
Expenditure by region[2]									
A35	main items of expenditure by GOR	5.1	5.1	5.1	5.1	5.1	5.1	5.1	5.1
A36	main items as a percentage of expenditure by GOR	5.2	5.2	5.2	5.2	5.2	5.2	5.2	5.2
A37	detailed expenditure by GOR	5.3	5.3	5.3	5.3	5.3	5.3	5.3	5.3
..	(housing expenditure in each tenure group)	-	-	-	-	-	-	5.4	5.4
..	expenditure by type of administrative area	-	-	5.4	5.4	5.4	5.4	5.5	5.5
A38	expenditure by urban/rural areas (GB only)	5.4	5.4	5.5	-	-	-	-	-
Household income									
A40	Income by household composition	8.1	8.1	8.1	8.1	8.1	8.1	8.1	8.1
A41	Income by age of HRP	8.2	8.2	8.10	-	-	-	-	-
..	by age of head of household	-	-	8.2	8.2	8.2	8.2	8.2	8.2
A42	Income by income group	8.3	8.3	8.3	8.3	8.3	8.3	8.3	8.3
A43	Income by household tenure	8.4	8.4	8.4	8.4	8.4	8.4	8.4	8.4
..	Income by economic status of HoH	-	-	8.5	8.5	8.5	8.5	8.5	8.5
..	Income by occupational grouping of HoH	-	-	8.6	8.6	8.6	8.6	8.6	8.6
A44	Income by Region	8.5	8.5	8.7	8.7	8.7	8.7	8.7	8.7
A45	Income by GB urban/rural areas	8.6	8.6	8.8	-	-	-	-	-
A46	Income by socio-economic class	8.7	-	-	-	-	-	-	-
A47	Income 1970 to 2002-03	8.8	8.7	8.9	8.8	8.8	8.8	8.8	8.8
..	Income by economic activity status of HRP	-	-	8.11	-	-	-	-	-
..	Income by occupation of HRP	-	-	8.12	-	-	-	-	-
Households characteristics and ownership of durable goods									
A48	Household characteristics	9.1	9.1	9.1	9.1	9.1	9.1	9.1	9.1
A49	Person characteristics	9.2	9.2	9.2	9.2	9.2	9.2	9.2	9.2
A50	percentage with durable goods 1970 to 2003-04	9.3	9.3	9.3	9.3	9.3	9.3	9.3	9.3
A51	percentage with durable goods by income group & hhld composition	9.4	9.4	9.4	9.4	9.4	9.4	9.4	9.4
A52	percentage with cars	9.5	9.5	9.5	9.5	9.5	9.5	9.5	9.5
A53	percentage with durable goods by UK Countries and Government Office Regions	9.6	9.6	9.6	9.6	9.6	9.6	9.6	9.6
A54	percentage by size, composition, age, in each income group	9.7	9.7	9.7	9.7	9.7	9.7	9.7	9.7
..	percentage by occupation, economic activity, tenure in each income group	-	-	9.8	9.8	9.8	9.7	9.7	9.7
A55	percentage by economic activity, tenure and socio-economic class in each income group	9.8	9.8	-	-	-	-	-	-
Trends in household expenditure (moved to Chapter 4)									
4.1	main items 1980 - 2003-04	6.1	6.1	6.1	6.1	-	-	-	-
4.2	as a percentage of total expenditure 1980 - 2003-04	6.2	6.2	6.2	6.2	6.1	6.1	6.1	6.1
..	by Region[3]	-	-	6.3	6.3	6.2	-	-	-

.. Tables do not appear in the 2003-04 report
1 Household reference person (HRP) replaced head of household (HoH) in 2001-02